The Legacy of the Global Financial Crisis

The Legacy of the Global Financial Crisis

Edited by

Youssef Cassis and Jean-Jacques van Helten

BLOOMSBURY ACADEMIC
LONDON • NEW YORK • OXFORD • NEW DELHI • SYDNEY

BLOOMSBURY ACADEMIC
Bloomsbury Publishing Plc
50 Bedford Square, London, WC1B 3DP, UK
1385 Broadway, New York, NY 10018, USA
29 Earlsfort Terrace, Dublin 2, Ireland

BLOOMSBURY, BLOOMSBURY ACADEMIC and the Diana logo
are trademarks of Bloomsbury Publishing Plc

First published in Great Britain 2021
This paperback edition published by Bloomsbury Academic in 2023

Copyright © Youssef Cassis and Jean-Jacques van Helten, 2021

Youssef Cassis and Jean-Jacques van Helten have asserted their right under the Copyright,
Designs and Patents Act, 1988, to be identified as Editors of this work.

Series design by Adriana Brioso
Cover image © Anton Petrus/Getty Images

Bloomsbury Publishing Plc does not have any control over, or responsibility for,
any third-party websites referred to or in this book. All internet addresses given
in this book were correct at the time of going to press. The author and publisher
regret any inconvenience caused if addresses have changed or sites have
ceased to exist, but can accept no responsibility for any such changes.

A catalogue record for this book is available from the British Library.

A catalog record for this book is available from the Library of Congress.

ISBN: HB: 978-0-7556-2662-5
PB: 978-1-3502-6143-3
ePDF: 978-0-7556-2664-9
ePub: 978-0-7556-2663-2

Typeset by RefineCatch Limited, Bungay, Suffolk NR35 1EF, UK.

To find out more about our authors and books visit
www.bloomsbury.com and sign up for our newsletters.

Contents

Figures

Tables

Contributors

Magnus Agustsson was appointed Chief Risk Officer of the SEB Group (Skandinaviska Enskilda Banken AB) in 2017. He joined the SEB Group as Baltic Head of Risk Management in 2009 and since 2011 has held various management positions in Group Risk. As Chief Risk Officer, he is responsible for all risks across the group, managed through Group Credits and Group Risk. He is also a member of the Group Executive Committee. Before joining SEB in 2009, Magnus was Head of Risk Methods at DEPFA and Head of Strategy at the Nordic Investment Bank. Throughout his career, Magnus has been responsible for managing and overseeing various roles including risk methodologies, risk classification, credit risk, valuations, economic capital, market risk, liquidity risk, strategy development, portfolio management and risk appetite. Magnus holds degrees in Mechanical Engineering and Economics from the University of Iceland.

Pervenche Berès is a member of the *Autorité des marchés financiers* committee on climate and sustainable finance. She was a Member of the European Parliament (MEP) from 1994 to 2019. From 2017 to 2019 she was S&D Spokesperson of the Committee on Economic and Monetary Affairs (ECON). Pervenche was rapporteur in 2018 on the European Investment Stabilisation Function, in 2015 on a budgetary capacity for the Eurozone and in 2014 on the economic governance framework of EMU. From 2009 to 2014, she was Chairwoman of the Employment and Social Affairs Committee and rapporteur of the temporary committee on the financial, economic, and social crisis (CRIS). She has been Chairwoman of the ECON (2004–09) and head of the French socialist delegation (June 1997–June 2004, June 2014–January 2017, March–July 2019). From December 1999 to October 2000, she was member of the Convention in charge of the EU Charter of Fundamental Rights and then of the Convention in charge of the EU Constitution (February 2002–July 2003). Between 2001 and 2008 she was also Member of Sèvres Municipal Council. A graduate of the Institut d'Etudes Politiques in Paris, Pervenche worked from 1981 to 1994 as administrator in the French National Assembly and from 1988 to 1992 as advisor on international and European affairs to the Speaker.

Jacques Beyssade is the Group Secretary General of the French banking group BPCE (Banques Populaires & Caisses d'Epargne) and a graduate of HEC, Paris. His career started at Crédit Lyonnais (later merged into Credit Agricole CIB) as a financial analyst in London before moving to Paris, New York, Seoul and Hong Kong as head of various business units in commercial and investment banking. In 2008, Jacques joined Natixis to identify and organize the assets to be run off by the bank. One year later, he was appointed Chief Risk Officer of Natixis and, from 2015 onwards, of the entire BPCE Group. From 2016, his responsibilities were expanded to Risk, Compliance and Permanent Control with the title of Deputy CEO. Aside from his banking career, Jacques is a foreign trade advisor to the French government and a deputy mayor of his village, Chouvigny.

Laurence Bogni-Bartholomé is the Group Chief Risk Officer at Lowell. She leads the Risk, Compliance and Internal Audit functions. Laurence has twenty-eight years of experience in risk and portfolio management, compliance and audit in banking, financial services and manufacturing. Prior to joining Lowell, Laurence was EMEA Head of International Risk Oversight at Wells Fargo Bank, leading the Corporate Risk second line of defence. Before that, she spent thirteen years with GE Capital where she held various Chief Risk Officer roles before taking up the position of EMEA General Manager/COO for the Leverage Finance business in charge of Risk, IT, Operations, Procurement and Change. She also served on several General Electric Company Boards in France, Italy, the UK and the Netherlands. Laurence holds a Master's degree in Banking and Corporate Finance from Aix-Marseille University and a Master's in Management Sciences, Finance and Tax from Paris Dauphine University. She is Six-Sigma certified.

Dorothee Bohle holds a chair in social and political change at the Department of Political and Social Sciences of the European University Institute, Florence. Her research is at the intersection of comparative politics and political economy with a special focus on East Central Europe. She is the co-author, with Béla Greskovits, of *Capitalist Diversity on Europe's Periphery* (2012), and of *Europe's New Periphery: Poland's Transformation and Transnational Integration* (in German; 2002). Her publications have also appeared in *Comparative Politics, Studies in Comparative International Development, West European Politics, Journal of Democracy, European Journal of Sociology and Review of International Political Economy,* among others. Her current work looks at the policy responses to the Great Recession in several European peripheral countries.

Gerald Braunberger is a graduate in Economics from Goethe University, Frankfurt, after which he joined the *Frankfurter Allgemeine Zeitung (FAZ)*. He covered Banking and Monetary Policy for seven years before becoming the paper's Paris correspondent in 1995. Retuning to Frankfurt in 2004, he joined the FAZ's Sunday edition for three years. From 2007 to 2019, Gerald was Chief Editor of FAZ's Financial Section and in April 2019 he was appointed Publisher. Gerald has edited and written various books on economic topics, among them a book on John Maynard Keynes.

Youssef Cassis is Professor at the Robert Schuman Centre for Advanced Studies, European University Institute, Florence, and Director of the European Research Council funded project on 'The Memory of Financial Crises: Financial Actors and Global Risk' (MERCATOR). He was previously Professor of Economic History at the European University Institute (2011–19), the University of Geneva (2004–10), and the University of Grenoble (1997–2004). His work focuses mainly on banking and financial history, as well as business history more generally. His most recent books include *Crises and Opportunities. The Shaping of Modern Finance* (2011), and, with Philip Cottrell,

Private Banking in Europe: Rise, Retreat and Resurgence (2015). He has also recently co-edited with Richard Grossman and Catherine Schenk *The Oxford Handbook of Banking and Financial History* (2016). In 1994, he was the co-founder/editor of *Financial History Review*, a long-serving member of the Academic Advisory Council of the European Association for Banking and Financial History (EBHA), and past President (2005–2007) of the European Business History Association.

Kārlis Danēvičs joined SEB Latvia in 2003 and currently serves as member of the SEB's Latvian Board, responsible for Compliance and Anti Money Laundering (AML). During the Baltic crisis, Kārlis was Head of Credits for SEB's Latvian operations. He worked as Chief Financial Officer of SEB Latvia, and was part of the management team between 2014 and 2017. Kārlis has acquired considerable experience during his years at SEB, having held the roles as Latvian Head of Industry and Corporate Analysis, Head of Credits and Head of Corporate Client Coverage. He has also lived and worked in Sweden, covering Country and Financial Institution risks and limit decisions. In addition to his SEB commitments, Kārlis is a frequent lecturer and he holds Board positions in several non-governmental institutions. For example, he is Chairman of the Board for SOS Children's Villages in Latvia. Kārlis is a graduate of Riga Business School and has participated in SEB's top management development programme, the Wallenberg Institute.

Charles Goodhart trained as an economist at Cambridge (undergraduate) and Harvard (PhD). He then began a career that alternated between academia (Cambridge, 1963–5; LSE, 1967–8; again from 1985 to date), and work in the official sector, mostly in the Bank of England (Department of Economic Affairs, 1965–6; Bank of England, 1968–85; Monetary Policy Committee, 1997–2000). He is now Norman Sosnow Professor Emeritus at the London School of Economics. Throughout his career he has worked as a specialist monetary economist, focussing on policy issues and on financial regulation both as an academic and in the Bank of England. He devised 'the Corset' in 1974, advised Hong Kong on 'the Link' in 1983, and Reserve Bank of New Zealand (RBNZ) on inflation targets in 1988. Charles notes that he has 'written more books and articles on these subjects throughout the last fifty or sixty years than any sane person would want to read'.

Patrick Honohan was Governor of the Central Bank of Ireland and a member of the Governing Council of the European Central Bank from September 2009 to November 2015. He is an Honorary Professor of Economics at Trinity College Dublin, a Nonresident Senior Fellow at the Peterson Institute for International Economics and a Research Fellow of the Centre for Economic Policy Research. Previously he spent twelve years on the staff of the World Bank, where he was a Senior Advisor on financial sector issues. During the 1990s, he was a Research Professor at Ireland's Economic and Social Research Institute. In the 1980s, he was Economic Advisor to Ireland's *Taoiseach* (Prime Minister) Garret FitzGerald. A graduate of University College Dublin, he received his PhD in Economics from the London School of Economics in 1978. Professor Honohan was elected a member of the Royal Irish Academy in 2002. His most recent book, *Currency, Credit and Crisis* (2019), provides an account of the financial crisis with a focus on Ireland.

Thomas Huertas is Adjunct Professor at the Institute for Law and Economics, Senior Fellow at the Center for Financial Studies and Fellow at SAFE (Sustainable Architecture for Finance in Europe), all at the Goethe University in Frankfurt. In addition, he is a non-executive director of Barclays Bank Europe. Formerly, Tom was a partner in EY's Financial Risk Practice and chaired the firm's Global Regulatory Network. From 2004 to 2011, he was an Executive Director of the UK Financial Services Authority as well as Vice Chairman of the Committee of European Bank Supervisors (2009–10), Alternate Chair of the European Banking Authority (2011), Vice-Chair of the European Systemic Risk Board (2011), Member of the Basel Committee on Bank Supervision (2009–11) and Member of the Resolution Steering Committee of the Financial Stability Board (2009–11). Earlier in his career, Tom was Chief Executive and Chair of Orbian plc, an internet-based supply chain finance company. He also held a number of senior positions at Citigroup, including Chief Executive and Chairman of Citibank AG (Germany). He holds a PhD in Economics from the University of Chicago and has published extensively on financial services regulation.

Ramon Marimon is Professor of Economics and Pierre Werner Chair at the European University Institute, on leave from Universitat Pompeu Fabra. He is Research Fellow of CEPR and NBER. His research is in Dynamic Macro-Finance and Contracts, Learning and Labour, with a special emphasis on European issues. He has been Secretary of State for Science and Technology in Spain (2000–02) and co-founder of UPF and of Barcelona Graduate School of Economics (Chair of the Board of Trustees 2011–18), and first Director of CREi (UPF) and of the Max Weber postdoctoral programme (EUI). He was the Scientific Coordinator of the Horizon 2020 project ADEMU, 'A Dynamic Economic and Monetary Union' (2015–18), President of the Society for Economic Dynamics (2013–15) and of the Spanish Economic Association (2004), Assistant and Associate Professor at the University of Minnesota and visiting professor in different US and European Universities. He has been an advisor to the European Commission on R&D policy. He has published in *Econometrica, Journal of Political Economy, American Economic Review, Review of Economic Studies, Journal of Economic Theory, Review of Economic Dynamics*, and others.

George Papaconstantinou is Professor and Director of Executive Education at the School of Transnational Governance of the European University Institute. As Greece's Finance Minister at the outset of the Eurozone crisis, he played a key role in the design and negotiation of Greece's support programme by the EU and the IMF and in the implementation of its associated economic, financial and structural policies. Subsequently, as Minister of Environment and Energy, he pursued policies to advance Greece's sustainable growth agenda. He holds a BSc from the London School of Economics, an MA from New York University and a PhD in economics from the London School of Economics. Before being elected to the Greek Parliament and subsequently the European Parliament, he had been a senior economist at the OECD, taught at the Athens University of Economics and Business and consulted for the European Commission and international think tanks. He is the author of *Game Over: The Inside Story of the Greek Crisis* (2016) and *Whatever It Takes: The Battle for Post-Crisis Europe* (2020).

Catherine R. Schenk FRHS, FRSA, is Professor of Economic and Social History at the University of Oxford. She completed her undergraduate and Master's degrees at University of Toronto before completing her PhD at the London School of Economics. She has held academic positions at Victoria University of Wellington, New Zealand, Royal Holloway, University of London and at the University of Glasgow. She was visiting professor at Nankai University, China, and Hong Kong University. She has also been a visiting researcher at the International Monetary Fund and at the Hong Kong Institute for Monetary Research and was Lamfalussy Senior Research Fellow at the Bank for International Settlements. She is an Associate Fellow in international economics at Chatham House. Her current European Research Council-funded project traces the dynamics of international bank networks during the twentieth century. Her most recent book (with W. Plumpe and A. Nutzenadel) is *Deutschebank: The Global Hausbank 1870–2020* (2020).

Agnieszka Smoleńska is a Visiting Fellow at the Robert Schuman Centre for Advanced Studies at the European University Institute (EUI) and a senior EU affairs analyst at Polityka Insight. She completed her PhD in EU cross-border banking regulation at the EUI in 2020. She holds a BA in European Social and Political Studies from University College London and an MA in European Interdisciplinary Studies from the College of Europe (Natolin). Previously, she worked at the European Commission and the European Parliament and has cooperated with Transparency International, the World Bank and Florence School of Banking and Finance. Her research interests span EU financial regulation and Economic and Monetary Union (EMU) as well as differentiated integration in finance.

Jean-Jacques van Helten is a Visiting Fellow at the Robert Schuman Centre for Advanced Studies & the Florence School of Banking and Finance at the European University Institute (EUI). For more than seventeen years, he was a Managing Director & Chief Risk Officer, EMEA, for the Bank of Montreal (BMO) Financial Group and more recently a non-executive member of the Board of BMO Europe, Dublin. Previously, he worked variously in a range of senior executive risk and capital markets business roles in major international investment banks in Europe, Australia, Asia and the UK with responsibility for market, liquidity and operational risks, and credit risk analytics. Jean-Jacques completed his undergraduate and Master's degrees along with his PhD in economics/economic history at the University of London, studied at the Goethe Universität, Frankfurt, and Freie Universität, Berlin, and has held academic research positions at La Trobe University and the University of London. His current research interests span EU's Capital Markets Union (CMU), financial regulation and post-GFC developments in risk management and corporate governance.

Acknowledgements

This volume grew out of a High-Level Policy Workshop on the Legacy of the Global Financial Crisis held at the European University Institute (EUI), Florence, on the tenth anniversary of that crisis in 2018. We explain in the Introduction why we decided to mark that anniversary with yet another commemorative workshop and in what respects we believe this book is different and makes an original contribution to the debate. The Workshop brought together many scholars, academics, banking practitioners, politicians, journalists, regulators, central bankers and students from across Europe and North America and the intensity of the debates at the conference is reflected in the wide range of contributors to this volume.

The editors would like to express their gratitude to Miguel Poiares Maduro, director the School of Transnational Governance, and Brigid Laffan, director of the Robert Schuman Centre for Advanced Studies, both at the EUI, for their intellectual and financial support, which made this Workshop possible. They would also like to thank the many people who contributed to the success of the event by chairing a session, presenting a paper and taking part in the debates. They are particularly grateful to Renaud Dehousse (president of the EUI), Stefan Grundmann (Humboldt University Berlin and EUI), Luc Thévenoz (University of Geneva), Adam Tooze (Columbia University), Andreas Gottschling (Crédit Suisse), Keishi Hotsuki (Morgan Stanley) and Stefano Cappiello (AMCO Asset Management Company). They would also like to thank Angelika Lanfranchi and Paula Gori, who dealt highly efficiently with all organizational issues.

Introduction: The Legacy of the Global Financial Crisis

Youssef Cassis and Jean-Jacques van Helten

This book's concept: an archipelago[1]

The Global Financial Crisis was arguably the most severe financial panic in modern history. Never before, even in the 1930s, did so many of the leading banks, in terms of both size and reputation, in so many advanced economies, find themselves at almost exactly the same moment requiring state intervention to save them from failing (Cassis 2011). However, as an economic downturn, the Great Recession that followed it was not comparable to the Great Depression of the 1930s in terms of the collapse of industrial production and international trade, and the rise in unemployment, partly thanks to the lessons drawn from history, though it undoubtedly was the most severe since then (Eichengreen and O'Rourke 2009).

The Global Financial Crisis, which includes the Great Recession and the euro crisis, was thus a historical event of momentous significance, reflected in the way its tenth anniversary in September 2018[2] was marked, with extensive coverage by both the specialized and the general press, symposia and colloquia, as well as the publication of a number of reflective commemorative books. These included, among others,[3] *Firefighting* (2018), a memoir by the three leading American protagonists in the crisis, Ben Bernanke, Tim Geithner and Hank Paulson,[4] and Adam Tooze's *Crashed* (2018), the first history of the event by a professional historian.

---

[1] Rather than a chronological or thematic analysis of the crisis, we use the concept of an 'archipelago' borrowed from John Foot (2018). This conjures up the image of a group of islands each with their own characteristics using quite different insights, views, fragments and personal perspectives of the Global Financial Crisis.

[2] The collapse of Lehman Brothers on 15 September 2008 is usually seen as the trigger of the financial panic. The suspension by BNP Paribas of two of its investment funds on 9 August 2007, because it could no longer value its assets, which marked the beginning of the 'credit crunch', has also been regarded as the beginning of the crisis.

[3] Other significant publications include Aliber and Zoega (2019), Arner et al. (2019), Ball (2018), D'Arista (2018), Goodhart and Tsomocos (2019), O'Halloran and Groll (2019).

[4] Ben Bernanke was Chairman of the Federal Reserve, Timothy Geithner was President of the Federal Bank of New York and, from 20 January 2009, Secretary of the Treasury, Henry Paulson was Secretary of the Treasury until 20 January 2009.

This present book, the outcome of a conference held at the European University Institute in Florence on 9 November 2018, is part of this effort to better understand and draw lessons from the shock that threatened the world financial system ten years earlier.

The emphasis of this book is on the Global Financial Crisis' legacy, which, according to the *Oxford English Dictionary* is 'something left or handed down by a predecessor'. The definition is broad but suggests some different perspectives, notably what is left from the past, including what is remembered from it. This of course includes, to a certain extent, the lessons drawn from the crisis. But the legacy also introduces a dynamic dimension: the nature of what has been left from the past – whether it is an asset or a liability; and its transformative character – what can be done, and what has been done, with this inheritance?

The legacies of the Global Financial Crisis should thus be distinguished from its consequences. Banks' failures or near failures were a consequence of the financial crisis. The legacy of the crisis, however, relates to the condition of the banking system in general and the systemically important banks in particular, especially in terms of risk management and regulation, as well as the mechanisms put in place to cope with future crises. Lessons drawn from the crisis are part of its legacy. One thinks of the monetary and fiscal policies pursued to prevent the recession from turning into a depression – and the extent to which this legacy differs from that of the Great Depression. A long-term legacy can be a decisive advance in macroeconomics, as with Keynesianism, clearly a legacy of the Great Depression. But legacies can also be social, cultural and political in nature, and thus harder to pick up on: to what extent has such a significant financial crisis led to changes in professional behaviour, or the emergence of a new business ethics? The same is true of the social and political legacies of the crisis: should growing inequalities and the rise of populism be seen as a legacy of the Global Financial Crisis, or are they part of a much broader phenomenon?

One of our objectives in publishing this book is the transmission of the experiences of the Global Financial Crisis from one generation to the other – from the generation who experienced it first hand to its successor, made up of people who are now taking the reins and have mostly learnt from it by hearsay. Historian Jan Assmann makes an interesting distinction between a 'communicative memory' and a 'cultural memory'. Communicative memory refers to the fairly recent past, to memories that exist in everyday life and which can be shared by contemporaries, and whose transmission cannot go beyond three to four generations (eighty to 100 years). Cultural memory is a more formalized and institutionalized type of memory, however: it can go back several hundred years and sometimes turn into myth; it is mediated in 'texts, icons, rituals, and performances of various kinds' (Assmann 2008).

The legacy of the Global Financial Crisis is thus in many respects embodied in people's memory of it – both in terms of personal memories of the crisis, still vivid in this early post-crisis stage, and its collective memory. The two are closely interrelated. It is true that strictly speaking, only individuals have a memory and can remember. However, starting with the pioneering work of the French sociologist Maurice Halbwachs in the 1920s (Halbwachs 1925, 1950), several studies have shown how a person's memory is clearly shaped by socio-cultural factors, and how social groups or nations can construct a shared past, through media, institutions and practices, in a process that bears some resemblance to that of individual memory, especially in the selection of versions of the past (Erll 2010). The memory of the Global Financial Crisis, for individuals, groups, societies, or nations, has clearly been read through the memory of the Great Depression, which has itself been reconstructed by various stages of mediation, through the process of historical writing, the evolution of economic thought and the changing ideological and political climate.

This book is also different in its conception. The legacy and memory of the Global Financial Crisis are transmitted by a wide range of actors, all of whom have been involved in one aspect or another of the crisis, including reflecting and commenting on it, and who offer different perspectives on the event. So far as we are aware, this is the only book that brings together academics, themselves coming from various disciplines (economics, history, law, and politics), senior journalists, politicians, central bankers and regulators, as well as banking practitioners – mostly banks' Chief Risk Officers (CROs) – with some overlap between professional activities, for example between academics and central bankers, academics and politicians, regulators and banking practitioners. The book is edited jointly by an academic historian, Youssef Cassis, Professor at the European University Institute, and an experienced banker, Jean-Jacques van Helten, former Chief Risk Officer EMEA of the Bank of Montreal and now at the European University Institute. Academics, journalists (in a different way) and policymakers (to a lesser extent) have had many opportunities to write about the crisis. With rare exceptions, usually through interviews, the voice of banking practitioners has rarely been heard, even though they have been at the core of events.

Another of the objectives of the book is to gather different views on the same aspect of the crisis. Three main themes have been defined for that purpose: one general, offering perspectives on the Global Financial Crisis taken as a whole, and two more specific, looking respectively at national experiences, and at the architecture of control. Dealing with national experiences necessitated to make choices, we decided to concentrate on small countries, which have attracted less attention in the press and the literature but whose experiences form an important part of the legacy of the Global Financial Crisis nonetheless.

This does not mean ignoring the better-known experiences of the larger countries: these are discussed in the first part of the book, which offers broad perspectives on the crisis. The third part, on the architecture of control, discusses one of the main legacies of all major financial crises: the new regulatory frameworks and banks' risk and governance structures that are set up in their wake.

A diversity of perspectives makes for a different type of book, in both style and content. Banks' senior executives do not write like academics or journalists. They are also interested in different aspects the crisis and its legacy. We have deliberately not tried to harmonize all chapters therefore into a standard academic style – hence the concept of an archipelago – and believe that this gives the book its unique configuration and perspective.

Part I of the book offers general perspectives on the Global Financial Crisis by two economists, Charles Goodhart, emeritus professor at the London School of Economics and former member of the Bank of England's Monetary Policy Committee, and Ramon Marimon, professor at the European University Institute; one historian, Catherine Schenk, professor at Oxford; one journalist, Gerald Braunberger, economics editor of the *Frankfurter Allgemeine Zeitung*; and one politician, Pervenche Berès, Member of the European Parliament (Party of European Socialists) and Chair of its Committee on Economic and Monetary Affairs during the crisis.

Charles Goodhart, who also gave the conference's keynote speech, approaches the legacy of the Global Financial Crisis from the perspective of macroeconomic policy, which he judges to have been suboptimal in the ten years following the crisis, pushing advanced economies into a debt trap. Interestingly, one way of reversing the shift into debt and making equity finance more attractive would be to address what has been considered as one of the main causes of the Global Financial Crisis, namely senior executives' misaligned incentives and responsibilities.

For Ramon Marimon, this legacy consists in the changes cum lessons inherited from the crisis, in particular the new era of central banking inaugurated by Ben Bernanke; the relationship between a country's fiscal capacity and the level of its stimulus package; and the importance of linkages in crises, especially the financial-monetary-fiscal linkage, which explains the difference between a relatively short crisis in the United States and a longer one which turned into the Eurocrisis in the eurozone (or euro area).

Catherine Schenk reflects on the Global Financial Crisis from the perspective of using, remembering and forgetting the past – in this instance first and foremost the Great Depression of the 1930s, which played a crucial role in the response to the crisis in 2008. The role of historians in analysing the past and creating the understanding on which policy decisions are made represents an important legacy of all financial crises.

Gerald Braunberger discusses the interplay between the memory of the Global Financial Crisis and four major economic and financial changes taking place in its aftermath: slow growth, combined with low inflation and low interest rates; a new phase of financial liquidity, benefiting asset managers; a lack of liquidity in asset markets, leading to spikes in volatility; and the rise of inequality and populism.

For Pervenche Berès, from the perspective of the European Union, the legacy of the Global Financial Crisis is a mixed balance of successes and failures: in other words, the pre-crisis problems that have been fixed (for example the role of the ECB) and those that have not been fixed (for example social inequalities) in the subsequent ten years.

Part II is devoted to national experiences (Hungary, Greece, Ireland, Iceland, Cyprus and the three Baltic countries) and brings together a political scientist, Dorothee Bohle, professor at the European University Institute in Florence; a central banker and economist, Patrick Honohan, former Governor of the Bank of Ireland; a politician and economist, George Papaconstantinou, former Greek Finance Minister and now professor at the School of Transnational Governance of the European University Institute; and a banking practitioner, Magnus Agustsson, Chief Risk Officer of the Swedish financial Group, Skandinaviska Enskilda Banken (SEB).

Dorothee Bohle considers the political legacy of the Global Financial Crisis. She seeks to explain the differing extents to which right-wing and left-wing nationalists have challenged the pre-crisis neo-liberal and integrationist consensus. Comparing the cases of Hungary and Greece, she argues that to be successful, the answer must be both politically and economically viable, and that these conditions have favoured the right-wing rather than left-wing answers to the crisis.

Patrick Honohan reflects on the uncertainty of one important legacy of the Global Financial Crisis, the management of systemic crises, looking in particular at the vexed issue of bail-in or bailout. Analysing the highly contrasting cases of Ireland, Iceland and Cyprus, he suggests that such a choice is context specific and in no way as clear cut as often assumed.

Magnus Agustsson's account of SEB's strategy during the crisis in order to fulfil its commitment towards the banks that it had acquired in the 1990s in Latvia, Lithuania and Estonia, together with Kārlis Danēvičs' eyewitness report from Riga during the 'Great Baltic Depression' constitute a legacy of the Global Financial Crisis in the form of a unique account to be transmitted to the next generation.

George Papaconstantinou's view from Greece also extends to Europe by showing how Greece acted as a conduit between the Global Financial Crisis of 2007–09 and the ensuing Euro crisis. Narratives of the crisis form an integral part of changing memory and legacy. Papaconstantinou shows how the example of Greece modified this narrative by shifting the focus from the irresponsible attitude of over-leveraged bankers to the irresponsible attitude of over-indebted governments.

Part III deals with the regulatory legacy of the Global Financial Crisis, a theme addressed by a regulator, Thomas Huertas, a former member of the Executive Committee at the UK's Financial Services Authority, the erstwhile regulatory body of the British financial services industry and now global regulatory network coordinator at Ernst & Young; a lawyer, Agnieszka Smoleńska, Research Associate at the Robert Schuman Centre for Advanced Studies of the EUI in Florence; and two banking practitioners, Jacques Beyssade, former Deputy CEO in charge of Risk, Compliance and Control at Group BCPE (since 2019 Secretary General), and Laurence Bogni-Bartholmé, Chief Risk Officer of Group Lowell.

Thomas Huertas underlines the enormous effects of expectations in economics and finance, including financial stability. The Global Financial Crisis could arguably be attributed to, amongst other causes, the rapid change in expectations regarding businesses considered 'too big to fail', as represented by the collapse of Lehman Brothers. Two of the main legacies of the Global Financial Crisis are usually considered to be the reforms intended to make banks less likely to fail, and to make banks resolvable or 'safe' to fail. The authorities will have to fulfil these expectations.

Agnieszka Smoleńska provides a comprehensive survey of a major legacy of the Global Financial Crisis: the new EU post-crisis regulatory framework for the banking sector. Her analysis emphasizes the distinct character of this new regime which combines elements of bank regulation and corporate governance, which marks a new departure from pre-crisis EU law.

Jacques Beyssade contrasts two facets of the regulatory legacy of the Global Financial Crisis. One is expressed in an accumulation of stricter rules imposed by regulators, which tend to amount to 'more of the same'. The other and ultimately more important one is expressed in codes of conducts and ethics guiding bankers' behaviour, from junior staff to top executives.

Laurence Bogni-Bartholmé considers the legacy of the Global Financial Crisis through the strengthening of banks' and financial institutions' balance-sheet, liquidity and performance. She suggests that this has been achieved through the development of a more holistic risk management; an enhanced risk and corporate governance; and an embedded risk culture – though the banking sector remains exposed to future downturns.

The legacy of the Global Financial Crisis

Readers will thus find much food for thought in the book's thirteen chapters – from different perspectives, with different points of view, with focuses on different aspects of the crisis and its legacy. The second part of this introduction will bring these various threads together, as well as other insights that have been expressed elsewhere, to offer a more synthesized view of the Global Financial Crisis' legacy. We will consider three main issues: risk and governance; regulation; and culture, society and politics. A third and final part will briefly reflect on some connections between the Global Financial Crisis and the still ongoing COVID-19 Crisis.

Risk and governance

More than anything, the financial crisis of 2007–09 revealed a pattern of excessive risk-taking and inadequate capital and liquidity buffers within the financial industry, together with very material shortcomings in the prudential framework notably in Europe and in the United States. At the time, sustained financial market exuberance saw banking assets, credit and profits grow faster than economic activity. This was the heyday of mergers and acquisitions, leveraged buy-outs and in 2007 the bold hubristic acquisition of ABN Amro by the Royal Bank of Scotland, together with Banco Santander and Fortis. In July of the same year Chuck Prince, then CEO of Citibank, noted that global liquidity was enormous and that only a significant disruptive event could create difficulty in the expanding leveraged buyout market; meanwhile he declared: 'As long as the music is playing, you've got to get up and dance . . . and we're still dancing.'

As part of the prevailing business model underpinning this exuberance, banks relied heavily on short-term wholesale markets to fund their expansionary activities, often operating with thin capital and liquidity buffers. Their incentive structures focused on short-term revenue gains over long-term strategic, sustainable business objectives and, critically, the appropriate pricing of risk in transactions. Risk management and control did not feature significantly in bank compensation structures. At times, the risk function was often regarded as little more than an impediment to business growth. This was particularly evidenced by a lack of risk discrimination in credit markets where credit standards were relaxed notably in the sub-prime mortgage market in the US marked by the advent of non-income verification mortgage loans, also known as 'liar loans'.

Revenue-generation from complex products that were heavily reliant on 'black box' modelling included structured securitizations like RMBS and over-the counter (OTC) derivatives. Misaligned incentives between the lenders, originators and the rating agencies in the securitization markets contributed to the sub-prime mortgage crisis.

The risk analysis of these products had been mostly focused on the risks related to short-term price changes in market factors rather than on the risk of unexpected changes in the credit quality of the loans underlying the structured securities.

As set out elsewhere in this book, regulators have responded to the Global Financial Crisis in myriad ways, but mainly by demanding enhanced capital and liquidity standards, stronger supervision and more explicit resolution and recovery frameworks as part of the EU's Bank Recovery and Resolution Directive (BRRD). Stakeholder scrutiny of banks has intensified, and as part of the legacy of the Global Financial Crisis, banks have drawn lessons in terms of their operating environment and have been improving their governance and risk-management practices. These lessons are still being learnt, as noted in Jacques Beyssade's personal testimony of his experiences as a front-line executive in risk management.

One area that *has* changed for the better in the post-financial crisis era has been governance and risk management in banking. In 2008–09, no one would have thought that risk functions could have changed as much as they have in the last ten years. The countless regulations that emerged from the global financial crisis triggered a long overdue change in risk functions in banks. As a result of more detailed and demanding capital, leverage, liquidity and funding requirements as well as much higher standards for risk reporting, such as BCBS 239,[5] banks sought to establish best-practice principles spread across overarching governance and infrastructure, risk-data-aggregation capabilities, risk-reporting practices and supervisory reviews.

Among others, stress testing emerged as a major supervisory tool in parallel with the rise of expectations for detailed bank risk-appetite statements (RAS). Annual internal capital adequacy assessment process (ICAAP) and the internal liquidity adequacy assessment process (ILAAP) reporting were established by the banks and reviewed by supervisors during the annual Supervisory Review and Evaluation Process (SREP). Banks also invested in strengthening their risk cultures and involved their boards more closely in key strategic risk decisions. Banks delineated their three lines of defence and embedded risk-related controls in business processes and procedures.

The post-financial crisis regulated banking landscape, principally led by Basel III, has dictated that banks assess and carefully review their risk frameworks, establish firm-wide risk taxonomies and assess the risk reward impact of strategic decisions on day-to-day business activities.

What was once, pre-crisis, a regulatory and compliance driven function, led by quantitative assessments, has become a more proactive participant in holistic, top-down business strategy underpinned by regular risk and control monitoring processes. As traditional business models are disrupted, not least by crises, the need to manage risk appetites, to develop effective risk frameworks, controls and policies, and to provide advice to boards is higher than ever. This trend has been exemplified over the last ten years by Chief Risk Officers joining the C-suite of executives that have direct reporting and independent access to boards.

---

[5]   BCBS or Basel Committee on Banking Supervision's standard number 239, "Principles for effective risk data aggregation and risk reporting".

A bank culture that sought ever greater market share, profits and bonuses invariably leads to exposures in high-risk activities. By 2008–09, these developments created a breakdown in corporate governance and risk management practices. One of the legacies of the Global Financial Crisis therefore has been the widespread recognition among regulators, supervisors, and financial institutions that, as Beyssade notes, 'Culture and control should go together'.

Since 2008–09, however, elements of a strong risk culture have become more commonplace in financial institutions and include timely information sharing, rapid elevation of any emerging risks, and the willingness to review and challenge practices. In 2016, the FCA introduced the Senior Managers and Certification regime to encourage a change in culture in organizations and strengthen market integrity by making individuals accountable for conduct and competence. The appointments of senior executives like CROs are reviewed and pre-approved by the regulator before candidates take up their roles. The process of 'review and challenge' by boards of executive decision-making has become one of the key aspects of governance monitored by regulators of whether a culture of control and vigorous independent oversight is genuinely embedded in a bank or not.

Additionally, the use of tools such as independent risk-culture surveys by consultants provides a deeper understanding of nuances of risk culture across the organization and ensures sufficient accountability, ownership and involvement from all stakeholders. Increasingly, risk management is also linked to overall performance management objectives. In short, a bank's risk culture can be actively shaped, monitored and sustained by committed organizations.

Post-COVID, with a political focus on banking as a critical actor in mitigating the impact of the pandemic, the implementation and maintenance of an effective, enterprise-wide risk-management framework will remain critical.

Regulation

Financial crises are invariably followed by increased prudential or regulatory oversight. The 1929 stock market crash, along with the ensuing Great Depression, led the US Congress to become concerned that commercial banking operations and the prevailing payments system were incurring losses from particularly volatile equity markets. The Banking Act of 1933 (known as the Glass-Steagall Act) sought to restrict the use of bank credit for speculation and to direct bank credit into what was broadly held to be more productive uses, such as industry, commerce and agriculture. It effectively separated commercial banking from investment banking.

Likewise, the aftermath of the Global Financial Crisis saw a slew of reforms implemented across the international banking regulatory framework. As outlined in this book by Smoleńska and Honohan, these reforms included among others materially increased capital requirements, introduced new liquidity and leverage requirements, and boosted the requirement in terms of loss-absorbing capacity of major banks. Following this wave of reforms, the banking industry did register a significant increase in the amount and quality of equity capital. This has been mostly achieved through capital increases.

By introducing bail-in mechanisms for banks' liabilities, as noted by Honohan, taxpayer liability in support of insolvent banks via government bailouts was reduced. At the same time, to further limit excessive risk-taking, regulators also constrained the variable and deferred components of managers' compensation and introduced bonus clawback clauses.

The introduction of stricter capital and liquidity requirements inevitably also affects the ability of banks to generate an adequate return on their equity. Since the Global Financial Crisis, banks have had to consider the high compliance costs associated with the new regulatory framework.

In fact, a recent report by the ECB highlights the impact on overall profitability in the still highly fragmented EU banking sector[6] challenged not only by stricter regulation but also by high non-performing loan impairments, ongoing pressure on revenues from the post-crisis economic environment and low interest rates. These developments are, if anything, likely to be exacerbated following the COVID pandemic.

Both Papaconstantinou and Smoleńska draw attention to the so called 'doom loop' at work during the 2010–12 sovereign debt crisis in countries such as Greece, Spain, Portugal and Italy. The workings of this 'doom loop' are fairly straightforward: a deterioration of the sovereign creditworthiness directly contributes to a decrease in the value of banks' holding of government bonds. This in turn reduces banks' solvency, which leads them to cut back on their lending activities if their regulatory capital is negatively affected by the decrease in the market value of their sovereign bond portfolios.

The current prudential regulatory framework's capital and liquidity requirements actually provide a strong incentive for banks to hold domestic government bonds, and consequently there have been a number of proposals aimed at limiting this vicious circle between sovereign debt and banks.

Indeed, in 2015 the Basel Committee set up a task force to critically discuss the existing proposals and come up with possible amendments to the regulatory treatment of sovereign exposures, including the introduction of risk weights for domestic sovereign bonds and limits for bank limits of holdings of domestic sovereign bonds. These proposals and other ongoing regulatory debates only reinforces that after 10 years, the regulatory wave 'which the crisis had triggered and which sought to correct ex post the pre-crisis shortcomings never seems to have ended' (Gortsos 2015).

Culture society and politics

The socio-cultural and political legacies of the crisis are harder to identify. Nevertheless, the effects of a global financial crisis, followed by a deep recession and, in Europe, a currency crisis, reach far beyond the economic domain. But should these effects be considered as a legacy of the crisis? Increased inequality is a case in point. There is clear

---

[6] ECB – *SSM thematic review on profitability and business models. Report on the outcome of the assessment*, September 2018.

evidence that inequalities have continued to rise in advanced economies, with austerity policies affecting the poorest, and monetary policies (low interest rates and quantitative easing result in higher stock market returns) benefiting the richest. Ten years after the collapse of Lehman Brothers, this could be considered either as a legacy of the crisis or as trend that was accelerated by the crisis – with in both cases the possibility of a reversal taking place in the medium to long term.

The same can be said about populism, the rise of which has undoubtedly been fuelled by the socio-economic impact of the crisis, but very unevenly from country to country: it is a complex phenomenon that cannot be directly and solely attributed to the Global Financial Crisis. Dorothee Bohle provide an insightful framework of analysis by identifying four policy responses to the crisis: a left-wing one, which aims to reduce inequality, and a right-wing one, which tolerates it; and within left and right, an international integrationist current and a sovereign nationalist one (see Figures 6.1 and 6.2). The result show that mainstream neoliberal responses favouring international integration and tolerating inequality remained largely dominant in Europe's peripheral (that is, smaller and poorer) countries – the resilience of neoliberalism, the integrationist right, appears as puzzling as the failure of social-democracy, the integrationist left. The success of the nationalist right, as in Hungary, and the failure of the nationalist left, as in Greece, are the result of a set of specific conditions amongst which the financial crisis played a significant role.

The Global Financial Crisis did not leave a lasting legacy on the international financial order. The weight of East Asia in world finance had been steadily growing since the beginning of the new century (China) and before (Japan, the Asian Tigers), but ten years after the Global Financial Crisis, New York and London remained firmly in place at the top of the hierarchy of international financial centres (GFCI 2018). Here again, we have a long-term trend which was somewhat accelerated by the crisis, but not in a way comparable to the effects of a major war. In the past, major conflicts have had devastating effects on such centres as Amsterdam (Napoleonic Wars), Frankfurt (Austro-Prussian War), or Berlin (Second World War).

On the other hand, the Global Financial Crisis *did* have a profound effect on Europe – the main area of interest in this volume. The crisis was an extremely violent shock, which tested to the limit the strengths and weaknesses of Europe's monetary Union, and ultimately of the European Union itself, and resulted in mixed legacies. Pervenche Berès provides an engaged assessment of the situation ten years after the initial shock. On the credit side, she sees a series of institutional improvements in the fields of macro and micro supervision and regulation, as well as economic governance,[7] together with the European Central Bank acting as 'a major federative institution'. These points are well documented in Agnieszka Smoleńska's chapter. On the debit side, there are mainly missed opportunities – to address the issues of social inequalities, of long-term

---

[7]   In particular, the establishment of the European Systemic Risk Board (ESRB) at macro level, and the three European Supervisory Authorities (ESAs) at micro level; the creation of the banking union anchored in the Single Supervisory Mechanism (SSM), Single Resolution Board (SRB) and European Deposit Guarantee Scheme (EDGS); and the establishment of the European Stability Mechanism (ESM) in order to address the Greek crisis.

investment, to question the stability pact, to establish the EU's much vaunted Capital Markets Union[8] to reform economic governance.

A more enduring legacy, included in Berès's overall balance sheet, is the economic and social divergence within the European Union, in particular between its core and periphery, which has been aggravated by the Global Financial Crisis. This point, and more specifically the case of the GIPS (Greece, Italy, Portugal and Spain), is discussed in a more technical way by Ramon Marimon in his analysis of the debt and stimulus packages and the role of linkages in crises, above all the financial-monetary-fiscal linkage. It is also discussed in an political economic way by George Papaconstantinou, who shows how the focus on fiscal rather than banking issues during the Greek crisis extended beyond Greece, forcing weak European economies in particular to adopt austerity policies during a recession.

Ultimately, when considering the legacy of the Global Financial Crisis, the question must be: what has really changed after the crisis? What difference, if any, did it make? Here, comparisons with the Great Depression are difficult to avoid, though they are not as obvious as might appear at first sight. One point is clear: the Great Depression was an epoch-changing moment in history in a way that the Global Financial Crisis and the Great Recession cannot claim to be.

In terms of economic policy, the Great Depression marked a break with the nineteenth century's predominantly laissez-faire attitude, which continued throughout the 1920s despite the break of the First World War. There were differences between countries, but this was clearly a general trend. The break is particularly visible in the far higher level of state intervention in the economy, including widespread nationalizations, in a number of countries, and Keynesian contra-cyclical economic policies aiming at ensuring full employment; a steep deglobalization, with the introduction of exchange controls and the collapse of international capital flows; a much more tightly controlled financial sector, sometimes described as 'financial repression' or 'boring banking'; a new monetary order established in 1944 at Bretton Woods. Beyond these specific though far-ranging measures, the legacy of the Great Depression can be characterized by the emergence of a new zeitgeist, favouring state intervention and financial stability, that was to last for nearly half a century.[9]

The Global Financial Crisis has left no such legacy. The massive state intervention that followed the collapse of Lehman Brothers, including the quasi-nationalizations of banks in several countries, was destined to prevent the collapse of the international financial system and to prevent the Great Recession turning into a new Great Depression, not as a break with the neo-liberal order of the preceding thirty years or so. The state retreated once these two risks had been avoided.

Interestingly, the regulatory measures introduced after the crisis, which are discussed above and in great detail (for the European Union) in Agnieszka Smoleńska's

---

[8] EU 'A New Vision for Europe's Capital Markets. Final Report of the High Level Forum on the Capital Markets Union', June 2020.

[9] There is a huge literature dealing with the transformations brought about by the 'Thirty Years War' of the twentieth century. Here are four very different books: Van der Wee (1986), Hobsbawm (1994), Crafts and Toniolo (1996), Judt (2005).

chapter, went beyond those introduced during the Great Depression – with the possible exception of the Glass-Steagall Act of 1933, which profoundly transformed the American banking system. Altogether, banking legislation during the Great Depression was more timid in most European countries.[10] Recent regulations have been more intrusive and required far more regulatory compliance, governance and enhanced control and oversight by risk officers. This appears to be the main legacy of the Global Financial Crisis: a set of banking regulations and improved risk management resulting in better capitalized and probably safer banks, not a transformed financial system.

The culture has changed only partly, especially outside banks. The incentives to take risks with other people's money have not been entirely eradicated, top bankers' packages, including bonuses – though they have been capped in the European Union in 2014 – have remained over-inflated, mainly though not only in the United States. There have been many suggestions to reform the industry's incentive structure, including one in Charles Goodhart's chapter proposing to distinguish between a class of 'insiders' within the firm's top managers, who would be subject to multiple liabilities, and a class of 'outsiders', who would retain limited liability. However, they have all remained suggestions. Banks might have been tamed, though not to the same extent as their forerunners during the Great Depression, but other players, such as asset managers, have risen to new prominence, as underlined by Gerald Baumgartner, and the shadow banking system based in part on hedge funds is alive and kicking.

The other compelling comparison is with the financial instability of the early 1970s, marked by the return of financial crises (secondary banking crisis in Britain, collapse of the Herstatt Bank in Germany, failure of the Franklin National Bank in the United States), the end of Bretton Woods, the oil shock, the first recession since the Second World War, and a period of 'stagflation'.[11] The crisis of the 1970s marked another epochal change: the beginning of the gradual dismantling of the legacy of the Great Depression, with the mounting challenge to Keynesianism by monetarism, a wave of financial liberalization starting in the 1980s and culminating in the repeal of the Glass-Steagall Act in 1999, and more generally the advent of a neo-liberal view of the economy and of society advocating a smaller state and the strengthening of market mechanisms.

This is a strong legacy, which has not been matched by that of the Global Financial Crisis. There have been contestations but no undoing of the main tenets of the neo-liberal order – which had differed between countries and had seen shifting attitudes and policies over the years. Globalization has been dented but has not ended and, as we have seen, the financial system has remained fundamentally unchanged. This might be a good thing or a bad thing, but in terms of legacy, it is in sharp contrast with previous global financial shocks.

---

[10] There was no banking law in Britain; universal banking survived in Germany despite the country having suffered the most severe banking crisis of the 1930s, as well as in Austria and Switzerland, though not in Italy and Belgium; France enacted a separation between commercial and investment banking, but the separation existed de facto if not *de jure* since the 1880s.

[11] In addition to the books dealing with post 1945 Europe quoted above, see more specifically on the 1970s Ferguson et al. (2010).

How to explain this contrast? As far as the Great Depression is concerned, it should be borne in mind that the shock of the Great Depression was far more extreme than that of the Global Financial Crisis; on the other hand, the legacy of the Great Depression has to be viewed in its proper context. It was the result of an exceptional historical period marked by two world wars, the redrawing of international boundaries, a devastating economic crisis, massive political upheavals and shifts in ideological outlooks – the 'Thirty Years War' of the twentieth century. Many of the measures of state intervention that characterize the third quarter of the twentieth century came into effect after the Second World War, especially in Europe. On a smaller scale, the same is true of the 1970s crisis: it was a broad phenomenon, and posed new economic challenges: stagflation, the recycling of the petrodollars, the decline of the old industries and the end of the Fordist model of production and regulation.

The Global Financial Crisis was a financial crisis of huge proportions, which caused the outbreak of a deep recession and led to a sovereign debt crisis in the eurozone. But it was not accompanied by other major economic or political mutations. Avoiding a catastrophe required decisive action, but the tools were developed drawing on the experience of the Great Depression and from advances in macroeconomics. Finance might have become dangerously overgrown, but the passage to a post-industrial society was already well underway and heavily relied on the industries of the third industrial revolution, information technology and bio technologies – financial technology (FinTech) really took off after the Global Financial Crisis and without much connection to it. In this context, it is not surprising that, ten years after the outbreak of the Global Financial Crisis, its legacy should primarily consist in an improved supervision, regulation, and management of the financial system, above all the banks, rather than in a turning point in economic or even financial history.

But will the same conclusion be reached on its fifteenth or twentieth anniversaries, by September 2023 or 2028? A tenth anniversary is still a short- to medium-term distance to the past and history does not stop there. The legacies of the Great Depression and the crisis of the 1970s took longer to unfold. What could make the Global Financial Crisis part of an epochal moment is the COVID-19 crisis, which broke out just over eleven years after the collapse of Lehman Brothers, but when the scars of the Global Financial Crisis had not entirely healed. The two crises are, of course, different, but they also present some similarities, especially in terms of policy responses. A brief discussion of the coronavirus crisis should help put the legacy of the Global Financial Crisis into a different perspective.

The COVID-19 Crisis

There has been much debate on whether the current coronavirus pandemic and the Global Financial Crisis are comparable. What are the similarities, notably in terms of policy responses, between a fast-moving and unprecedented health pandemic that has engulfed the world, causing untold human as well as economic misery, and a much slower-moving financial crisis after 2007 that to all intents and purposes impacted mainly the developed world?

Thus, following the sub-prime problems in 2006, European financial institutions only started to have problems in the summer of 2007, with Bear Stearns rescued in early 2008 and Lehman's collapse in September 2008. For the most part, the Global Financial Crisis unfolded gradually, even if widespread panic followed the collapse of Lehman Brothers. The pandemic and its impact globally, however, have been much more dramatic.

Interestingly, both crises were initially viewed as specifically local events. In the case of the Global Financial Crisis, it was the US's sub-prime mortgages that were seen as idiosyncratic to that country's real estate market and unlikely to impact Europe whilst the outbreak of the coronavirus in a Wuhan 'wet market' was seen as a largely containable public health problem akin to SARS that, at worst, would have only a limited regional impact.

However, one of the key outcomes of the Global Financial Crisis in terms of policy responses, as underlined by Catherine Schenk, has been the increased recognition that when faced with a global crisis, a massive intervention by government is needed and that ideally, this intervention should be international and coordinated to be really effective. As noted by Schenk, 'the mobilization of the G20 in November 2008 seemed to signal finally the acceptance beyond lip service of the wider governance of the global economy'.

Following the COVID-19 outbreak and in recognition of Draghi's remark[12] during the eurozone crisis that the 'ECB would do whatever it takes' to support the euro, governments have acted not only 'to flatten the [corona-virus] curve' and to address public health concerns, but also to stave off long lasting economic scarring by providing a wide range of guarantees, loan repayment moratoria and other fiscal measures to support financial and non-financial businesses.

In terms of monetary policy, central banks responded rather quicker to the COVID-19 crisis than during the Global Financial Crisis albeit not quite in the same coordinated manner as outlined by Schenk. Policy responses have varied in size and scope, ranging from outright moratoria to state guarantees of varying modest degrees underpinning businesses or supporting employment via various furlough schemes. For example, during March 2020, the FRB and ECB were ahead of governments by lowering interest rates, extending loan facilities, or lowering collateral standards for those seeking central bank emergency funding, such as that offered by the Pandemic Emergency Purchase Programme (PEPP). Macro-prudential policies including lower capital buffers and provisions on non-performing loans (NPLs) were eased if covered by government guarantees.

An important difference between the two crises is that COVID-19 did not originate in the financial sector, which is in healthier shape than it was a decade ago as a result of post-crisis changes to manage systemic risk, as discussed earlier in this introduction.

Thus the Fed drew upon the lessons learnt during the Global Financial Crisis when global liquidity was constrained at times and in March 2020 made dollar swap lines available for up to six months to a larger number of central banks than ten years ago to

---

[12] Mario Draghi, Speech at the Global Investment Conference in London 26 July 2012 (https://www.ecb.europa.eu/press/key/date/2012/html/sp120726.en.html).

ensure ongoing functioning of the international dollar-dependent financial markets. The European banks alone borrowed $130 billion within days after the swap line was reopened and as noted by Schenk, this time the geographic spread of Fed support was not only increased beyond the 2008 scheme but it also included a new repurchase ('repo') facility.

In March 2020, the ECB announced that it would buy an additional €120 billion under its asset purchase programme (APP) or QE and within a few days it then launched the €750 billion PEPP, which will last until the coronavirus crisis period is over. The PEPP is 'a new temporary asset purchase programme of private and public sector securities to counter the serious risks to the monetary policy transmission mechanism and the outlook for the euro area posed by the outbreak and escalating diffusion of the coronavirus, COVID-19'.[13] Unlike the APP, the assets to be bought under the PEPP will also include commercial paper issued by non-financial corporations.

Critically, the ECB in early March 2020 announced that banks could use the capital and liquidity buffers they have accumulated in recent years to lend to consumers, businesses and other banks, noting that as European banks had built strong capital positions in the wake of the Global Financial Crisis to withstand exogenous shocks like COVID-19, they should now be able to support the economy. This change amounts to €120 billion in new capital to be used to absorb losses or finance up to €1.8 trillion of lending. The regulator instructed banks to use their additional capital to support the economy and not to increase dividends or share buybacks at least until October 2020.[14] But as the crisis deepened, the ECB announced the following month the launch of pandemic emergency long-term refinancing operations (PELTROs), which will provide liquidity to banks and money market funds until September 2021.

At the time of the Global Financial Crisis, liquidity facilities and large-scale asset purchases (LSAP) or QE were introduced only progressively by the Fed throughout the crisis in a measured response to the turmoil in the financial markets: this time, however, the rapid and overwhelming response (often daily) by regulators to the alarming speed with which the pandemic and its impact spread globally reflected the lessons learned and experience gained from the financial crisis.

Banks are now part of the solution to the COVID-19 crisis, rather than part of the problem: governments have relied on the banks as the transmission agents of choice to distribute crisis loans and grants to businesses and organisations. At the same time, the EU banking sector remains highly fragmented, characterized by low profitability and operational capabilities that will undoubtedly be severely tested. As the COVID crisis continues, vulnerabilities could emerge in banks' balance sheets and government guarantees come to an end, many of the expanding number of COVID-19 crisis loans may have to be extended or will not be repaid. Notwithstanding that banks now have more flexibility on what loans to classify as non-performing and can also set aside less capital to cover losses from non-performing loans, at some stage these supportive measures will need to be unwound.

[13] See https://www.ecb.europa.eu/press/pr/date/2020/html/ecb.pr200318_1~3949d6f266.en.html
[14] See. https://www.iif.com/Portals/0/Files/Databases/COVID-19_regulatory_measures.pdf

At that point, the non-performing loans that arise from the COVID-19 crisis will be added to the banks' existing legacy portfolios of NPLs dating from the Global Financial Crisis, especially if the post-COVID recovery is slow and unevenly spread across sectors within the economy. Regulators may then need to have a moratorium on implementation of yet further structural reforms, recognize some of the recent 'regulatory fatigue' prevalent in the financial sector occasioned by, for example, MIFID II, and consider that the financial sector can now also be a positive agent for change once the worst of the pandemic is over.

Despite their differences, there are obvious connections between the two crises and the legacy of Global Financial Crisis – what was remembered of and learned from it – appears to have been of some use during the coronavirus crisis. And these lessons might be of even greater use if banks were to be more severely tested by the COVID-19 crisis. At the same time, and somewhat paradoxically, there is a risk that the coronavirus crisis could lead us to forget the Global Financial Crisis. The fact that banks are safer in 2020 than 2008 and part of the solution to the crisis rather than the cause should not conceal the fact that bankers' reckless behaviour was a major contributory factor in the outbreak of the Global Financial Crisis. This memory must not fade, as the same could happen again.

The legacy of the Global Financial Crisis could also change in another way, by morphing with that of the COVID-19 crisis. The two crises have followed each other in relatively short succession, with problems raised by the former not yet solved by the time of the outbreak of the latter: think, for example, of bank's non-performing loans, the sequels of austerity policies, or the level of public debt. We might be soon talking of the dual crisis of the early twenty-first century and reflect on its wide-ranging legacy regarding, in particular, social inequalities, the environment and the role of the state – as well as a more efficient financial system.

References

Aliber, Robert Z., and Gylfi Zoega, eds. 2018. *The 2008 Global Financial Crisis in Retrospect: Causes of the Crisis and National Regulatory Responses*. London: Palgrave Macmillan.

Arner, Douglas W., Emilios Avgouleas, Danny Busch and Steven L. Schwarcz, eds. 2019. *Systemic Risk in the Financial Sector: Ten Years After the Great Crash*. Waterloo, ON: Centre for International Governance Innovation.

Assmann, Jan. 2008. 'Communicative and Cultural Memory.' In Astrid Erll and Ansgar Nünning (eds), *Cultural Memory Studies: An International and Interdisciplinary Handbook* 109–18. Berlin/New York: Walter de Gruyter.

Ball, Laurence M. 2018. *The Fed and Lehman Brothers: Setting the Record Straight on a Financial Disaster*. Cambridge: Cambridge University Press.

Bernanke, Ben, Timothy F. Geithner and Henry M. Paulsen Jr. 2018. *Firefighting: The Financial Crisis and its Lessons*. New York: Penguin Books.

Cassis, Youssef. 2008. *Crises and Opportunities. The Shaping of Modern Finance*. Oxford: Oxford University Press.

Craft, Nicholas, and Gianni Toniolo. 1996. *Economic Growth in Europe since 1945*. Oxford: Oxford University Press.

D'Arista, Jane. 2018. *All Fall Down: Debt, Deregulation and Financial Crises*. Cheltenham, UK: Edward Elgar Publishing.

Eichengreen, Barry, and Kevin O'Rourke. 'A tale of two depressions: what do the new data tell us?' *Vox-EU*, 2009, several updates.

Erll, Astrid. 2010. 'Cultural Memory Studies: An Introduction.' In Astrid Erll and Ansgar Nünning (eds), *A Companion to Cultural Memory Studies*, 1–15. Berlin/New York: de Gruyter.

Ferguson, Niall, Charles S. Maier, Erez Manela and Daniel J. Sargent, eds. 2010. *The Shock of the Global: The 1970s in Perspective*. Cambridge, MA and London: The Belknap Press of Harvard University Press.

Foot, John. 2010. *The Archipelago: Italy since 1945*. London: Bloomsbury.

Global Policy, 9, 51, 2018, Special Issue: Ten years after the Global Financial Crisis

Goodhart, Charles A.E., and Dimitrios P. Tsomocos, eds. 2019. *Financial Regulation and Stability: Lessons from the Global Financial Crisis*. Cheltenham, UK: Edward Elgar Publishing.

Gortsos, Christos V. 2015. 'The crisis-based European Union financial regulatory intervention: are we on top of the prudential wave?' *ERA Forum* 16 (1): 89–110.

Halbwachs, Maurice. 1925. *Les cadres sociaux de la mémoire*. Paris: Presses universitaires de France.

Halbwachs, Maurice. 1950. *La mémoire collective*. Paris: Presses universitaires de France.

Hobsbawm, Eric. J. 1994. *Age of Extremes: The Short Twentieth Century 1914–1991*. London: Michael Joseph.

Judt, Tony. 2005. *Postwar: A History of Europe since 1945*. London: William Heinemann.

O'Halloran, Sharyn, and Thomas Groll. 2019. *After the Crash: Financial Crises and Regulatory Responses*. New York: Columbia University Press.

Tooze, Adam. 2018. *Crashed: How a Decade of Financial Crises Changed the World*. London: Allen Lane.

Van der Wee, Herman. 1986. *Prosperity and Upheaval: The World Economy 1945–1980*. New York: Viking.

Part One

Perspectives on the Global Financial Crisis

1

Moral Hazard and Equity Finance: Why Policy has been Sub-optimal since the Global Financial Crisis

C.A.E. Goodhart

Introduction

Whereas this chapter was written before the coronavirus pandemic struck, I see no reason to amend or alter any of its contents and arguments. Its thesis is that macroeconomic policy remained sub-optimal in the years between the Great Financial Crisis and the onset of COVID-19. The main reason why this has been so is that there has been a generalized failure to appreciate the moral hazard that was introduced into the modern capitalist economy by the legal institution of limited liability for all equity holders. The incentive structure induced by limited liability has led corporate managers, notably bank managers, to seek excessive risk and leverage in the pursuit of return on equity (RoE), egged on by shareholders. There has been a tendency to accuse bankers of moral failings; whereas there is little evidence that bankers are significantly different from other humans, except, perhaps, in having better numerical and computational skills. An associated failing has been to anthropomorphize banks, and treat them as if they were human beings, whereas non-sentient institutions banks have no emotions and cannot make decisions; only bankers can do that. While the policy measures of requiring banks, especially larger banks (SIFIs), to hold significantly more equity capital, has been correct and helpful, the failure to deal with the underlying moral hazard has meant that bankers still have a strong incentive, in pursuit of RoE, to avoid or evade, and manipulate, the regulations, rather than internalize the optimal level of social risk-taking. Section 1 gives a fuller analysis of the implications of the moral hazard inherent in limited liability for all equity shareholders.

This has been one of the factors, amongst several, which has led to investment ratios remaining low, and a surplus developing for the non-financial corporate sectors, in many of our countries, despite the extraordinarily expansionary monetary policies and the high corporate profitability enjoyed by the corporate sectors in most advanced countries. This is documented and further described in Section 2. Again, whereas the expansionary monetary policy was certainly a great improvement on doing nothing, nevertheless it has been accompanied by relatively low investment, stagnant productivity and low wage growth.

This has also led our economies to fall into a debt trap. Although the leverage ratios of banking sectors, and of households in those countries most affected by the Global Financial Crisis, have been pared back, the debt ratios of non-financial corporates and of the public sector have, in many, perhaps even most, cases risen sharply during the last ten years. Such debt ratios have grown so large that it will be difficult for central banks to raise interest rates significantly, or fast, without increasing debt service payments to a level that will potentially place corporate solvency at risk, or in the case of the public sector, be yet another factor leading to the need for increased taxation, with worsening intergenerational inequality. This is discussed in Section 3.

I conclude in Section 4 by suggesting alternative policies which could help to extract us from this debt trap. This has two main planks, both of which involve institutional change, with the purpose of bringing about a major shift in the financial structure of our economies towards equity finance, and away from debt finance.

The first institutional change would be to eliminate the fiscal advantage that debt finance currently enjoys over equity finance. This has already been proposed, and suggestions made as to how this might be introduced first, in the Mirrlees' book, *Tax By Design: The Mirrlees Review* (2011), and, second, in the paper on 'Destination Based Cash Flow Taxation' (often otherwise called 'Border Taxation', see Auerbach et al. 2017a and b).

The second institutional change would involve introducing a legal distinction within equity finance, whereby there are separate categories of shareholders. The first category would involve insiders, i.e. those who have both inside information and the ability either to influence or control the decisions which the corporations makes. These would have multiple liability, possibly, in the case of the CEO, unlimited liability. The second category would be outsiders, who have neither inside information, nor the ability to influence or to control corporate decisions. They would retain limited liability, as at present. The case for doing this is set out in greater length in the associated paper by Professor Rosa Lastra and myself, 'Equity Finance: Matching Liability to Power' (*Journal of Financial Regulation*, March 2020). Again, an alternative would be to require the same set of insiders to be paid primarily in bail-inable debt; see T. Huertas, 'Pay to Play' (2019).

1. The moral hazard of limited liability

A consequence of limited liability for shareholders is that the return to their investment, as a function of the profitability of the firm in which they have an equity share, is flat when the company is doing badly or becomes insolvent, but slopes upwards strongly when the public company is doing well. This is shown graphically in Figure 1.1 below.

With a return structure of this kind, the shareholders are led to prefer a riskier strategy, as shown in the figure, with an even chance of an outcome of A and B receiving a return equal to the mean profit to the corporation of AB, rather than a completely safe policy, as shown in the diagram at point C. So, shareholders have an innate preference to encourage management to take on riskier activities. Such shareholder

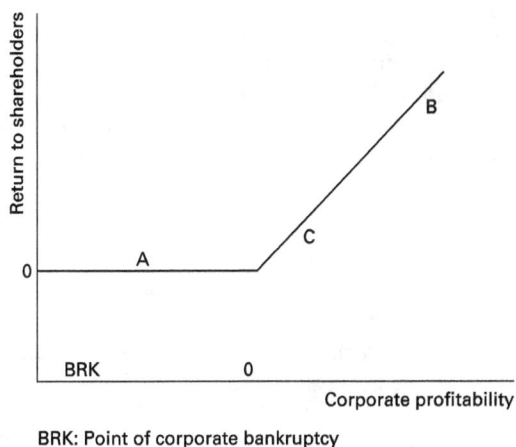

Figure 1.1 Corporate bankruptcy.

preference for risk is somewhat abated by loss aversion; see, for example, Kahneman (2012). But that, in turn, is reduced by appropriate diversification, so that the loss involved on any single portfolio holding is limited. So, the implication is that limited liability naturally leads shareholders to push management to adopt riskier strategies than would be socially optimal.

In earlier decades, before the 1990s, this pressure on management was mitigated by the fact that managers were primarily paid by a cash salary unrelated to equity valuation. Moreover, other considerations, such as reputation and pride in developing a successful company over the long term, had the effect of constraining managers willingness to take on risk. But one of the other possible incentives on managerial behaviour, as a result, was to spend resources on activities that might bolster managerial reputation and personal comfort, rather than maximizing profits. Such considerations involved size and spending money on managerial perks, including not only such perks as company planes and chauffeur-driven cars, but also fancy, prestigious architecture, head offices, etc. The cry went up, as a result, that managerial incentives should become better aligned with the interests of shareholders, possibly one of the worst ideas developed by academic economists in recent decades!

Partly in response to public attitudes then, about soaring managerial pay and perks, President Clinton introduced measures in 1993,

> when he effectively set a $1 million limit on directors' pay by making anything above that level non-tax deductible for companies. However, in the small print of his legislation, was a clause that specified payments with performance conditions were exempt from the $1 million rule. That effectively meant company boards boosted all salaries to $1 million and paid bonuses and extras in stock options that directors could cash in for shares at a later date. This prompted an explosion in executive awards . . .
>
> Hargreaves 2018: 77

The result of such alignment of managerial incentives with those of shareholders, in some large part done consciously, resulted in there being the exact same incentive on management to give priority to policies that would maximize equity valuation; naturally this would generally lead them to pursue additional risk. Moreover, the expected lifetime incumbency of most CEOs is relatively short – five years or less – and that means that the incentive on them is to maximize short-term equity valuations. This can most easily be achieved by accepting a riskier financial structure, e.g. buybacks to increase leverage and raise RoE, reducing employee headcount and cutting out such longer-term investment, notably in R&D, the return on which was unlikely to become clear for a long time.[1]

So, the criticism of modern capitalism has several facets; it is argued that it leads to managers assuming excessive risk, being overpaid and failing to undertake sufficient long-term investment, especially R&D. The first two criticisms, excessive risk and excessive pay, were particularly levied at banks and other financial intermediaries in the aftermath of the Global Financial Crisis. There have been a variety of proposals aimed at checking or preventing such malfunctions. One set of such proposals has focussed on limiting the business structures of banks and other financial intermediaries. Examples of such proposals include narrow banking in various guises, ringfencing of core retail financial structures and a variety of other regulatory measures. A recent addition to this set is by Conti-Brown (2012), arguing for the abolition of limited liability for SIFIs, unless they become very highly capitalized.

Another set of responses, aimed more widely at the general governance structure of (public) corporations, has considered such remedies as two-tier governing boards, as can be seen in the German system, and changing the statutory duty of governing boards, for example as argued by Schwarcz (2014).

A third, and final, set of proposals, including those in the accompanying paper by myself and Rosa Lastra, would adjust the link aligning the interests of shareholders and managers, by imposing additional duties on managers, either through tougher legal requirements (see Kokkinis 2018), or by changing the incentive and remuneration terms for management.

2. Why has non-financial corporate investment been so low?

Ever since the financial panic accompanying the Global Financial Crisis abated in 2009, conditions for the corporate sectors in most advanced economies have become extremely favourable. The share of corporate profits in national income over the years 2010–17 has increased strongly in most countries, Italy being an exception, and has become much higher than during the years 1990–2005.

---

[1]　There is a counter-argument pointing to the high stock market valuations of tech companies which during their early lives can be expected to pay out nothing; with the implication that this shows that shareholders and management do give proper full valuation to longer-term future returns. But the prospects for such companies are inherently risky, and it is the lure of potentially massive future returns, with an offsetting significant probability of total collapse, that attracts investors, rather than the long-term nature of their activities per se.

During these same recent years interest rates, both real and nominal, have declined sharply, and equity valuations have increased in a continuing bull market, except in Japan. Under these circumstances, one might have expected that fixed investment would have increased strongly. Instead, however, investment ratios in western economies have remained stagnant, although the investment ratio in China has remained elevated. The result is that the non-financial corporate sectors in several advanced western economies have been in surplus in recent decades. The main exception is China, where investment has continued apace, largely financed by higher debt.

During the last thirty or so years, there has been a major demographic shift and sweet spot, whereby the working population has increased sharply relative to their dependents, the young below twenty, and the old above sixty. With increasing expectations of both longer lives and higher working incomes, this has led to a strong increase in the personal sector savings ratio in most countries. With both the non-financial corporate sector and the personal sector being net savers and in surplus, the inevitable counterpart, in order to keep our economies in balance, has had to be, on a worldwide basis, an increase in the public sector deficit. Of course, in individual countries, such as Germany and certain oil-producing countries, the combined surplus of the corporate and personal sectors can be matched and off-set by the deficit of the Rest of the World to them, i.e. by their positive current account balance. But that just shifts the matching need for public sector deficits worldwide onto those countries running current account deficits. In this respect, the accusations of President Trump that the US deficit was in some large part a consequence of the policies followed by current account surplus countries has some merit.

Even though the demographic sweet spot will now be rapidly disappearing in most western countries and in China, as it already has in Japan, it will be difficult to cut back on public sector deficit finance, especially given the need for pensions and health care of the massively expanding cohorts of the elderly, so long as the investment ratios of the advanced economies remain so low.

So, a key question is what has caused such investment ratios to be so low, despite the otherwise favourable circumstances that have seemed to have held during recent years? There are several competing explanations, none of which are mutually exclusive, and all of which may have played some role in this. There are, perhaps, four main candidates as explanations. These are:

1. Growing corporate concentration and monopolization
2. Technology
3. Managerial incentives
4. Cheap labour

Growing corporate monopolization

There is some evidence, mostly relating to the United States, that there has been an increasing degree of concentration and monopolization in the corporate sector; see, for example, Autor et al. (2017a and b) and Philippon (2019). If so, then that would lead to higher profit margins, a greater share of profits in national income than otherwise, and lower investment. In a NBER Working Paper, Liu et al. (January 2019) have argued that the continuation of very low interest rates has itself led to greater market concentration, reduced dynamism and slower productivity growth. Also, see the references to the earlier literature on the relationship between lower interest rates and the rise in industry concentration and higher corporate profit share, included in footnote 2 on page 5 of that paper.

Technology

The leading sector currently comprises technological companies, which rely much more on human capital than on fixed capital in the form of steel, buildings, heavy machinery, etc. The development of software, for example, requires a lot of human skills and effort, but relatively little fixed investment. Insofar as technology is shifting the balance towards human capital and away from fixed investment, the ratio of expenditures on fixed capital to total revenues and output is likely to decline, possibly quite sharply.

Managerial incentives

As already noted, in Section 1, the alignment of managerial incentives with those of shareholders enjoying limited liability is likely to lead to a focus by managers on maximizing short-term equity values. This can be done most easily by buybacks, i.e. using profits to increase leverage by substituting debt for equity; but short-term profitability can also be enhanced by cutting back on longer-term fixed investment and R&D. This line of argument has been stressed by Smithers in several books (see Smithers 2009 and 2013).

Labour has become cheap

The combination of globalization and the demographic sweet spot has led to an unprecedented jump in the available global supply of workers within the world trading system. Why invest in expensive equipment at home, in order to raise productivity, when one can increase output at lower cost by shifting production abroad, e.g. to China or Eastern Europe, or employ immigrants? Meanwhile competition from such potential outsourcing, and inward migration, has reduced the power of private sector trade unions, and held down real wages over the last few decades. Under these conditions, investment has migrated to those countries where labour has been particularly cheap, and has taken the form of labour-using and capital-saving techniques.

What the balance might be between these four explanations is not easy to discern, and I make no attempt to do so here. But I think that all these potential explanations have merit, perhaps particularly the final two, that managerial incentives have been, from the point of view of society as a whole, misaligned, and that investment in most western economies has been held down by the shift of production to China and Eastern Europe.

The trends of globalization and of demography are now beginning to reverse. Populism and protectionism have become powerful political influences in the context of economies where real wages have stagnated over the last thirty years. Meanwhile, the demographic sweet spot, leading to a massive increase in the workforce and fall in dependency ratios, is on the verge of reversing sharply, as has already happened in Japan. This will have the effect of raising real wages in most western economies, and that is likely to lead business owners to invest more in order to raise productivity and to hold down unit labour costs.

But insofar as the low investment ratio has been due to the short-termism of managers, owing to the incentive structure under which they operate, this particular cause of low fixed investment will continue.

What has happened over the last decade has been that a combination of exceptionally low interest rates – combined with low fixed investment, and an incentive to issue debt rather than equity – has led to a massive increase in leverage and debt ratios for most countries and most sectors. There are a few exceptions to the generalized increase in debt ratios. Thus the banking sectors in most economies have reduced leverage under the influence of stronger regulation. The personal sectors in those countries most hit by the housing boom/bust cycle, e.g. US/UK/Ireland/Spain, have mostly reduced their debt ratios, and debt ratios in Germany have generally gone down. But for the rest, debt ratios have generally increased, though the balance between the rising ratios for the corporate, personal and public sectors have varied from country to country.

This has been leading the advanced economies of the world into a debt trap. We turn to this next.

3. The debt trap, and how to escape it

As noted above, debt ratios – that is, the ratio of debt to GDP – have been rising for most sectors in most countries (with the exception of the banking sector and Germany), and now stand at a level considerably higher than at the time of the Global Financial Crisis in 2008–09. This has not, so far, led to any great difficulties for debtors, because the decline in interest rates has, more or less exactly, offset the increase in the debt ratios, leaving debt-service payments roughly constant as a ratio to GDP. Thus the debt-service ratio for the public sectors has, in most countries, remained roughly constant and, similarly, with profits remaining high, the debt to surplus ratio for non-financial corporates has remained stable. But the rising debt ratios could make servicing such debt increasingly uncomfortable as and when nominal real interest rates rise, and corporate profitability declines. Indeed, the increase in debt ratios has been so great that there is a danger that we have *already* entered a debt trap.

The debt trap operates as follows. The financial fragility of an over-indebted world economy is such that it may well preclude any sharp or significant rise in nominal interest rates, out of a (possibly justified) fear that any such increases in rates would lead to financial difficulties among major sectors so extensive that a further recession might be provoked. This would, in turn, have adverse fiscal consequences. But if rates, therefore, have got to be kept low, with only gradual increases, that will lead to financial conditions under which borrowers will consider it still advantageous to raise further debt, thereby possibly increasing debt ratios further still.

So how could we get out of this debt trap? The best, and most attractive, way of doing so is by faster real growth. If real growth is greater than the level of real interest rates, then, with a zero sectoral deficit, the debt ratios would inevitably be falling. Indeed, if real growth is sufficiently high relative to real interest rates, the sectoral deficit can become higher, whilst still allowing for a fall in debt ratios.

The problem that the world, and particularly most advanced economies, face is that the conjuncture is highly unlikely to be conducive to growth in excess of real interest rates. This is for several reasons:

First, there is going to be a strong increasing demand for public sector expenditures to provide pensions and healthcare and support for the sharply increasing proportion of the aged in our economies, as life expectancies have risen and could rise yet further. The prospect for such additional public expenditure in future decades is concerning, see the Office for Budget Responsibility (OBR), *Report on Fiscal Sustainability* 2018, pp. 75–85, especially Box 3.3. Meanwhile the taxable capacity of those of working age is limited: see Heer et al. (2018).

Second, meanwhile demography is bringing about not only a decline in the rate of growth of, but in many countries, e.g. in Europe and China, an absolute decline in the number of workers. Even if productivity were to return to the more favourable growth rates of the decades up to 2008, such declines in the workforce mean that aggregate real output will continue to grow at a slow rate. The growth of output per worker in Japan has been rising rather faster than the growth of output per worker in most other advanced economies (see Table 1.1 below).

But, nevertheless, the growth of real output in aggregate in Japan has been slow, at about 1 per cent per annum, because of the declining workforce there in recent years. Similar problems will weigh heavily on many European countries and China over future decades, though the US and UK are in a slightly more favourable position, in part because of inward migration in recent decades.

Table 1.1 Percentage change for GDP per hour worked.

	USA	Germany	UK	France	Japan
2010	2.83%	2.47%	2.16%	1.31%	3.27%
2011	0.16%	2.06%	0.32%	0.89%	0.23%
2012	0.26%	0.62%	−0.53%	0.20%	0.94%
2013	0.38%	0.78%	0.25%	1.35%	2.06%
2014	0.44%	1.02%	0.17%	0.95%	0.08%
2015	0.75%	0.58%	1.67%	0.77%	1.50%
2016	0.26%	1.42%	−0.55%	0.05%	0.28%
2017	1.00%	0.89%	0.77%	0.97%	0.92%
Sum	**6.08%**	**9.84%**	**4.01%**	**6.49%**	**9.28%**

Source: OECD.

And third, real interest rates have become exceptionally low, partly because demographic pressures, particularly in China, have led to savings 'gluts', while investment ratios outside of China, as earlier argued, have remained extremely low, partly under the influence of the globalized availability of additional cheap labour. Both these factors are going into reverse. As the dependency ratio rises, personal sector savings ratios are likely to decline, unless governments consciously restrict the future generosity of their pensions and medical assistance for the aged, which could be politically challenging. At the same time the recovery in the power of labour, as workers become scarce, and taxation rises to meet extra public sector expenditures, will lead to rising real unit labour costs. In order to offset that, corporates are likely to increase their investment demand. So, the likelihood is that the balance between investment and saving, i.e. the demand and supply of loanable funds, may well lead to a recovery in real interest rates. If so, forthcoming pressures may lower growth rates, at the same time as real interest rates rise, making it increasingly difficult simply to grow out of current high debt ratios.

If we cannot grow out of the current high debt ratio levels, then debtors could meet claims on them by failing to pay back as much initially as implicitly promised. Again, there are three ways of doing so.

The first, and simplest, way of reducing the real debt burden is through (unexpected) inflation; note that inflation expectations are currently 'well anchored' and held at low levels, around 2 per cent. Such anchoring of inflationary expectations depends, considerably, on investor confidence that central banks will be able to maintain their inflation target into the foreseeable future. But will they? Over the last two and a half decades since inflation targetry became generally adopted, nominal and real interest rates have trended downwards. This has made central banks the best friend of indebted Ministers of Finance and their bosses (Prime Ministers). If nominal interest rates are now on a rising track again, even if gradually, this will put them in conflict with the immediate desires and interests of Ministers of Finance and other politicians, as has already been evident in certain countries, such as the US and Turkey. In almost every country, the central bank's independence was brought about by an act of the legislature; the exception is the euro area, where the independence of the ECB is enshrined in a common Treaty. Whereas the independence of the ECB would be hard to revoke, the independence of other central banks can be reversed by a further Act. If the politicians find that central bank policies to achieve price stability get in their way of objectives for faster growth and lower taxes, they may seek to end, or sharply reduce, the independence of those banks. If so, that vaunted independence might ultimately prove a somewhat weak reed as protection against a more inflationary future.

The second is through renegotiation. The ECB's independence is more solidly based. In their case, debtors – including national member governments – would not be able to get out of their commitments by inflating them away. The same would be true in those other countries where central bank independence (CBI) holds firm. In such cases, when the pressure of debt service becomes too great, the next possible alternative is renegotiation of promised cash flows to ease the debt service burden. Such renegotiations generally go under the heading of 'Extend and Pretend', whereby the cash flows in the form of regular interest payments are either reduced and/or pushed further back in time, thereby alleviating the immediate cash flow burden on the debtor.

Normally, this is done in such a way that, although the present value of the debtors' future cash flows is reduced, the accountants feel able to leave the nominal value of such debt unchanged on the books of the creditors. In this way, debtor relief need not necessarily be accompanied by any reduction in the apparent financial strength of creditors. That is, of course, 'smoke and mirrors', but since much finance depends on confidence and trust, 'smoke and mirrors' can be a beneficial device.

The final mechanism for debtor relief is straight default, either partial or total, writing down the nominal amounts of cash flows to be paid back to creditors. Such default, of course, prevents the debtor involved from accessing credit markets for a period of time. But the history, for example of sovereign default, implies that memories are relatively short, so that a prospective recovery of the defaulting debtor need not prevent a return to financial markets for very long. Nevertheless, in such circumstances, where there is a clear-cut default, the creditor involved has to take an offsetting immediate hit to their own balance sheet. Thus, default can have far greater systemic effects than renegotiation; the problems of the 'doom loop' between banks and sovereigns is a case in point. So, both because of the costly implications of default for borrowers, and the widening systemic effect of such default on creditors, default by borrowers is an extreme, and unhappy, response to excessive debt burdens, perhaps more so than either renegotiation or a slightly higher rate of inflation. Nevertheless, all these three alternatives, i.e. inflation, renegotiation and default, are costly and undesirable.

So, if growing out of debt seems improbable, and failing to meet commitments by one, or another, form of default on debtor promises, is also highly undesirable, what else could be done? The argument here is that what could be done, should have been done, and has not been done, is to revise the balance of (re)financing dramatically towards equity finance, and away from debt finance. This is perhaps easiest to see in the case of corporate finance.

Households borrow primarily on fixed interest mortgages, in order to buy houses. This too could be switched more onto an equity basis. During periods when housing prices were expected to rise at a rate faster than the CPI, financial institutions might be glad to provide an equity element to housing finance, but borrowers might be resistant. But the regulators might adjust the required loan to value ratio to give an advantage to equity finance, rather than fixed interest finance, for mortgage borrowing, in some large part on the grounds that it would protect the borrower. On the other hand, equity finance for housing would require the development of future markets for housing prices wherein lenders could hedge their inflation risk exposure. While difficult, this could probably be done. During periods when housing prices were expected to fall, relative to the CPI, even if only temporarily, lenders would not be happy to take out such equity finance. In such circumstances the public sector might have to provide a backstop for equity finance for housing. Over the very long run, technical innovation in building houses has lagged severely behind innovation in most other manufacturing production. Moreover, much of the price of housing relates to land values, and land is in fixed supply. Partly as a result, again over such very long periods, housing prices have generally trended above the CPI. If that should remain in future, a government-provided equity finance backstop, along the lines of 'Help-to-Buy' would actually provide, in the medium term, a profitable opportunity for the public sector.

Finally, the public sector itself could turn to a more equity-based form of finance by offering nominal income bonds, in place of fixed interest debt. While such issues have been advocated from time to time quite frequently during recent years, they have yet to be taken up on any large scale. But given the uncertainties about productivity and the availability of labour over future decades, it might well be a propitious moment for yet a further reconsideration.

There are two main problems that need to be addressed fairly soon, if there should be any sustained shift by the corporate sector to equity finance. The first of these is that debt finance has, at least for the corporate sector, considerable fiscal advantage over equity finance. This would have to be rectified and equity finance made as advantageous for corporates as debt finance already is, if there were to be any success in introducing such a shift. We discuss this below.

The second problem is that the combination of limited liability for all equity holders, and the alignment of the incentives of managers with their equity shareholders, has led to a tendency towards short-termism and low investment, as noted earlier, and discussed further in the associated paper by Goodhart and Lastra (2020), and also by Huertas (2019).

Levelling the net fiscal advantages of debt and equity

There are two main sets of proposals, of which I am aware, that address the issue of removing the fiscal advantage of debt for corporates and levelling the playing field between equity and debt finance. These are, first, the Allowance for Corporate Equity (ACE), included in the Mirrlees Review (2011), and the second is the proposal for 'Destination-based Cash Flow Taxation' (DBCFT), now more usually described as Border Taxes, as described in the Oxford University Centre for Business Taxation, paper of the same title, (WP17/01), January 2017. These are further described in order below.

Allowance for corporate equity

The ACE is an attempt to replicate the tax benefits of debt for equity financed projects –by introducing an explicit (through imputed) allowance against equity that is also tax deductible, just like interest expenses. There are two issues with the implementation of the ACE that the Mirrlees Review addresses. First, equating debt to equity could be done by removing the tax deductibility of interest expenses, but this would have to be done globally. Otherwise, firms would simply relocate to other destinations that continued to allow tax deductibility. Second, introducing the ACE would mean a loss of tax revenue. While it would be tempting to raise the corporation income raising tax to compensate for that lost revenue, the Mirrlees Review suggests instead accepting the loss of tax revenue from this particular source and balancing it off against a review of the nation's tax structure as a whole. Thus, in an internationally competitive context, it would not be viable to remove the tax deductibility of interest payment for (say) UK firms unilaterally. So, in order to level the fiscal advantages of debt and equity, the normal return component of profits would equally have to go untaxed, thereby narrowing the corporate tax base. Although such a reform was introduced in Belgium in 2008, its main drawback is that it would have a significant revenue cost, unless the corporate tax was raised considerably in lieu.

The problem with the latter would be that it would raise corporate tax rates in the UK probably well above those ruling in other countries, and thereby increase the incentive for multinational firms to shift taxable profits, or even activity, outside the UK. So, the Mirrlees Review suggest that the authorities should accept that they can get less revenues from such corporate taxation and offset this by raising taxation elsewhere as part of a larger overall adjustment of the tax system.

In my own view, the benefit of rebalancing debt and equity as a source of finance is big enough, in the context of excessive leverage that the world has inherited, to make the introduction of such rearrangement of the tax base worthwhile. Nevertheless, political resistance to any further increases of taxation elsewhere has been such that there has been no indication, as far as I am aware, of any willingness by the Treasury or any Chancellors of the Exchequers, in the years since the Mirrlees Review was published, to give active consideration to this proposal. Whether a future crisis involving enhanced concerns about excessive leverage of non-financial corporations might reinvigorate discussion of this issue remains to be seen.

Destination-based cash flow Taxation (DBCFT)

This is best described in the Executive Summary of the paper mentioned above, as follows:

> The DBCFT has two basic components.
>
> - The 'cash *flow*' element gives immediate relief to all expenditure, including capital expenditure, and taxes revenues as they accrue.
> - The 'destination-based' element introduces border adjustments of the same form as under the value added tax (VAT): exports are untaxed, while imports are taxed.
>
> This is equivalent in its economic impact to introducing a broad-based, uniform rate Value Added Tax (VAT) – or achieving the same effect through an existing VAT – and making a corresponding reduction in taxes on wages and salaries.
>
> The paper evaluates the DBCFT against five criteria: economic efficiency, robustness to avoidance and evasion, ease of administration, fairness and stability. And it does so both for the case of universal adoption by all countries and the more plausible case of unilateral adoption.
>
> In contrast with existing systems of taxing corporate profit, especially in an international environment, the DBCFT and VAT-based equivalent have significant attractions:
>
> - A central motivation for the DBCFT is to improve economic efficiency by taxing business income in a relatively immobile location – that is, the location of final purchasers of goods and services (the 'destination'). The DBCFT should not distort either the scale or the location of business investment and eliminates the

tax bias towards debt finance by assuring neutral treatment of debt and equity as sources of finance.

- Taxing business income in the place of destination also has the considerable advantage that the DBCFT is also robust against avoidance through inter-company transactions. Common means of tax avoidance – including the use of inter-company debt, locating intangible property in low-tax jurisdictions and mispricing inter-company transactions – would not be successful in reducing tax liabilities under a DBCFT.
  Here however the distinction between universal and unilateral adoption is important. With adoption by only a subset of countries, those not adopting are likely to find their profit shifting problems to be intensified: companies operating in high tax countries, for instance, which may seek to artificially over-price their imports, will face no countervailing tax when sourcing them by exporting from related companies in DBCFT countries.
- By the same token, the DBCFT provides long term stability since countries would broadly have an incentive to adopt it – either to gain a competitive advantage over countries with a conventional origin-based tax, or to avoid a competitive disadvantage relative to countries that had already implemented a DBCFT. It would also be resistant to tax competition in tax rates.

Given all these attractions and benefits of a DBCFT, one might reasonably ask why it has not already been adopted? It was seriously considered by the incoming Trump administration in 2017, but then dropped. There are, however, numerous drawbacks.

- It would represent a major change in the direction and assignment of taxation. As with any such major change, it would have large groups of sizeable losers and winners. Losers usually are more vocal in remonstrating than winners are in support.
- The main losers would be importers. It would be seen, and subject to objection, as equivalent to a temporary devaluation. There may be some query whether it is acceptable under WTO rules.
- It would (temporarily) raise domestic inflation, especially of goods/services with a high import content.
- While the intention is to combine the rise in VAT with a reduction in taxes on labour income, there is no certainty that this would, or could, be done so as to leave labour real post-tax incomes unchanged.
- Even more seriously, the poor (e.g. old, unemployed, sick) would not be protected, and, absent a general re-rating of benefits would lose. So the scheme could be attached as potentially highly regressive.
- Since investment is pro-cyclical and volatile, as are corporate losses, DBCFT tax receipts would be more procyclical and volatile than with the current forms of corporate tax (Hebous et al. 2019).
- It could generate schemes for fraudulent loss-making.

Thus, to introduce DCBFT without provoking a political storm would probably have to involve reworking much of the structure of transfer payments, as well as taxes on wages and salaries. So, it would be a massive exercise, which would dampen the enthusiasm for such a reform of most Ministers of Finance.

Rather than do this, they might prefer to explore other channels for dealing with the tax avoidance mechanisms that so many international corporations can now put in place.

While the benefits of a DBCFT are clear, the costs of making such a large jump to a new, and untried, system create a sizeable hurdle and have so far prevented its acceptance.

Reforming the incentive structure for corporate managers

Current criticism of modern capitalism has several facets; it is argued that it leads to managers assuming excessive risk, being overpaid, and failing to undertake sufficient long-term investment, especially R&D.[2] The first two criticisms, excessive risk and excessive pay, were particularly levied at banks and other financial intermediaries in the aftermath of the GFC. There have been a variety of proposals aimed at checking or preventing such malfunctions. One set of such proposals has focussed on limiting the business structures of banks and other financial intermediaries. Examples of such proposals include narrow banking in various guises, ringfencing of core retail financial structures, and a variety of other regulatory measures.

Our proposal, instead, is to apply a distinction between a class of 'insiders', who should be subject to multiple liability, and 'outsiders', who would retain limited liability, as at present. So, for the ordinary shareholder there would be no change. Such a scheme obviously involves making a distinction, which must be inevitably somewhat arbitrary, between 'insiders' and 'outsiders'.

Our basic proposal is that there should be two separate categories of equity investors: 'outside' investors who maintain limited liability, as now; and 'insiders', who should have varying degrees of further liability, as outlined below. But how do you distinguish between these two categories? In principle, the distinction is straightforward. 'Insiders' have access to significantly greater information about the working of the enterprise than 'outsiders', and the potential to use that information to prevent excessively risky actions. In practice, of course, the distinction is not so easy to make. 'Insiders' would include all of the Board of Directors, including the externals. For employees, we would suggest a two-fold categorization, by status within the company, and by scale of remuneration. Thus any employee on the Executive Board, or who was Chief of a Division would be included. But the key players in a company are frequently indicated by the scale of their remuneration rather than by their formal position. So any employee who was earning a salary in excess of, say, 50 per cent of that of the CEO, would also be assessed as an 'insider'. Nevertheless, if the potential sanction of multiple liability arising from failure was regarded as severe, there could be attempts to adjust titles and

[2] In an article entitled 'Rethink the purpose of the corporation' (*Financial Times*, 12 December 2018), Martin Wolf criticizes the mantra of shareholder value maximization, affirming that in the cases of highly leveraged banking, the Anglo-American model of corporate governance does not work. He refers to a number of books – including Colin Mayer's 2018 *Prosperity* – which suggest that capitalism is substantially broken.

salaries so as to avoid being categorized as an 'insider'. So, the regulatory authority should have the right to designate anyone in a particular company as being an 'insider', subject to judicial review.

Large shareholders are also in a position to access inside information, and to exert influence on the course that a company might follow. So any shareholder with a holding greater than, say, 5 per cent of the company, should also be regarded as an 'insider'. There is no particular key threshold, above which a large shareholders should be regarded as an 'insider'. It is arguable that one should give shareholders holding between 2 and 5 per cent of the value of the shares the ability to choose whether to count as an 'outsider', or as an 'insider'. If they want to count as an 'outsider', they would have to give up all voting rights, and not participate in policy discussions, e.g. at AGMs.

The base to which the liability should apply would be the remuneration of all those counted as 'insiders', cumulated from the date that they took on that role. This would apply to all forms of remuneration, except those provided in the form of bail-inable debt, with all subsequent transactions in such debt having to be notified. This would apply to the directors and employees. Shareholders would be liable according to the par value of their shares.

Not all 'insiders' are equal, however. In particular, the CEO has much more information and power than any of his subordinates, other members of the Board, or the auditors. One might think that the CEO's liability could be three times the accumulated relevant value of remuneration (ex bail-inables) from the time that he or she had taken up that role. Board members and chief officers of the company might have two-times liability, and every other 'insider' employee a single liability equal to their accumulated revenue. Similarly, large shareholders with greater than 5 per cent holdings might have double liability, i.e. for an additional twice par value of their shares, while 'insider' shareholders, between 2 and 5 per cent, might be liable to pay in an additional par value of their shares, as in the American National Bank system before the 1930s.

That raises two further questions. The first is what should happen when an 'insider' ceases to play that role, e.g. an employee leaves the company, or a large shareholder sells their shares. The second is that an 'insider' may be aware that the company is entering dangerous territory, but cannot persuade management to change direction. In that case, how could they avoid being sanctioned for a policy that they would not themselves advocate?

In the first case, of departure from the role of 'insider', it would seem appropriate to taper the liability according to the degree of 'insider' knowledge and power. Thus, if it was agreed that the CEO should have a three-times extra liability, then that liability would decline at a constant rate over the following three years, leaving the CEO with zero further liability exactly three years after they had left. By the same token, those with a two-times additional liability should have it taper at a constant rate until they were free of any further liability after two years; and so on for those with a one-time additional liability.

Then we come to the second issue, which is the question of how those with additional liability can avoid sanction in those cases where they have opposed the policy, but have failed to succeed in changing it. Our suggestion in this case is that those in such a position should address a formal, but confidential and private, letter to the relevant regulators, setting out their concerns about the policy being followed. The regulator would have to formally acknowledge receipt of such letters, and they could then be used in mitigation, or often abandonment of any sanction, should the company then fail. Moreover, in the event of the company failing, for the reasons indicated in such a letter(s), this would in turn act as a form of accountability for the regulators. All such letters would have to be made publicly available in the event of failure. It would be a legal offence for the regulator then not to publish any such letter.

There is a more difficult question, of whether the regulator, having received such a private confidential letter of warning, perhaps from the auditor, or an unhappy employee, should make it public. In our view, such warnings need to be investigated further by an independent body, such as the regulator or a financial ombudsman before being made publicly available, since in many cases, they may well be groundless with the maintained policy of the company being appropriate. But if the regulator, after investigation, should feel that the warnings had merit, the first step would then be to have a private discussion with management on the merits of the case, and, if management remained unmoved, the next stage would be to publish the warning (anonymously) together with the regulator's own assessment, at the same time offering management the opportunity to state publicly their own side of the case. When the latter process had been completed, 'outsiders' would then be as well informed as 'insiders' on the merits of the issue.

Note that it puts regulators in the firing line for at least severe reputational damage, if they receive such warnings, fail to act upon them, and the warnings prove prescient.

The purpose of the exercise is to provide appropriate sanctions for failure on those with 'insider' knowledge and power. The particular illustrative numbers chosen in the above section are, obviously, somewhat arbitrary. But the exercise can be calibrated to impose appropriate sanctions for all such 'insiders', whether large shareholders, key employees or regulators. We think that this would be a better form of governance.

4. Conclusions

Despite favourable macro-economic conditions, corporate investment has remained low for the last decade. One of the several reasons for this has been that the structure of corporate governance privileges buy-backs, to raise the return on equity, over longer-term fixed investment. This, in turn, has been one of the factors leading to a generalized, but not universal, increase in debt ratios. The effects of this have been masked until now by declining nominal, and real, interest rates, leaving debt service ratios roughly constant. But interest rates are now rising from their effective lower bound.

We find ourselves in a debt trap. Debt ratios have become so high that any sharp, or major, increase in interest rates would precipitate a new recession. But the current low level of rates still encourages further debt accumulation. Faster real growth is not an option; indeed currently adverse demographic trends are likely to slow growth further, absent a productivity miracle. Unexpected inflation may well ensue, as populist politicians put pressure on central banks to go easy on the achievement of inflation targets, and central bank independence withers. There will be debt defaults and renegotiation.

But none of the above will be pleasant. The proposal made here, instead, is to shift the balance of finance from debt to equity finance. This will require a number of key reforms. Two such reforms are highlighted. The first is to remove the fiscal advantage of debt vis-à-vis equity. The second is to change the structure of corporate governance so as to apply greater sanctions and penalties to management in the event of corporate failure.

References

Auerbach, A. 2017a. 'Border Adjustment and the Dollar.' *AEI Economic Perspectives*, February.

Auerbach, A. 2017b. 'Demystifying the Destination-Based Cash-Flow Tax.' *Brookings Papers on Economic Activity*, Fall, pp. 409–32.

Auerbach, A., M.P. Devereux, M. Keen and J. Vella. 2017a. 'Destination-Based Cash Flow Taxation.' *Oxford University Centre for Business Taxation Working Papers*, No. 17/01.

Auerbach, A., M.P. Devereux, M. Keen and J. Vella. 2017b. 'International Tax Planning Under the Destination-Based Cash Flow Tax.' *National Tax Journal*, Vol. 70: 783–801.

Autor, D., D. Dorn, L.F. Katz, C. Patterson and J. Van Reenen. 2017a. 'The Fall of the Labor Share and the Rise of Superstar Firms.' MIT Working Paper, 2 May.

Autor, D., D. Dorn, L.F. Katz, C. Patterson and J. Van Reenen. 2017b. 'Concentrating on the Falling Labor Share.' *American Economic Review Papers & Proceedings* 107 (5): 180–5.

Barbiero, O., E. Farhi, G. Gopinath and O. Itskhoki. 2018. 'The Macroeconomics of Border Taxes', *NBER Working Papers*, No. 24702.

Conti-Brown, P. 2012. 'Elective shareholder liability.' *Stanford Law Review* 64: 409–69.

Goodhart, C.A.E., and R. Lastra. 2019. 'Equity Finance: Matching Liability to Power.' *Journal of Financial Regulation*, published online 11 March 2019, fjz010, https://doi.org/10.1093/jfr/fjz010.

Hargreaves, D. 2018. *Are Chief Executives Overpaid?* Cambridge: Polity Press.

Hebous, S., A. Klemm and S. Stausholm. 2019. 'Revenue Implications of Destination-Based Cash-Flow Taxation.' *IMF Working Paper* WP/19/7, January 15.

Heer, B., V. Polito, and M.R. Wickens. 2018. 'Population Aging, Social Security and Fiscal Limits.' CESifo Working Papers, 7121/1028, June.

Huertas, T. 2019. 'Pay to Play', available at SSRN: https://ssrn.com/abstract=3336186 or http://dx.doi.org/10.2139/ssrn.3336186, 17 February.

Kahneman, D. 2012. *Thinking, Fast and Slow*. London: Penguin Books.

Kokkinis, A. 2018. *Corporate Law and Financial Instability*. London: Routledge.

Liu, E., A. Mian and A. Sufi. 2020. 'Low Interest Rates, Market Power, and Productivity Growth.' NBER Working Paper 25505, January.

Mayer, C. 2019. *Prosperity: Better Business Makes the Greater Good*. Oxford: Oxford University Press.

Mirrlees, J. 2011. *Tax By Design: The Mirrlees Review*. Oxford: Oxford University Press.

Office for Budget Responsibility. 2018. *Fiscal Sustainability Report*, found at https://obr.uk/fsr/fiscal-sustainability-report-july-2018/

Philippon, T. 2019. *The Great Reversal: How America Gave Up on Free Markets*. Cambridge MA and London UK: Belknap Press of Harvard University Press.

Schwarcz, S.L. 2014. 'The Governance Structure of Shadow Banking: Rethinking Assumptions About Limited Liability', *90 Notre Dame Law Review* 1 (2014); also available at http://ssrn.com/abstract=2364126

Smithers, A. 2009. *Wall Street Revalued: Imperfect Markets and Inept Central Bankers.* Chichester: John Wiley & Sons.

Smithers, A. 2013. *The Road to Recovery: How and Why Economic Policy Must Change.* Chichester: John Wiley & Sons.

Wolf, M. 2018. 'Rethink the purpose of the corporation', *Financial Times*, 12 December.

2

The Global Financial Crisis Ten Years On: Using and Forgetting the Past?

Catherine R. Schenk

Financial crises recur in part because memories fade.

Geithner, Bernanke and Paulson 2019

The historical perspective of modern bankers is notoriously short. In the financial services sector, compensation schemes based on share-price movements or profits from annual deal-making reinforce this short-termism. It is salutary, however, that the trader Greg Lippman, famous for predicting the end of the securitized mortgage debt boom (and making billions for Deutsche Bank when the system collapsed) based his Big Short on a longer-term data set than his competitors (Lewis 2011; Schenk 2020a). By looking at disaggregated US property prices back beyond the customary ten to fifteen years, he was able to surmise the impact of a slowing down in re-mortgaging for the pyramid of debt. The past is not always prologue, but it should clearly not be ignored. Policy-makers, on the other hand, are more open to reflection, even if only to decide that 'this time is different'. Understanding what is different is as important as understanding what might be the same as past episodes. However, just at the time of the Global Financial Crisis, Macmillan (2008) reminded us that 'the past can be used for almost anything you want to do in the present'. Historians may rail against their own irrelevance most of the time, but the past is often a recourse in times of crisis for policy-makers, although their use of the past may be selective.

The past, of course, is not neutral territory. Forgetting in the context of this paper is not restricted to personal recollection, although sometimes this can be important. For example, in 1973 when the Bretton Woods pegged exchange rate ended, there were no traders or bankers in the market that could personally remember a time of floating exchange rates forty years earlier and this led to mistakes both of governance of banks and increased operational risks in foreign exchange markets (Schenk 2014). Rather than personal memory, this chapter addresses how interpretations of the past by historians were used in the Global Financial Crisis across four dimensions: monetary policy; fiscal policy; currency wars; and international cooperation. In the case of 2008, there was a clear leap of imagination to the 1930s Great Depression by the public and among policy-makers, which should open up the scope for other uses of the past.

The shadow of the 1930s

Reflecting on ten years after the Global Financial Crisis, it is important to remember that Europe was at war ten years after the 1929 stock market crash associated with the Great Depression. The war the world began to fight twelve years after the Global Financial Crisis is against a virus pandemic, which might have economic effects as great as the 30 years of war that cast such a shadow over most of the twentieth century. In 2020, policy-makers remembered from 2008 the importance of monetary and fiscal expansion, although the threat to the global trade system arising from American and British policy seems to signal some forgotten features of 1930s depression, which descended into nationalist protectionism. Unlike after 2008, the increase in government borrowing to support advanced economies through the pandemic is unprecedented since the Second World War. The outcome for global inequality and international cooperation remains to be seen.

The plethora of memoirs of the 2008 financial crisis over the following ten years speaks to the urge among policy-makers to impress their views of the unfolding events on the public memory. They also often draw on their own understanding of the past. British Chancellor of the Exchequer in 2008, Alistair Darling, remembered in his 2011 memoir that he was 'influenced hugely by Keynes' thinking' in the 1930s about the importance of government spending for maintaining employment in the great depression. In 2009, the Chief Economist at Moody's Economy.com remarked that 'The most fundamental lesson of the Great Depression for today's crisis is that government must be extraordinarily aggressive . . . in times of crisis, it must be overwhelming and everywhere' and lamented that 'policymakers in the current crisis were slow to heed this lesson' (Zandy 2009). US Treasury Secretary Tim Geithner (2014) remembered in January 2009 'starting to read Liaquat Ahamed's *Lords of Finance* [2009, subtitled 'The Bankers Who Broke the World'], the history of the policymakers whose mistakes helped create and prolong the Great Depression but I had put it down after a few chapters. It was too scary.' Nevertheless, the 1930s looms large in the first few pages of his book as he contextualized the crisis and explained to the reader his plans to bail out banks and insurance companies to prevent 'a worldwide financial meltdown, and a much deeper economic crisis'. Bernanke's (2015) memoir predictably makes the strongest case for a policy-maker relying on his understanding of the great depression, since he was a scholar of the period. He recalls finding Friedman and Schwartz's (1963) classic account of the 1930s US depression 'fascinating', inspiring him to become a 'Great Depression buff' (2015: 33). In his 2002 address at Friedman's ninetieth birthday he extolled the virtues of *A Monetary History*, concluding

> Let me end my talk by abusing slightly my status as an official representative of the Federal Reserve. I would like to say to Milton and Anna: Regarding the Great Depression. You're right, we did it. We're very sorry. But thanks to you, we won't do it again.
>
> Bernanke 2002

As the tenth anniversary of the onset of the financial crisis of 2008 loomed, there were also many academic reflections on both the causes of the crisis and the progress made in the decade that had intervened (Anheier and Haley 2018 et al.; King 2018; Goodhart and Tsomocos 2019; O'Halloran and Groll 2019). There were certainly many candidates for blame: why were governments so complacent, regulators so blind, bankers so greedy and home-buyers so irresponsible? After the immediate crisis, a reinvigorated focus on macro-prudential supervision turned attention to macroeconomic indicators that might trigger systemic fragility. In effect, these policies were designed to make it easier for central bankers or finance ministers to remove the punch bowl before the party got out of hand and the house was trashed, a conception of the responsibilities of a central banker first developed in the US economic boom in the 1950s.[1] At the same time, a swathe of micro-prudential rules was used to restrain the excesses of individual institutions; higher capital requirements, more extreme stress testing, reintroduction of 1930s regulations to protect retail deposit institutions from the risks of investment banking (Schenk 2020c). This process itself promoted the 1930s crisis as a comparator in the public discourse.

In sum, understandings of the causes of the 1930s financial crisis and the global great depression that followed were core to the response to the crisis in 2008. That both the Chair of the Federal Reserve Board (Bernanke) and the head of Obama's Council of Economic Advisers (Romer) were scholars of the interwar depression no doubt increased the accessibility of historical lessons to inform policy (Eichengreen 2015; Bordo and Landon-Lane 2010).

Breaks with the past

There were differences as well as similarities between these two episodes. The 1930s financial crisis followed rather than anticipated the economic collapse for many countries outside the United States. The drop in world agricultural prices and slow growth in many regions began in the middle of the 1920s, whereas the financial crisis in Europe and the US started in 1930–1. The historically specific cycle of war debts and reparations created special conditions for capital flight and contagious banking failures. The collapse of the Credit Anstalt in Austria in May 1931 is commonly blamed for sparking off the European financial crisis after the French acted on political as well as financial motives to withdraw their funds (Aguado 2001). Although the blame for the European financial crisis has since been shifted (Marcus 2018), when the Bank of England was preparing for the looming sovereign debt banking crisis in 1970s, they started with an internally commissioned analysis of the Credit Anstalt crisis.[2] This report convinced them of the importance of international cooperation to cope with

---

[1] The punch bowl analogy is usually attributed to Fed Chair William McChesney Martin in the mid-1950s during a period of credit expansion and inflationary pressure. Although the direct quotation cannot be tracked down, it is attributed to him by Canby Balderston (1957). Balderston was Vice-Chair of the Fed. The phrase is also used to describe the character of a central banker in *Annual Report of the Federal Reserve Bank of Philadelphia*, 1956, p. 19. Balderston was on the board of the Philadelphia Fed.

[2] E.M. Drage, Creditanstalt Crisis of 1931, 30 December 1977. Bank of England Archives, 3A143/1.

the contagious effects of bank crises and the need to keep central bank balance sheets unencumbered. The use of the interwar depression is certainly not restricted to the 2008 Global Financial Crisis.

Despite the differences between the 1930s and 2008, the strongest historic lesson drawn by economic historians such as Bernanke and others was the need to avoid monetary contraction in the wake of banking crises. Friedman and Schwartz (1963) blamed the depth of the depression on a critical policy mistake by the Fed: the failure to expand the money supply in the wake of the US banking crisis. The reasons for the mistake include a lack of understanding of how monetary policy works, a confusion between indicators of monetary conditions and a stubborn adherence to the gold standard until 1933. This conclusion was victorious in a broad debate on the causes of the Great Depression during the 1980s that pitted Keynesians against monetarists (Romer 1992; Temin 1976; Wheelock 1989). The debate over the monetary causes of the depression in the US continues, with Parent (2019) going so far as to suggest that the widespread misinterpretation of the Fed's monetary policy should be a 'warning against making use of history for economic policy purpose'. The past is constantly liable to reinterpretation by historians, but Friedman and Schwartz (writing in the 1960s about the 1930s) seemed to provide a clear lesson to policy-makers in 2008 that expansive monetary was required. This diagnosis drove central bankers to inject an extraordinary amount of liquidity into national and international money markets in what was obliquely dubbed 'unconventional monetary policy'. The unconventional soon become conventional as more central banks adopted it and as the policy persisted through the first post-crisis decade, ready to be renewed when the 2020 pandemic struck.

Eichengreen (2015) has pointed to other lessons. Fiscal expansion was an important element initiating the recovery from the Great Depression through, for example, the New Deal in the US, but he is critical of the subsequent rolling back of fiscal policy that prompted recession in 1937–8. For him, this was a lesson that was forgotten: 'in both cases [1930s and 2010s] the desire to restore normal fiscal and monetary policies before normal economic conditions had returned was heavily responsible for the disappointing state of the economy' (2015: 326). In a 2009 address, Romer (2009), as head of Obama's Council of Economic Advisers, pointed to the need for significant fiscal expansion as her first 'crucial lesson from the 1930s'. She also referred explicitly to 'The 1937 episode is an important cautionary tale for modern policymakers' not to curtail fiscal stimulus too soon. This was not a lesson forgotten, but one ignored.

International cooperation

Coordinated international efforts at fiscal expansion were also short-lived. British Prime Minister Gordon Brown and others recognized the need for cooperation and the commitments made at the G20 leaders meeting Washington DC in mid-November 2008 was a landmark occasion, but the political will to sustain government spending through the ensuing slump soon evaporated amid fears that deficits would rise too quickly and might lead to inflation or unsustainable levels of debt. In 2010, the G20 in

Toronto committed to cutting their deficits. After not learning from the 1930s, this appears to be a lesson that governments may have learned from 2008 for the COVID-19 crisis in 2020, which was met in many countries with unprecedented levels of government spending (and borrowing) in peacetime.

The efforts at cooperation in the 1930s were less successful than the 2000s: the World Economic Conference of 1933 (described by the economist Edwards (2017) as 'an almost forgotten episode in US monetary history') failed to bring about cooperation either to stabilize exchange rates or keep open goods markets. Before the conference, Sir Arthur Salter, UK bureaucrat and economist, warned that 'one thing at least is clear, if we enter this Conference without a plan we shall certainly come out of it without a remedy'.[3] Three weeks into the twelve-week schedule, Roosevelt suddenly announced that the talks were too biased toward exchange-rate policy and not enough toward controlling inflation and promoting recovery. With the US unwilling to participate in exchange rate stabilization, the meeting ended early. In November 2008, there was more consensus among the G20 on the causes of the crisis and, therefore, its likely solutions in the short term at least, partly because of common perceptions of the way policy failures in the 1930s worsened the international depression. What should be remembered from the 1933 conference is the importance of having a clear agenda and basis for agreement and that the US president should play a constructive (or at least not destructive) role in international cooperative initiatives. Thirty years later, in 1965, US Treasury Secretary Fowler (1965) called for an international monetary conference to make 'substantial improvements' to the twenty-year-old Bretton Woods system, but he echoed Salter's warning in 1933 by recognizing that 'to meet and not succeed would be worse than not meeting at all'. His European counterparts may have remembered 1933 when they advised that they would not attend such an event because there was no consensus on the diagnosis of the problem or firm proposals for a solution (Schenk 2010). The second lesson of the 1933 debacle (the importance of the US president's engagement) has become even more clear in many international fora dealing with e.g. climate change (Paris Agreement), trade (WTO) and health (WHO).

Charles Kindleberger's insight about the importance of the world's largest creditor, the United States, playing a leadership role in resolving global problems has also been influential (Kindleberger 1973; Temin and Vines 2013). He argued that when the American government turned away from international cooperation after 1919 and did not sustain open markets and countercyclical international lending, this worsened the global depression. The Americans learned this lesson relatively quickly and took a very different role in the reconstruction of the international economy after the Second World War, building their vision of post-war trade and payments into their negotiations with the UK over wartime support for the allied cause. From the Atlantic Charter signed dramatically by Churchill and Roosevelt in the North Atlantic off Newfoundland in 1941, through Lend-Lease and then the White Plan for the International Monetary Fund, the wartime American administration was committed to freer trade and payments and deliberate institutionalization of monetary cooperation. They found

---

[3] Quoted in The World Economic Conference, World Affairs, 96(1) March 1933, p. 6.

general agreement from the UK and other European states on the principle if not on the detail.

The establishment of the IMF as a forum for international cooperation is unprecedented and to some extent *sui generis*, coming as it did after thirty years of war among the richest countries in the world and evolving at a time of existential challenge to capitalism posed by the ensuing Cold War. Other organizations with more limited membership and mandates also emerged from the post-war settlement including the OECD and, from 1976, the G7. In terms of practical efforts at cooperation, other more private 'tinkering' efforts at central bank cooperation through the Bank for International Settlements should not be neglected (Toniolo 2005). Indeed, it was through the Gold Pool (Bordo, Monnet and Naef 2019) and central bank credits (Schenk 2010) that the Bretton Woods pegged exchange-rate system was sustained. In 2008, the US Federal Reserve Bank rushed to counter the liquidity shock in global dollar money markets by introducing bilateral swaps with central banks in Europe, Canada and Japan (and other regional financial centres from 2010) to provide dollar liquidity to banks in their jurisdictions (Tooze 2018). The records of the Federal Open Market Committee (FOMC) at the time express the concern by some members that memories of Fed swap systems of the past would be erroneously invoked to suggest that the Fed meant to intervene in exchange markets to manipulate the dollar exchange rate. But most accounts of the swaps set up in 2008 have forgotten an earlier iteration of the system.

The Fed central bank swap system was pushed on a reluctant set of European central banks from 1962 as a way to reduce their incentive to convert their dollar reserves to gold (Bordo, Humpage and Schwartz 2015). But the swaps were also meant to be available for other purposes, including affecting global offshore dollar liquidity. The Fed launched a special swap with the BIS in 1965 to do just that (McCauley and Schenk 2020). Figure 2.1 shows that from 1967 about half of the swaps offered by the Fed by

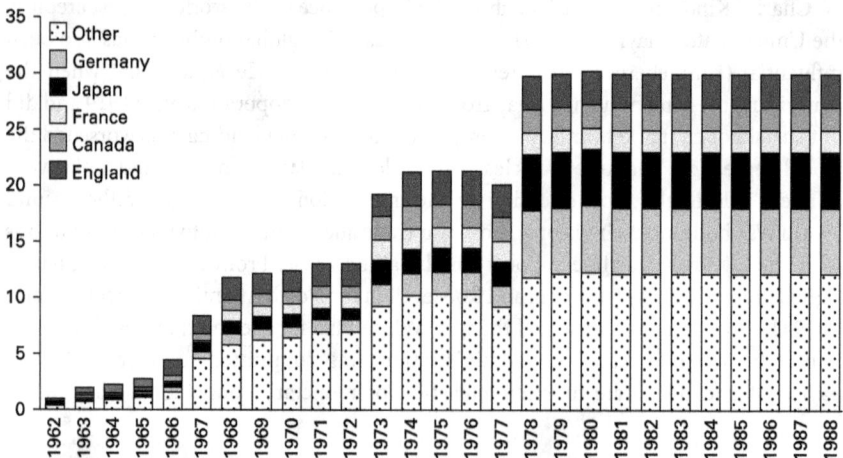

Figure 2.1 Federal Reserve swap lines 1962–88 (US$ billion).

value were to the central banks of the UK, Germany, Japan, France and Canada. The Bank of England was the largest participant in the 1960s and 1970s, but from the late 1970s Germany, Japan and Switzerland dominated.[4] Figure 2.2 shows the size of the early Fed swaps relative to the share of US GDP and the size of foreign exchange reserves. In the early 1970s the amount of swap facilities available was about the same value relative to US GDP as the swap facilities available on 18 September 2008 (*c.* $250 billion).[5]

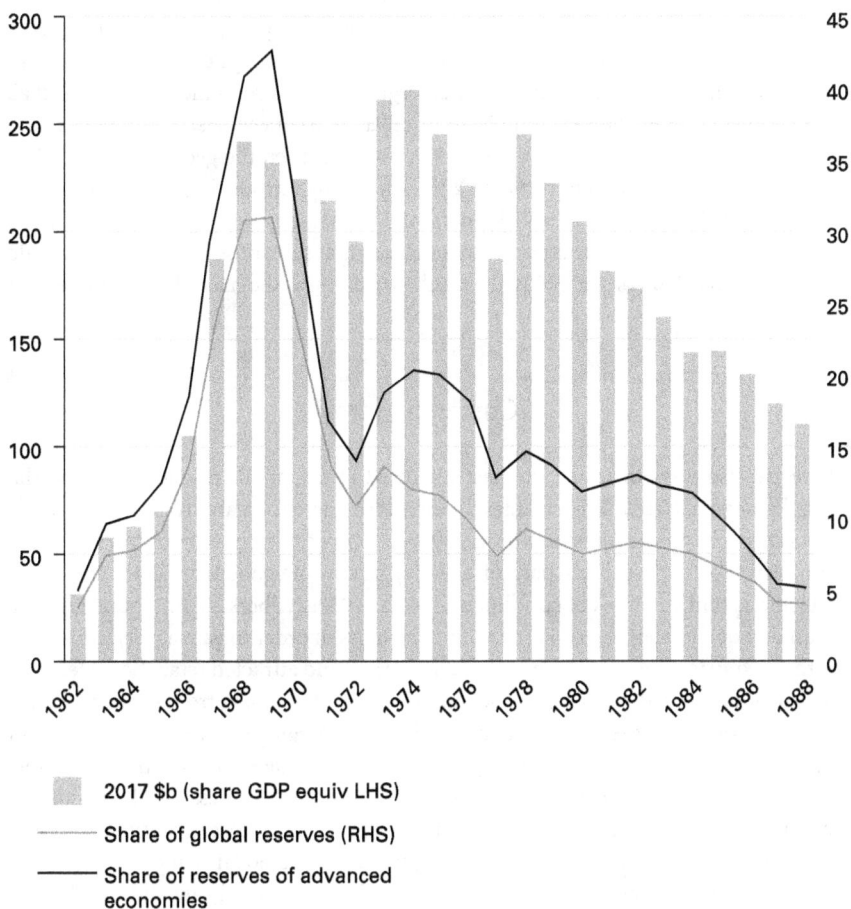

Figure 2.2 Fed's reciprocal swap lines in relation to US GDP (US$) and global reserves (%).

[4] By 1967 the Federal Reserve had entered into swap facilities with the central banks of the UK, the Netherlands, Canada, Japan, France, Germany, Belgium, Italy, Switzerland, Sweden, Mexico, Austria, Denmark, Norway and the Bank for International Settlements.
[5] The swap facilities were increased in steps during the rest of September, rising to $290 billion on 26 September and $620 billion on 29 September before pre-specified limits for most partners were lifted on 13 October 2008.

The earlier Fed swaps also amounted to between 15 and 40 per cent of global foreign-exchange reserves and so were an important supplement to global liquidity. In the 1960s, most Fed swaps were used to provide resources to influence exchange rates but the Fed also swapped dollars with the BIS against Swiss francs in order for the BIS to deposit dollars into banks in the Eurodollar market to depress interest rates there during seasonal periods of liquidity constraint. The aim was to avoid pressure from banks overseas trying to draw dollars out of New York to meet seasonal reporting requirements and thereby tightening domestic US dollar markets (McCauley and Schenk 2020). This function was largely forgotten, but it has a strong analogy with the operations from 2008 onward when the swaps were used by recipient central banks to provide dollar liquidity on an auction basis to their banks. These later swaps were criticized at the time for excluding many emerging market economies (Aizenman et al. 2011). In March 2020, the Fed swaps were reactivated to cope with similar strains in the global dollar market after the COVID-19 crisis. Moreover, the geographic spread of Fed support was increased beyond the 2008 scheme by introducing a new repurchase (repo) facility for foreign official holders of US Treasury and agency securities to enable them to access dollar liquidity without outright sales of securities in still fragile markets. Unlike 2008 or the 1960s, the Bank of Japan was the main drawer on the Fed swaps in 2020.

Currency wars

There are also ways in which the past was used in the public discourse around the Global Financial Crisis. This includes the claims of 'currency wars' from the 1930s that were echoed in political rhetoric of the 2010s. Competitive devaluations in the 1930s were believed to have been part of the 'beggar thy neighbour' policies that were emblematic of the failures of coordination in the 1930s (Albers 2020). Countries were accused of deliberately depreciating their currencies in order to gain a price advantage for their exports, which fed through to falling prices and attracted retaliation. Here, the equivalent in the 2010s was the impact on exchange rates arising from the quantitative easing of monetary systems, particularly in the US. Emerging market economies found their real exchange rates appreciating during the first stages of quantitative easing, which inflated asset prices and threatened the competitiveness of their exports. Bernanke's suggestion in May 2013 that the Fed would cease quantitative easing provoked a 'taper tantrum' that disrupted capital flows and dollar markets.[6]

Debate has continued over how important spill-overs actually are and the channel through which they operate. More consensus has landed on the side of a financial impact rather than through the trade channel. Nevertheless, the past was invoked by central bankers in emerging markets. Brazilian Finance Minister Guido Mantega declared in 2010 'we are in the midst of an international currency war...this threatens

---

[6] At the time the Fed was purchasing $85 billion in assets per month, reduced to $75 billion in December 2013. This decision was in line with Bernanke's statement in May 2013 that purchases would be reduced by the end of the year.

us because it takes away our competitiveness'. Four years later, Ragu Rajan, Governor of the Bank of India, warned that 'disregard for spillovers could put the global economy on a dangerous path to unconventional monetary tit for tat' (both quoted in Blanchard 2017: 283–4). The idea was also picked up by popular writers and captured the public imagination (e.g. Rickards 2011). The Fed's mandate is strictly limited to domestic and not international consequences of its policy, but it also disavows the importance of spillovers. In 2018, Fed Chair Jay Powell remarked that 'Monetary stimulus by the Fed and other advanced-economy central banks played a relatively limited role in the surge of capital flows to EMEs in recent years. There is good reason to think that the normalization of monetary policies in advanced economies should continue to prove manageable for EMEs' (Powell 2018). The differences between the 1930s and the 2010s also need to be highlighted. When sterling was devalued in 1931 it left a pegged exchange-rate regime, the gold-exchange standard, where the policy target was the exchange rate. In the 2010s the regime was a floating one, with most countries adopting inflation targeting, at least in theory.

In the interwar years, the spectre of currency wars after the devaluation of sterling and empire currencies in 1931 prompted retaliation in the form of trade controls that helped drive down the volume of world trade to the detriment of the world economy (Eichengreen and Irwin 2010). This reflected a view among countries like France (that did not want to devalue) that the exchange rate, and by extension monetary policy, was being used to gain an unfair advantage in world trade and that this justified retaliatory protectionist policies. The calls of currency wars in response to expansionary monetary policy in the US, Europe and Japan a decade ago did not themselves provoke a return to trade protectionism, but there was a softening in the IMF's view on capital controls. In 2011 the International Monetary and Financial Committee of the IMF called for a review of the management of capital flows. The so-called New Institutional View adopted in 2012 viewed controls on capital for specific short term purposes as acceptable, particularly for developing and emerging economies (IMF 2012).

The spillover from US monetary policy also launched a fresh look at how the international monetary system operates. Unlike the 1930s, the dominance of the US dollar in the 2000s enhances the influence of Federal Reserve monetary policy on global asset prices. In the inter-war period there was a more balanced distribution of monetary power between the dollar, the pound and the franc (Eichengreen and Flandreau 2009). The dominant role of sterling and the Sterling Bloc was balanced by the franc-led Gold Bloc while the Fed had success in actively promoting the use of the dollar as an international currency to challenge the pound. In the 2000s, by contrast, the US dollar dominated financial and commercial markets. Indeed, crises like 2008 and 2020 have increased demand for dollars, tightening liquidity in the world dollar market. Rey (2015/2018) has suggested that small open economies are vulnerable to global financial cycles driven in large part by US policy, which restricts their options to either capital controls or loss of policy sovereignty. In other words, the exchange-rate regime (fixed or floating) can no longer insulate an economy from the monetary policy in the hegemon. The IMF's efforts to try to encourage the US and others to consider the international impact of their monetary policy through multilateral surveillance gained little traction. Emerging market economies sought unsuccessfully to pressure Fed policy but this disappointment did not prompt tariff retaliation. Instead, after 2016 it was the US administration that began threatening to impose trade restrictions on its key trading partners including Mexico and Canada, China and the EU after identifying 'unfair' trade practices there.

Global governance

After 2008 the community of global governance was finally expanded to include the most important economies in the world, including China and Russia. Unlike after 1945, Cold War-style ideological barriers were not allowed to create distinctions. Indeed, cooperation seemed to get steadily more inclusive, culminating in the establishment in 2009 of the Financial Stability Board, which brought together all the multilateral financial institutions like the BIS, IMF, World Bank and OECD with the central banks and finance ministries of the G20. The mobilization of the G20 in November 2008 seemed finally to signal the acceptance beyond lip service of the wider governance of the global economy. The G20 had been formed at the end of 1999 after the rash of emerging market currency and financial crises highlighted the systemic risks from countries outside the G7. The possibility of linking wider governance directly to the IMF was rejected (G20 2008) and instead a separate organization was launched alongside the more exclusive G7. With the global scale of the 2008 crisis, the G20 took on greater traction. Even the relatively discreet and exclusive Bank for International Settlements gradually widened its governance (Schenk 2020b).

But as the geographic breadth of governance increased, so the effectiveness of multilateral policy-making arguably declined in pace and urgency. The onset of the European sovereign debt crisis in 2010, two years after the Lehman Brothers collapse, was a loud echo of the global crisis and demonstrated how much longer the repercussions would be felt (Tooze 2018). Ten years later, national electorates in rich countries were frustrated by the costs of restoring financial systems and the way that little seemed to have changed for the rich financiers. In many poor countries, armed conflict created huge populations of displaced persons seeking refuge. Public and academic focus turned toward inequality both within and between countries (Piketty 2014). These political as well as economic forces distracted energy from international or multilateral cooperation and germinated a new phase of political populism based partly on economic nationalism.

What was perhaps forgotten in this context was the challenge of effective governance at such a scale. As the urgency after a crisis recedes, so too does the impetus to pool sovereignty or overlook detailed differences in interests. After 2010, the coordination of fiscal expansion quickly dissolved partly due to fears that it would stoke inflation and unsustainable debt. Many believed at the time that they were learning historical lessons from eight centuries of financial crisis about the threshold of sustainable debt at 90 per cent of GDP from Reinhart and Rogoff (2010), later disputed by Herndon et al. (2014). When the European sovereign debt crisis emerged in 2010, enthusiasm for fiscal expansion evaporated. In this case looking beyond the 1930s might have been useful.

In the 1970s, the pressure to recognize the interests of a broader range of countries similarly drove efforts to include more developing economies and primary product producers into global governance. In the 1940s and 1950s, the global system had mainly been directed by the US and the UK. This broadened out to the G10 in the 1960s, where the plans for international monetary reform were hammered out.[7] By the early 1970s the problems of unequal development had greater prominence and primary product producers, especially OPEC, became more influential. The United Nations launched its New International Economic Order in 1974 and the IMF's Committee to Reform the International Monetary System expanded its membership to include a range of developing economies. The Committee of 20 (1972–4) became unwieldy and the inability to generate consensus on broad issues led the group to fragment into technical sub-committees (Williamson 1977; Schenk 2017). In the end, their proposals were not fully heeded. This included their suggestion to reduce the world's dependence on the dollar as the main international currency. Elaborate proposals for a substitution account were pursued but American interest in the project waned as the dollar strengthened and years of intensive planning were abandoned in 1982 (McCauley and Schenk 2015). Likewise, the UN's NIEO aiming 'to eliminate the widening gap between the developed and the developing countries' quietly faded away in the wake of the ruptures in the global economy in the 1970s.

Conclusions

In conclusion, it is clear that the Global Financial Crisis of 2008 led to widespread public as well as policy references to the Great Depression of the 1930s. Mostly, this comparison was made to judge the severity of the economic impact of the financial crisis (Eichengreen and O'Rourke 2012) but we have seen that the 1930s was also an inspiration (or spectre) for policy-makers. Certainly, the interwar depression, with its visible impact on employment, trade, income and wealth distribution has loomed large in the public imagination, particularly since it was followed by the resumption of armed conflict in Europe and then a second world war. Beyond this public imagination, the 1930s was embedded in how many policy-makers active in the 2000s learned their economics. In the 1980s, economic history was still a required part of many university economics programmes. Explaining the American interwar depression became a test case for the new breed of monetarists against the incumbent Keynesians and this elevated the debate of the causes of the depression into mainstream economics at a time when many of today's policy-makers were learning their craft. As we seek to reform or restore the global international order, we should also broaden our appreciation of the past. This chapter has suggested that there may yet be important historical lessons to be drawn, for example, from the breadth of central bank cooperation in the 1960s and from the 1970s when the world entered a new international

---

[7] The G10 was formed of countries contributing to the General Arrangements to Borrow in 1962; originally USA, Canada, UK, Belgium, Netherlands, West Germany, France, Italy, Sweden, Japan. Switzerland joined in 1964.

monetary regime but the aspiration to engage a broader range of countries in global governance was ultimately disappointed. While each era has its own special characteristics, the role of historians in analysing the past remains an important part of creating the implicit or explicit foundations on which policy decisions are made – so long as the contested and changing understanding of history is also recognized.

References

2008 Financial Crisis: A Ten-Year Review, *Annual Review of Financial Economics*, 10, 2008.

Aguado, I.G. 2001. 'The Creditanstalt Crisis of 1931 and the Failure of the Austro-German Customs Union Project.' *Historical Journal* 44 (1): 199–221.

Ahamed, L. 2009. *Lords of Finance: The Bankers Who Broke the World*. New York: Penguin.

Aizenman, J., Y. Jinjarak and D. Park. 2011. 'International reserves and swap lines: substitutes or complements?' *International Review of Economics & Finance* 20 (1): 5–18.

Albers, T.N.H. 2020. 'Currency devaluations and beggar-my-neighbour penalties: evidence from the 1930s.' *Economic History Review* **73** (1): 233–57.

Anheier H.K, and J.A. Haley, eds. 2018. 'Ten years after the Global Financial Crisis: an introduction.' Special issue of *Global Policy* 9 (51).

Canby Balderston, C. 1957. *The Effects of Federal Reserve Policy: Address at the Executives' Forum on Economics of Banking and Monetary Policy, Sponsored by the Miami Chapter of the AIB*, 4 February.

Bernanke, B. 2015. *The Courage to Act: A Memoir of a Crisis and its Aftermath*. New York: W.W. Norton and Co.

Bernanke, B. 2002. *Remarks by [Fed] Governor Ben S. Bernanke At the Conference to Honor Milton Friedman*, University of Chicago, Chicago, Illinois, 8 November.

Blanchard, O. 2017. 'Currency wars, coordination and capital controls.' *International Journal of Central Banking* 13 (2): 283–308.

Bordo, M., O.F. Humpage and A.J. Schwartz. 2015. *Strained Relations: U.S. Foreign-Exchange Operations and Monetary Policy in the Twentieth Century*. Chicago: University of Chicago Press.

Bordo, B., E. Monnet and A. Naef. 2019. 'The Gold Pool (1961–1968) and the Fall of the Bretton Woods System: Lessons for Central Bank Cooperation.' *Journal of Economic History* 79 (4): 1027–59.

Bordo, M., and J. Landon-Lane. 2010. 'The Banking Panics in the United States in the 1930s: Some Lessons for Today.' *Oxford Review of Economic Policy* 26 (3): 486–509.

Darling, A. 2011. *Back from the Brink: 1000 days at Number 11*. London and New York: Atlantic Books.

Edwards, S. 2017. 'The London Monetary and Economic Conference of 1933 and the end of the Great Depression.' *Open Economies Review* 28 (3): 431–59.

Eichengreen, B. 2015. *Hall of Mirrors: The Great Depression, the Great Recession and the Uses – and Misuses of History*. New York: Oxford University Press.

Eichengreen, B., and M. Flandreau. 2009. 'The rise and fall of the dollar (or when did the dollar replace sterling as the leading reserve currency?)' *European Review of Economic History,* 13 (3): 377–411.

Eichengreen, B., and D. Irwin. 2010. 'The Slide to Protectionism in the Great Depression: Who Succumbed and Why?' *The Journal of Economic History* 70 (4): 871–97.

Eichengreen, B., and K. O'Rourke. 2012. 'A tale of two depressions redux.' VoxEU https://voxeu.org/article/tale-two-depressions-redux

Fowler, H.H. 1965. Speech at Hot Springs Virginia, 10 July 1965. Congressional Record – Senate, 12 July 1965, pp. 16520–1.

Friedman, M. and A.H. Schwartz. 1963. *A Monetary History of the United States 1867–1960*. Princeton, NJ: Princeton University Press.

G20 Study Group. 2008. *The Group of Twenty: A History*, http://www.g20.utoronto.ca/docs/g20history.pdf

Geithner, T. 2014. *Stress Test: Reflections on Financial Crises*. New York: Random House.

Geithner, T., B. Bernanke and H. Paulson. 2019. *Firefighting: The Financial Crisis and its Lessons*. London: Profile Books.

Goodhart, C.A.E., and D.P. Tsomocos, eds. 2019. *Financial Regulation and Stability: Lessons from the Global Financial Crisis*. Cheltenham: Edward Elgar.

Herndon, T., M. Ash and R. Pollin. 2014. 'Does High Public Debt Consistently Stifle Economic Growth? A Critique of Reinhart and Rogoff.' *Cambridge Journal of Economics* 38 (2): 257–79.

IMF. 2012. 'The liberalization and management of capital flows: an institutional view.' Washington D.C: IMF.

Kindleberger, C.P. 1973. *The World in Depression, 1919–1939*. London and New York: Penguin.

King, M. 2018. 'Lessons of the Global Financial Crisis.' *Business Economics* 53: 55–9.

Lewis, M. 2011. *The Big Short: Inside the Doomsday Machine*. London and New York: Penguin.

Macmillan, M. 2008. *The Uses and Abuses of History*. Toronto: Viking Canada.

Marcus, N. 2018. *Austrian Reconstruction and the Collapse of Global Finance, 1921–1931*. Cambridge, MA: Harvard University Press.

McCauley, R.N., and C.R. Schenk. 2015. 'Reforming the International Monetary System in the 1970s and 2000s: Would a Special Drawing Right Substitution Account Have Worked?' *International Finance* 18 (2): 187–206.

McCauley, R.N., and C.R. Schenk, 2020. 'Central Bank Swaps Then and Now: Swaps and Dollar Liquidity in the 1960s.' BIS Working Paper 851.

O'Halloran, C., and T. Groll, eds. 2019. *After the Crash: Financial Crises and Regulatory Responses*. New York: Columbia University Press.

Parent, A. 2019. 'We did not repeat the errors of the past: Lessons Drawn from the Fed's Policy During the Great Depression', in Sharyn O'Halloran and Thomas Groll (eds), *After the Crash: Financial Crises and Regulatory Responses*, New York: Columbia University Press.

Piketty, T. 2014. *Capital in the 21st Century*. Cambridge, MA: Harvard University Press.

Powell, J. 2018. Speech at high-level BIS/SNB/IMF meeting, Zurich, May 2018.

Reinhart, C., and K. Rogoff. 2010. 'Growth in a time of debt.' *American Economic Review* 100 (2): 573–8.

Rey, H. 2015/2018. 'Dilemma not Trilemma: The Global Financial Cycle and Monetary Policy Independence.' NBER working paper 21162.

Rickards, R. 2011. *Currency Wars: The Making of the Next Global Crisis*. London: Portfolio.

Romer, C. 2009. 'Lessons from the Great Depression for Economic Recovery in 2009.' Speech at the Brookings Institution, Washington, D.C., 9 March 2009. https://www.brookings.edu/wp-content/uploads/2012/04/0309_lessons_romer.pdf

Romer, C. 1992. 'What Ended the Great Depression?' *Journal of Economic History* 52: 757–84.

Salter, A. 1933. Quoted in The World Economic Conference, *World Affairs*, 96 (1): 6.

Schenk, C.R. 2020a. 'Globalisation and Crisis 1989–2020.' In W. Plumpe, A. Nuzenadel and C. Schenk, *Deutsche Bank: The Global Hausbank, 1870–2020*. London: Bloomsbury.

Schenk, C.R. 2020b. 'The governance of the Bank for International Settlements 1973–2020.' In C. Borio, S. Claessens, P. Clement, R.N. McCauley and H.S. Shin (eds), *Promoting Global Monetary and Financial Stability: The Bank for International Settlements 1973–2020*, 46–93. Cambridge: Cambridge University Press.

Schenk, C.R. 2020c. 'The global financial crisis and banking regulation: Another turn of the wheel.' *Journal of Modern European History* 19(1): 8–13.

Schenk, C.R. 2010. *Decline of Sterling: Managing the Retreat of an International Currency 1945–1992*. Cambridge: Cambridge University Press.

Schenk, C.R. 2014. 'Summer in the City Banking Failures of 1974 and the Development of International Banking Supervision.' *English Historical Review* 129 (540): 1129–56.

Schenk, C.R. 2017. 'Coordination failures during and after Bretton Woods.' in M. Qureshi and A. Ghosh (eds), *From Great Depression to Great Recession: The Elusive Quest for International Policy Cooperation*. Washington, D.C.: IMF.

Temin, P. 1976. *Did Monetary Forces Cause the Great Depression?*, New York: W. W. Norton.

Temin, P., and D. Vines. 2013. *The Leaderless Economy: Why the World Economic System Fell Apart and How to Fix It*. Princeton, NJ: Princeton University Press.

Toniolo, G. 2005. *Central Bank Cooperation at the Bank for International Settlements 1930–1973*. Cambridge: Cambridge University Press.

Tooze, A. 2018. *Crashed: How a Decade of Financial Crises Changed the World*. London: Penguin.

United Nations. 1974. *Declaration on the establishment of a new international economic order*. New York: UN.

Williamson, J. 1977. *The Failure of World Monetary Reform 1971–1974*. London: Nelson and Sons.

Wheelock, D.C. 1989. 'The Strategy, Effectiveness and Consistency of Federal Reserve Monetary Policy 1924–1933.' *Explorations in Economic History* 26 (4): 453–76.

Zandy, M. 2009. *Financial Shock (Updated Edition): Global Panic and Government Bailouts–How We Got Here and What Must Be Done to Fix It*. Harlow: PH Professional Business.

3

On Volatility, Economic Slow-Motion and Populism: The Global Financial Crisis and Beyond

Gerald Braunberger

Now there is no part of our economic system which works so badly as our monetary and credit arrangements; none where the results of bad working are so disastrous socially; and none where it is easier to propose a scientific solution.

John Maynard Keynes (1923)

The hockey stick

They call it the 'financial hockey stick'. After analysing data sets on twenty-five different indicators for seventeen advanced economies going back to 1870, economists Òscar Jordà, Moritz Schularick and Alan M. Taylor find that after almost a century of stability, loans by banks to the non-financial sector began after 1950 to grow systematically faster than GDP around the world. 'The ratio of aggregate private credit to income in advanced economies has surged to unprecedented levels over the second half of the 20th century', they write. This growth in credit was concentrated in mortgage loans as opposed to unsecured lending (short-term as well as long-term) to businesses. But there is more. The 'hockey stick' in mortgage lending was accompanied by a similar pattern in real house prices, because after the Second World War, house prices have grown faster than inflation around the world.

The authors also find that as economies have become more leveraged, the standard deviation of output growth has become smaller, consistent with a phenomenon that has been coined the 'Great Moderation'. In a speech in 2004, Ben Bernanke hypothesized three potential causes for the Great Moderation: structural change in the economy; improved economic policies in part thanks to central bank independence; and good luck. At the helm of the Federal Reserve a couple of years later, Bernanke realized that the Great Moderation had ended brutally in the Great Financial Crisis.

Was this an inevitable sequence of events? Many financial crises are preceded by private credit booms, but only one in four credit booms is followed by a financial crisis. Economists like Schularick think that they can tell a 'good' credit boom, which supports economic growth, from a 'bad' one, which degenerates into a crisis. What are the typical ingredients of a 'bad' credit boom? There is a strong growth of property loans accompanied by rising property prices and a growing tendency of banks to refinance property loans not by deposits, but by the sale of short-term marketable debt.

Hyun Song Shin has demonstrated in a series of highly illuminating papers the building-up of a 'banking glut' in the years prior to the outbreak of the Global Financial Crisis. European banks – names like Deutsche Bank, Barclays or Société Générale come to mind – had enlarged their presence in the US market by attracting household savings via the wholesale funding market. For years, US money market funds had been happily buying short-term paper of European origin. At the height of the Crisis in 2008, foreign currency assets and liabilities of BIS-reporting banks were $18 trillion compared to $7 trillion in 2000 (Bruno and Shin 2014). The Global Financial Crisis obliged banks to reduce their international business – either due to regulation or due to conviction.

As the Global Financial Crisis confirms, 'bad' credit booms quite often are a cause of a severe banking crisis. A study published by the International Monetary Fund covering the years between 1970 and 2011 counts no less than 147 banking crises in the world. Sure, most of them had been regional or local in scope. They caused little pain for the global economy. The Global Financial Crisis, however, threatened to shatter the foundations of the global financial system. Any analysis of the soundness of today's financial system has to return to lessons that can be drawn from that crisis.

Our understanding of money and debt markets has benefitted from recent work by Bengt Holmström (2014) and Gary Gorton (2018). 'I will argue that "no questions asked" is the hallmark of money market liquidity; that this is the way money markets are supposed to look when they are functioning well', Nobel Prize winner Holmström wrote. 'A defence of obfuscation may sound unpalatable given the long shadows cast by the financial crisis, yet imposing transparency requirements on debt markets may make panics more likely. People often assume that liquidity requires transparency, but this is a misunderstanding.' Gary Gorton sums up nicely:

> Financial crises are runs on short-term debt. Whatever its form, short-term debt is an inherent feature of a market economy. A run is an information event in which holders of short-term debt no longer want to lend to banks because they receive information leading them to suspect the value of the backing for the debt, so they run. When runs are system-wide they threaten the solvency of the entire financial system requiring either public or private intervention. Runs, which most likely follow credit booms, are integral parts of movements in the macro-economy.

Modern economists confirm what was already known to Hyman Minsky and Charles Kindleberger, scholars of a former generation: an economy based on credit seems all too capable of creating its very own shocks.

Therefore, preserving the memory of the Global Financial Crisis is crucial. Because it may happen again. A couple of weeks after the outbreak of the coronavirus pandemic, Schularick wrote on Twitter: 'And the effect of the crisis will likely be more leverage. The ride on the financial hockey stick continues.' When holders of short-term debt began to question the value of the backing for the debt of international banks during the Crisis, the Federal Reserve worked in conjunction with other central banks around the globe to stop the panic that temporarily shut down money markets. On 12 December 2007, the Federal Reserve opened a dollar swap line with the European Central Bank and the Swiss National Bank, which gave European banks access to dollar loans supplied by their central banks. After the collapse of Lehman Brothers in mid-September 2008, the Federal Open Market Committee of the Fed authorized a $180 billion expansion of its swap lines, extending them to the central banks of Japan, England, and Canada. From 24 September to 29 October 2008, the Fed extended its dollar swap lines to Australia, Norway, Denmark, New Zealand, Brazil, Mexico, Korea and Singapore. In March 2020, the Fed entered into temporary swap lines with various foreign central banks once more in order to ease the strains in international markets for short-term dollar funding. Here we go again.

Economic slow-motion

There is, however, a much broader story to be told. The Global Financial Crisis has fostered a regime of 'economic slow-motion' in the developed countries characterized by a combination of low growth, low inflation and low interest rates. This regime will – assuming that the coronavirus pandemic does not cause long-term damage to the world economy – remain in place as long as the digital revolution is not able to produce a sustainable and significant boost to productivity. In our memory, the Crisis appears as a game-changer; however, things are not that simple, because fundamental forces have been at work for many years.

Low growth is mainly the result of changes in demography and little improvement in productivity. A short but deep recession and misallocations of capital before and after the Global Financial Crisis have contributed to that lack of growth.

Low inflation is partly explained by the export of deflation by emerging countries (China) to developed nations. 'The world economy has changed in ways which imply that global factors play a greater role in price dynamics', Kristin Forbes concludes.' Key changes include greater trade flows, the greater heft of emerging markets and their impact on commodity prices, and the greater use of supply chains to shift production to cheaper locations. The increased role of these global factors could also reduce the bargaining power of local workers' (BIS 2019). According to estimates by the Bank of International Settlements, globalization could have reduced the inflation rate in developed countries by roughly 1 percentage point. Whether globalization takes during the COVID-19 crisis remains to be seen.

As we have learnt in recent years, even 'ultra-loose' monetary policy, including negative nominal interest rates and quantitative easing, seems unable to stimulate inflation significantly. It appears that banking regulations after the Global Financial Crisis have contributed to the inefficiency of monetary policy: although central bank money ('base money') has virtually exploded since 2008, growth of broad money has been, until recently at least, modest. The traditional money multiplier no longer works. Credit growth has been much smaller since the 2008 Crisis than it was before.

Today, many people think that the currently very low interest rates are artificial. And at least some people do remember much higher interest rates in the 1980s. But it is possible that such rates were the exception and not the rule. In recent work, Paul Schmelzing (2020) has described a long historical trend of 800 years of falling real interest rates for safe assets. Schmelzing concludes: 'Against their longterm context, currently depressed sovereign real rates are in fact converging "back to historical trend" – a trend that makes narratives about a "secular stagnation" environment entirely misleading, and suggests that – irrespective of particular monetary and fiscal responses – real rates could soon enter permanently negative territory.'

It cannot be disputed that real interest rates have been falling in the last thirty years due to fundamental as well as monetary influences. One fundamental influence is the slow (but seemingly unstoppable) transformation of a capital-based industrial economy into a knowledge-based service economy. In research undertaken before the Global Financial Crisis but not published until 2010, Charles Hulton had analysed the financial reports of Microsoft. 'The main result emerging from the analysis is that the company has a lot more capital than is apparent from its financial statements. Conventional accounting practice puts Microsoft's balance sheet assets at some \$70 billion in 2006, but the estimates of this paper reveal an additional \$66 billion in missing intangible capital. These additional assets cause shareholder equity to jump from \$40 billion to \$106 billion', Hulton wrote. Intangible capital, including R&D, workers' training, brand equity and organizational development, 'does not affect the current volume of output produced, and differs, in this regard, from tangible plant and equipment'. Instead, intangible capital items 'involve the development of specific products or processes, or are investments in organizational capabilities, creating or strengthening product platforms that position a firm to compete in certain markets'.

This transformation into 'Capitalism without Capital' (Jonathan Haskell & Stian Westlake) has not only seen a secular fall in the prices of many capital goods, but also far-reaching economic and societal consequences. Although the data base is open to much improvement, it appears that the growing importance of intangible capital and the decline of the price of many capital goods has transformed, on a global scale, business into a net-saving economic sector.

A rise in intangible assets reduces business demand for loans which encourage banks to expand their lending in the mortgage sector. 'In other words, banking today consists primarily of the intermediation of savings to the household sector for the purchase of real estate. The core business model of banks in advanced economies today resembles that of real estate funds: banks are borrowing (short) from the public and capital markets to invest (long) in assets linked to real estate', comment Jordà et al. (2014). 'The intermediation of household savings for productive investment in the business sector – the textbook description of the financial sector – constitutes only a minor share of the business of banking today, even though it was a central part of that business in the 19th and early 20th centuries.'

Demographics affect low interest rates, although their significance is hotly debated. One way to look at the topic is by examining the ratio of middle-aged to young people. The famous life-cycle model of Franco Modigliani and Richard Brumberg suggests that young people borrow money, while middle-aged people invest it for retirement. The retired live off their savings. The model explains why in young populations, the interest rate should be higher than in slowly ageing societies. In our world with few young people but many baby-boomers still investing in retirement, demography favours low interest rates, whereby higher life-expectancy incites additional savings: excess demand for savings increases the price of bonds which, in turn, reduces yields. Recent work suggests of the real long-term interest rate by −1.7 to −0.4 percentage point in the eurozone between 1990 and 2030 due to demographics alone (Papetti 2019).

Demographics is one feature of Larry Summers' spectrum of secular stagnation (2016), which goes back, at least, to work done by Alvin Hansen before the Second World War: 'The economies of the industrial world, in this view, suffer from an imbalance resulting from an increasing propensity to save and a decreasing propensity to invest. The result is that excessive saving acts as a drag on demand, reducing growth and inflation, and the imbalance between savings and investment pulls down real interest rates. When significant growth is achieved, meanwhile – as in the United States between 2003 and 2007 – it comes from dangerous levels of borrowing that translate excess savings into unsustainable levels of investment (which in this case emerged as a housing bubble).'

Low productivity growth is also quoted as one reason for low interest rates. The reason is simple: lower productivity growth means less business investment, therefore a lower demand for capital. This in turn causes lower interest rates. The transformation from a capital-based industrial economy to a knowledge-based economy supports this view, as productivity growth in manufacturing usually exceeds productivity growth in services. We could add the well-known story of supply-side headwinds told by Robert J. Gordon. He thinks that the low-hanging fruits of the Industrial Revolutions of the past and the present have already been picked and all that remains is 'Stasis in the Office', 'Stasis in Retailing' and a 'Decline in Business Dynamism'.

Schmieding and Pickering (2020) suggest other origins for the long-lasting deceleration of productivity growth: 'Gains from post-war reconstruction were exhausted by the mid-1950s.Even before Donald Trump the pace of expansion in global trade had already eased. Whereas the fall of communism in Europe in 1990 and the concurrent economic liberalization of China provided another big boost to global trade, the regions themselves rather than their trading partners reaped most of the resulting gains in productivity. Mounting institutional rigidities, regulatory capture, and the rise of organised special interest groups in a largely settled political and economic environment impaired the supply potential of many economies. While the pace of technological change has been breath-taking in the last two decades, the diffusion of such innovations has been slow. Wide regional disparities, which partly reflect a failure of governments to adequately enhance the provision of public goods such as education, infrastructure and competent administration equitably across regions, have probably contributed to the slowing of technological diffusion.'

All in all, long-term real interest rates have fallen considerably over the last thirty years. Various attempts have been made to calculate the factors that have led to this decline. 'Although there is huge uncertainty, under plausible assumptions we think we can account for around 400 basis points of the 450 basis points fall', suggest Lukasz Rachel and Thomas D. Smith (2017). 'Our quantitative analysis highlights slowing global growth expectations as one force that may have pushed down on real rates recently, but shifts in saving and investment preferences appear more important in explaining the long-term decline. We think the global saving schedule has shifted out in recent decades due to demographic forces, higher inequality, and, to a lesser extent, the glut of precautionary saving by emerging markets. Meanwhile, desired levels of investment have fallen as a result of the falling relative price of capital, lower public investment, and an increase in the spread between risk-free and actual interest rates.'

Only few economists, however, would try to explain the recent fall in interest rates with secular forces alone. Two additional explanations are at hand. Possibly, real interest rates have fallen further as a result of the economic damage linked to the Global Financial Crisis and become negative at least for a short while (Holston et al. 2016). This should not come as a surprise. 'In the traditional view of the business cycle, a recession consists of a temporary decline in output below its trend line, but a fast rebound of output back to its initial upward trend line during the recovery phase', write Valerie Cerra and Sweta C. Saxena. 'In contrast, our evidence suggests that a recovery consists only of a return of growth to its long-term expansion rate – without a high-growth rebound back to the initial trend (see chart, bottom panel). In other words, recessions can cause permanent economic scarring.'

Monetary policy

There remains monetary policy. 'Is the monetary policy regime just a sideshow in the long-run evolution of real interest rates?', BIS-economists Claudio Borio, Piti Disyatat and Phurichai Rungcharoenkitkul ask (2019). Their answer is a straight 'no'. Following a line of thought that can be traced back at least to John Maynard Keynes, they refuse to think that changes in interest rates can be fully explained by the analysis of savings and investment. They insist on the relevance of financial factors and argue 'that monetary policy may play a more important role than commonly thought in long-run real economic outcomes, including real interest rates.'

For decades central banks have become ever more active, and since the outbreak of the Global Financial Crisis their policies have been even more expansionary than before. Over ten years ago Schularick and Taylor (2019) presciently observed: 'And yet it may be plausibly argued that the postwar ascent (especially since the 1970s) of a regime of fiat-money-plus-lender-of-last-resort could have also encouraged the expansion of credit to occur. Aiming to cushion the real economic effects of financial crises, policymakers have effectively prevented the periodic deleveraging of the financial sector seen in the olden days, resulting in the virtually uninterrupted growth of leverage we saw up until 2008.'

Since the Global Financial Crisis, at least central banks offer insurance against macroeconomic disasters. The scheme can be described as follows:

Liquidity and deflationary spirals self-generate endogenous risk and redistribute wealth. Monetary policy can mitigate these effects and help rebalance wealth after an adverse shock, thereby reducing endogenous risk, stabilizing the economy, and stimulating growth. The redistributive channel differs from the classic Keynesian interest rate channel in models with price stickiness. Central banks assume and redistribute tail risk when purchasing assets or relaxing their collateral requirements. Monetary policy (rules) can be seen as a social insurance scheme for an economy beset by financial frictions. As with any insurance, it carries the cost of moral hazard. Redistributive monetary policy should be strictly limited to undoing the redistribution caused by the amplification effects and by moral hazard considerations.

Brunnermeier and Sannikov 2012

Central banks became the only game in town, thereby stretching – some might say *over*stretching – their mandates.

This does not match the traditional view where the interest rate policies of central banks, in order to preserve the stability of the price level, merely follows fundamental economic trends. The origins of this tradition can be found in Knut Wicksell's classic work *Geldzins und Güterpreise* (1898). Economic equilibrium is secured if the money rate of interest equals the fundamental ('natural') rate of interest. Ideally, the central bank adapts its money rate to the long-term fundamental economic trend, which, also ideally, defines the long-term interest rate.

This is a simplified economic model, of course, and in reality the central bank might not restrict itself to the mere role of a trend-follower. And yet, it is as easy as it is seductive to overestimate the influence of central banks on long-term interest rates. The empirical relevance of the venerable expectations theory of the term-structure of interest rates – i.e. the explanation of long-term interest rates by the short-term interest rates set by central banks – is shaky at best. And numerous empirical studies show an impact of quantitative easing on the ten-year-yields of Treasuries of about 100 basis points. Monetary policy plays a role in the fall of interest rates, as do financial market regulations. But there are also fundamental forces at work. And with regard to the future: high public and private debt – in part another consequence of the Global Financial Crisis – will contribute to low interest rates as long as a massive restructuring of debt remains taboo for politicians.

Market trends

The Global Financial Crisis is remembered first and foremost as a banking crisis. However, it ushered in a second phase of liquidity which benefits asset managers at the expense of banks. The Global Financial Crisis was preceded by a 'first phase of global liquidity' (Shin 2013), which was used by banks to develop their international business. As noted above, at the height of the Global Financial Crisis in 2008, foreign currency assets and liabilities of BIS reporting banks were $18 trillion, compared to $7 trillion in 2000 (Bruno and Shin 2015). The Global Financial Crisis obliged banks to reduce their international business – either due to regulation or conviction. The expansionary monetary policy during and after the Global Financial Crisis created a 'second phase of global liquidity' which allowed asset managers and shadow banks to expand their international business.

Although the Global Financial Crisis had its origin in the US, and many elements of the crisis can be described as characteristics of the American capital market based financial system such as the securitization of assets or the importance of rating agencies, the capital-market-based financial system was strengthened after the crisis while the European-bank-based financial system was weakened.

Whereas the 'first wave' took place in developed nations – the Global Financial Crisis has been aptly named a 'transatlantic crisis' – the 'second wave of global liquidity' has also affected emerging economies. The 'second wave' is at the origin of the recent sharp rise of foreign currency liabilities of emerging market governments and corporates.

European banks find it increasingly difficult to finance long-term projects (other than property) such as infrastructure. They have been replaced by asset managers. The consequences of the rise of asset managers for financial stability need further research, because their vulnerability can also necessitate bailouts. When in 2008 US money market funds were in danger of 'breaking the buck', the Treasury announced a programme to insure the holdings of publicly offered money market funds in order to protect investors. When, in the same year, the ailing Dresdner Bank became a threat to the reputation of Allianz as an 'indestructible' insurer and asset manager, Dresdner Bank was rapidly sold to Commerzbank, which itself later had to be bailed out by the German government.

From what we can recall, the Global Financial Crisis shook deregulated financial markets to their core. Today, changes in market structure are also bound to provoke volatility and worries about financial stability. Black swans have become frequent since the Global Financial Crisis: there has been an astonishing amount of daily spikes in volatility in recent years which are in stark contradiction to the traditional idea of a Gaussian ('normal') distribution. So-called 'flash crashes' can be observed in all sorts of asset markets (gold, copper, Brent oil, exchange rates, yields, equity). One particular interesting episode took place shortly after the outbreak of the coronavirus pandemic. It affected one of the (presumably) most liquid financial markets in the world: the market for US Treasuries.

According to an interesting analysis by three authors from BIS (Schrimpf et al. 2020), for a two-week period in mid-March 2020, government bond markets – including that for US Treasuries – experienced uncharacteristic turbulence, sometimes selling off sharply in risk-off episodes when they would normally attract safe haven flows. 'Evidence in the US Treasury market points to forced selling of treasury securities by investors who had attempted to exploit small yield differences through the use of leverage', the authors write. This is reminiscent of behaviour that had been observed in the market for convertible bonds prior to the Global Financial Crisis. And they conclude: 'Even though government bonds are safe assets, large holdings by leveraged investors may detract from orderly market functioning and may necessitate interventions by the central bank.'

The most important reason for these spikes in volatility is a lack of liquidity in asset markets since the Global Financial Crisis. There are two principal origins for this.

First, a change in market conditions. Central banks have bought substantial amounts of government, corporate and mortgage bonds. Forty-two per cent of Japanese government bonds are owned by the Bank of Japan. At the moment, the largest 'ticket' that can be sold in the market for Italian government bonds – with a volume of more than €2000 billion, one of the largest bond markets in the world – is €10 million. If one or two big global asset managers decide to dump Italian bonds, there could be a spike in yields.

Regulations have reduced prop trading and market-making. Before the Global Financial Crisis, market-makers held 3 per cent of US corporate bonds. Recently they held 0.3 per cent. Exchange-traded funds (ETFs) are pro-cyclical. There are 1,600 companies on the MSCI Word index. When there is either strong demand or strong supply by investors, some markets for underlying equity are becoming illiquid.

Second, a change in investor behaviour. Low interest rates provoke a chase for yields, but many promising asset classes (such as private equity) are not very liquid. Low interest rates make high-rated government bonds unattractive. This leads to a lack of diversification in many multi-asset-portfolios because investors find it difficult to replace traditional government bonds with a liquid alternative. Short volatility strategies have become very popular, but again they can become a drain on liquidity in strained market conditions.

As the Global Financial Crisis and further academic research (Brunnermeier and Sannikov 2014) have demonstrated, a combination of rapidly shifting investor sentiment and market illiquidity can create liquidity spirals and doom loops. They can cause mayhem in financial markets and deep recessions. This memory of the Global Financial Crisis is still alive.

The threat of populism

According to relatively recent research (Funke et al. 2015), financial crises followed by deep recessions tend to provoke populist movements which benefit right-wing parties more than their left-wing counterparts. The authors write: 'After a crisis, voters seem to be particularly attracted to the political rhetoric of the extreme right, which often attributes blame to minorities or foreigners. On average, far-right parties increase their vote share by 30% after a financial crisis. Importantly, we do not observe similar political dynamics in normal recessions or after severe macroeconomic shocks that are not financial in nature.'

Low interest rates, whatever their origin, go hand in hand with high asset prices because, theoretically, an asset price equals the expected discounted payoff. Since the Global Financial Crisis we have seen a growing dispersion of yields between safe and liquid assets (bank accounts, high-rated government bonds) and on the other hand, either risky assets (listed equity) or illiquid assets (private equity, property, infrastructure). Although the empirical evidence is not entirely clear, the dispersion of yields seems to have contributed to not just the inequality of wealth but also to the inequality of income.

In some countries, real rates on safe assets have become negative. This is not just a short-term experience during a severe crisis: There is little hope that the real rates of safe assets will be significantly positive in a foreseeable future. If people regard the growing inequality of wealth/income as unfair and negative real rates on their safe assets as an expropriation, they might be tempted to listen to the siren call of populism.

Eventually the independence of central banks will be put at risk: in our memory of the Global Financial Crisis, central banks appear as heroes, while today they are often seen as villains. This is especially the case in a country like Germany, where many people think that the government, represented by the central bank, has to secure a positive real interest rate at all costs. 'Being in close interaction with the financial sector may lead to negative connotations, given the loss of trust in finance after the crisis', Ernest Gnan and Donato Masciandaro (2020) suggest. 'Some criticize central banks for favouring the interests of the financial sector. This assertion is particularly critical have after the global financial crisis been more heavily involved in banking supervision.'

Another oddity has emerged. 'The German experience in the financial crises of the past decade stands out in that there is no one story to tell. Whereas the Irish and Spanish crises can be explained in simple terms by boom-and-bust developments in real-estate markets, the German experience has no such simple explanation', says Martin Hellwig (2018). 'The underlying cause must be seen in the difficulties that arose when a traditional financial system was exposed to radical change in the 1990s.'

In 2009, the recession in Germany was deep but brief. The following eurozone crisis left the German economy almost untouched. According to a popular (although debatable) view, Mario Draghi's expansionary monetary policy ('whatever it takes') served highly indebted European countries but not Germany. A good many commentators, and not just right-wing populists, saw the central bank moving beyond the boundaries of its mandate. The recent judgement of the German Constitutional Court, which can be seen as a (albeit minor) restriction of the ECB's independence, was welcomed even in German quarters, where central bank independence was considered sacrosanct twenty years ago.

The growing mistrust of independent central banks is, however, much more general and not restricted to 'Swabian housewives' – often mentioned by Chancellor Merkel – for putting all their savings into a bank account. Central banks have been accused of having contributed to a pre-crisis financial exuberance. 'Moreover, central banks, alongside most others, failed to foresee or head off the Global Crisis and their focus on a narrowly construed price stability-oriented monetary policy made them ignore or insufficiently calibrate the perils of financial instability', Charles Goodhart and Rosa Lastra explain (2018). 'Although their immediate response in 2008/9 was exemplary, and did succeed in preventing another Great Depression, their record afterwards, from 2010 to 2016, was consistently one of failing to forecast the sluggishness of growth of either output or inflation, casting some doubt on their competence, economic understanding and capacities.'

Dani Rodrik (2018) agrees: 'Independent central banks have played a useful role in bringing inflation down in the 1980s and 1990s. But in a low inflation environment, their exclusive focus on price stability tends to impart a deflationary bias to economic policy.' A too-tight monetary is a particular concern of the so-called left-wing populism, a strand inside the populist movement, which is in favour of boosting economic growth with the help of expansionary monetary and fiscal policies. 'Central bankers motivated purely by inflation concerns will likely try to hit their target overwhelmingly from below. This may well create a tension with employment generation and growth. When the conflict becomes severe, the independence of the central bank can be called into question. In such circumstances allowing a certain degree of politicization of monetary policy may be the lesser evil', Rodrik concludes.

Gnan and Masciandaro echo another concern: 'Central banks scientific approach to policy may turn into the perception of being technocratic and remote from reality amidst the post-crisis skepticism against mainstream economics and the economics profession at large. Such criticism may be invigorated by failure to meet inflation targets, while side effects from an escalation of monetary easing become more wide-spread and visible.'

In May 2020 Adam Tooze, the most famed historian of the Great Financial Crisis, publicly declared the 'End of the Central Bank Myth' (Tooze 2020). He writes: 'For decades, monetary policy has been treated as technical, not as political. The pandemic has ended this illusion forever.' The Great Financial Crisis and the Corona Crisis may well be two nails in the coffin of central bank independence.

'The difficulty lies not so much in developing new ideas as in escaping from old ones', John Maynard Keynes once remarked. However – and particularly in the age of growing populism – it may turn out that central bank independence was not such a bad idea at all. Even if our monetary and credit arrangements may work badly, it might not be as easy to propose a scientific solution as the great Keynes had envisaged almost a century ago. It's not just old sins that cast long shadows. So does the Global Financial Crisis.

References

Borio, Claudio, Piti Disyatat and Phurichai Rungcharoenkitkul. 2019. 'What Anchors for the Natural Rate of Interest?' BIS Working Paper.

Brunnermeier, Markus, and Yuliy Sannikov. 2012. 'Redistributive Monetary Policy.' Jackson Hole Symposium.

Brunnermeier, Markus, and Yuliy Sannikov. 2014. 'A Macroeconomic Model with a Financial Sector.' *American Economic Review,* 104 (2)

Bruno, Valentina, and Hyun Song Shin. 2015. 'Cross-Border Banking and Global Liquidity.' *Review of Economic Studies.*

Cerra, Valerie, and Sweta C. Saxena. 2018. 'The Economic Scars of Crises and Recessions.' The IMF blog. URL: https://blogs.imf.org/2018/03/21/the-economic-scars-of-crises-and-recessions/

Forbes, Kristin. 2019. 'Has Globalization Changed the Inflation Process?' BIS Working Paper.

Funke, Manuel, Moritz Schularick and Christoph Trebesch. 2015. 'Going to Extremes: Politics after Financial Crises.' Cesifo Working Paper.

Gnan, Ernest, and Donato Masciandaro. 2020. 'Populism, Economic Policies and Central Banking: An Overview.' Vienna: Suerf.

Goodhart, Charles, and Rosa Lastra. 2018. 'Potential Threats to Central Bank Independence.' VoxEU. URL: https://voxeu.org/article/potential-threats-central-bank-independence

Gordon, Robert. 2015. 'Secular Stagnation: A Supply-Side View.' *American Economic Review.* 105 (5).

Gorton, Gary B. 2018. 'Financial Crises.' Yale Working Paper.

Hellwig, Martin. 2018. 'Germany and the Financial Crisis 2007–2017.' Max-Planck Institut für Gemeinschaftsgüter Working Paper.

Holmström, Bengt. 2014. 'Understanding the Role of Debt in the Financial System.' BIS Working Paper.

Holston, Kathryn, Thomas Laubach and John Williams. 2016. 'Measuring the Natural Rate of Interest: International Trends and Determinants.' San Francisco: Federal Reserve Bank of San Francisco.

Hulton, Charles R. 2010. 'Decoding Microsoft: Intangible Capital as a Source of Company Growth.' NBER Working Paper.

Jordà, Oscar, Moritz Schularick and Alan M. Taylor. 2016. 'Macrofinancial History and the New Business Cycle Facts.' NBER Working Paper.

Moggridge, Donald, ed. 1981. *The Collected Writings of John Maynard Keynes. Volume XiX: Activities 1992–1929.* Cambridge: Macmillan.

Papetti, Andrea. 2019. 'Demographics and the Natural Real Interest Rate: Historical and Projected Paths for the Euro Area.' ECB Working Paper.

Rachel, Lukasz and Thomas D. Smith. 2017. 'Are Low Real Interest Rates Here to Stay?' *International Journal of Central Banking,* 13 (3).

Rodrik, Dani. 2018. 'Is Populism Necessarily Bad Economics?' *American Economic Review,* 108, AEA Papers and Proceedings.

Schmieding, Holger, and Kallum Pickering. 2020. 'Economic Trends of the Decade: Productivity.' Hamburg: Berenberg.

Schrimpf, Andreas, Hyun Song Shin and Vladyslav Sushko. 2020. 'Leverage and margin spirals in fixed income markets during the Covid-19 crisis.' BIS Bulletin.

Schularick, Moritz, and Alan M. Taylor. 2009. 'Credit Booms Go Wrong.' VoxEu.

Shin, Hyun Song. 2013. 'The Second Phase of global Liquidity and its Impact on Emerging Economies.' San Francisco: Federal Reserve Bank of San Francisco.

Summers, Larry. 2016. 'The Age of Secular Stagnation.' *Foreign Affairs,* March–April.

Tooze, Adam. 2020. The End of the Central Bank Myth. *Foreign Policy,* 13 May.

Wicksell, Knut. 1898. Geldzins und Güterpreise. Jena: Fischer.

4

Lessons from the Great Financial Crisis in Perspective

Ramon Marimon[*]

The queen's question

On 5 November 2008, Queen Elizabeth II, whose personal fortune had just taken an estimated hit of £25 million, paid her first visit to the London School of Economics and bluntly asked: 'It's awful – Why did nobody see it coming?' A follow-up letter, signed by a group of leading UK economists and historians, concluded by saying:

> In summary, Your Majesty, the failure to foresee the timing, extent and severity of the crisis and to head it off, while it had many causes, was principally a failure of the collective imagination of many bright people, both in this country and internationally, to understand the risks to the system as a whole.

In fact, one of the brightest, Nobel Laureate Robert Lucas had said in his Presidential Address to the American Economic Association: 'My thesis in this lecture is that macroeconomics in this original sense has succeeded: Its central problem of depression prevention has been solved' (Lucas 2003). He was not alone, regarding asset bubbles; 'benign neglect' was the general attitude among academic macroeconomists, while central banks were simply focusing on inflation, based on the 'divine coincidence' argument, according to which maintaining a stable inflation would suffice to keep economic activity close to its potential (Blanchard et al. 2012).

In sum, under closer scrutiny, there is nothing unique or incorrect with Lucas' statement, nor did the financial crisis prove him wrong. The 'original sense' referred to the design and implementation of fiscal and monetary stabilization policies in economies facing business cycle fluctuations and possible inflationary pressures. On this, independent central banks, following macroeconomists' advice, have done their job: price stability has been a feature of advanced economies at the end of the twentieth century, as well as the first two decades of the twenty-first, financial crisis included.

[*] I want to thank Youssef Cassis and Jean-Jacques van Helten for their persistence and patience as editors and Chloe Larkou for her skillful research assistance work: they made this chapter possible.

However, in the fall of 2008 the period known as 'the great moderation' suddenly ended with a financial crisis at the core of the financial system of the advanced economies and rapidly spread through them. That is:

Lesson #1: In an integrated global financial market, a country's financial crisis is likely to become a *global* financial crisis – and very fast, if it is at the core of the international financial market[1].

Wasn't macroeconomic policy supposed to prevent it? Actually, no, since a financial crisis was by definition a finance issue. Finance theory is one of the main achievements of economic science: it is behind billions of daily financial transactions that use its pricing formulas, instruments, etc., to support a better allocation of risks and investments. In sum, it is behind the growth of developed and developing countries, but no engine of growth is perfect. Even if finance theory had been developed in universities and business-schools hand-in-hand with modern macroeconomic theory, at the beginning of the twenty-first century, it remained a different field. A highly leveraged financial sector (in US) or a highly indebted private sector (in some European countries) were not on the radar of macroeconomic policy, nor was their stability a target for central banks. Taken together, they were not part of Lucas' 'original sense'. Yet:

Lesson #2: A developed financial sector tends to be pro-cyclical, exacerbating the euphoria in good times and rushing away – as financial runs – to safer havens, in bad times.

The pro-cyclical nature of developed financial systems has aggregate macroeconomic effects; in particular, it nourished the seeds of the financial crisis during the 'Great Moderation'. As Acharya and Richardson (2009) said, 'there is almost universal agreement that the fundamental cause of the [2007–08] crisis was a combination of a credit boom and a housing bubble'.[2] Money and credit had been at the core of macroeconomics since its beginnings, but the complementarity, and explosive combination, between credit booms and housing bubbles, had only ever been at the margin. Unfortunately, it is true that there were no macro-financial instruments or policies that could have prevented the financial crisis from happening. Nevertheless, when the 2007–08 crisis struck, lessons from the past, from the 1930s crisis and recession, came to the rescue – in part.

---

[1] Note that this lesson also follows from Network Theory. All the lessons in this chapter are important, but the final three stand-out and are labeled 'Lessons for the future'.

[2] Acharya and Richardson (2009: 12). Claessens et al. (2014) add two features to Acharya and Richardson's list: 'the 2007–2009 crisis (...) shares at least four major features with earlier [crises] episodes: rapid increases in asset prices, credit booms, a dramatic expansion in marginal loans, and regulation and supervision that failed to keep up with developments' (p. xiii). That the housing bubble was not an exogenous event has been forcefully argued by Rajan (2010).

The financial and monetary side: lessons from the past and the new era of central banking

One key lesson from the past was that regulation and regulatory institutions could play a key role in preventing banking and financial crises. Truly revolutionary regulation – although it sounds like a contradiction in terms – took place in the US in the 1930s, with its two main pillars being the Securities Act of May 1933, which regulated the offering of securities and created the Federal Trade Commission (later the SEC), and the Banking Act of June 1933 (the so-called Glass-Steagall Act), which created the Federal Deposit Insurance Corporation (FDIC) in order to prevent bank-runs, and to separate commercial and investment banking. However, regulation and supervision failed to keep up with developments leading to the financial crisis. This was due, in part, to deregulations – for example, abandoning the functional separation of banking activities noted above – but mostly due to expansion of the unregulated non-banking financial sector. 'With the benefit of hindsight, we can say with confidence that the US and European financial systems in 2007 lacked two key shock absorbers – adequate capital to meet falls in asset values and defaults, and adequate holdings of high-quality liquid assets to meet a temporary liquidity shortfall' (Cecchetti and Schoenholtz 2017).

In the 2007–09 crisis, there was a regulatory response, not a revolution. The Dodd-Frank Wall Street Reform and Consumer Protection Act of 2010, established the Systemic Risk Council which allowed the regulation of the non-bank financial firms in the US. The 2010 Basel III agreement, which the US Federal Reserve endorsed in 2011 and the European Union in 2013, addressed capital requirements and liquidity concerns, as well as regulatory and supervision procedures to reduce systemic risk.

Unfortunately, the Dodd-Frank Act would have not discouraged the fragility of a highly leveraged financial system to common asset shocks, nor would it have prevented 'the enormous lending bubble specific to subprime mortgages in the United States' (Acharya et al. 2011: 22–3); Basel III, specifically designed to avoid excessive risk-taking, has been a long and unfinished process of implementation.

In macroeconomics and central banking, the main lesson from the past was the need to avoid the errors of the 1930s – in particular, the central bank must accommodate to the liquidity needs of the economy in times of crisis. In fact, Bernanke (1983) further develops the pioneer work of Friedman and Schwartz (1963) and concludes:

> Institutions which evolve and perform well in normal times may become counterproductive during periods when exogenous shocks or policy mistakes drive the economy off course. The malfunctioning of financial institutions during the early 1930's exemplifies this point.

These concerns became the drivers of Bernanke's research career (e.g. Bernanke 1995 and 2004). Two of his contributions are particularly relevant for the financial crisis. One is conceptual: to characterize a financial crisis as a period of unusual financial distress, which he identifies with the 'cost of credit intermediation'[3]. His other contribution was in monetary policy, and it can be paraphrased as:

> Lesson #3: If inside money collapses, outside money should quickly come to the rescue.

The end of the 'great moderation' brought to a sudden stop the large expansion of different forms of financial intermediation, which provided liquidity (inside money) to a very active, and creative, financial sector. Not only did the cost of credit intermediation skyrocket – for example, the cost of short-term borrowing in US increased by 500 basis points during the last months of 2008[4] – but there was also an effective asset-run on previously perceived safe (AAA) assets (Figure 4.1); in other words, assets that were liquid suddenly became illiquid.

Fortunately, Ben S. Bernanke himself, as Chair of the Federal Reserve Bank (2006–14), applied his policy lessons and in so doing started a 'revolution' in central banking. He not only adapted the basic policy instrument – the interest rate – to the crisis situation (Figure 4.2), but also began an unprecedented expansion of the Federal Reserve Bank (FRB) balance sheet, corresponding to an increase of the (outside) money supply and a range of non-conventional (quantitative easing etc) monetary policies. A battery of

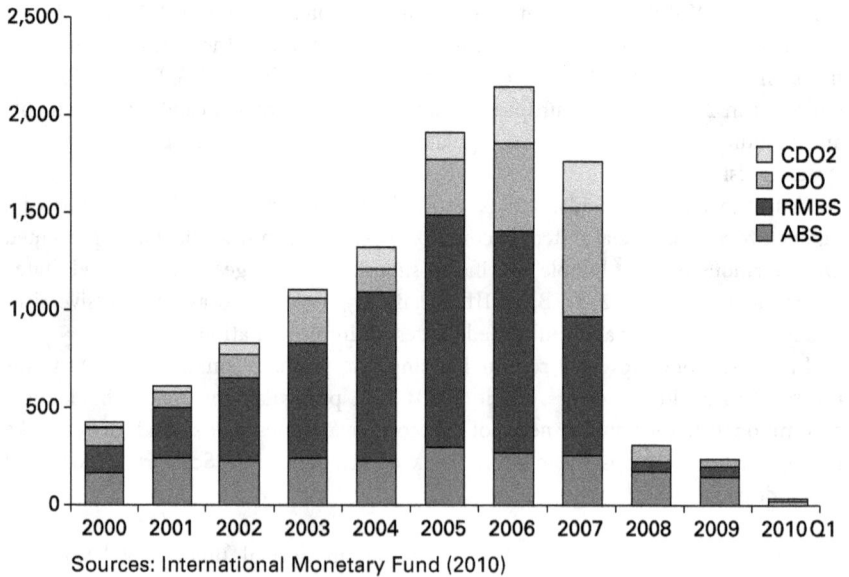

Sources: International Monetary Fund (2010)

Figure 4.1 The US 2007–08 asset run in private-label term securitization insurance market (billions of dollars).

---

[3] Romer and Romer (2017) have developed a new measure of financial distress based on Bernanke's characterization of a financial crisis and show how it traces the different patterns that the crisis followed in United States and European countries.

[4] See, for example, Bernanke (2013: Lecture 3).

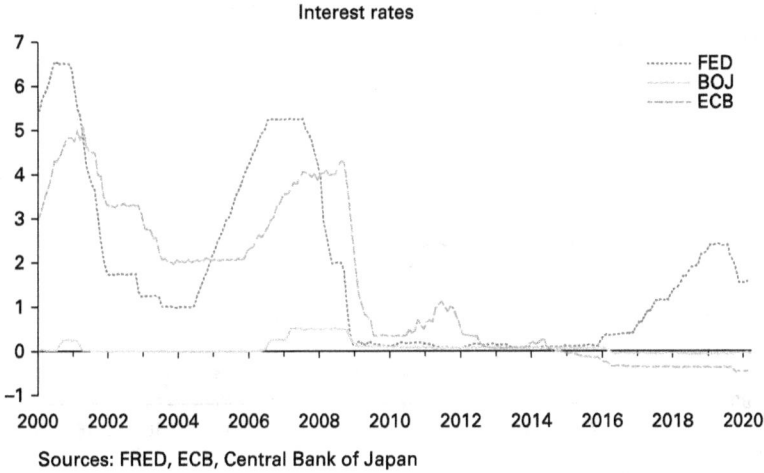

Figure 4.2 Central banks fighting the financial crisis (and beyond) with their traditional instrument: the interest rate.

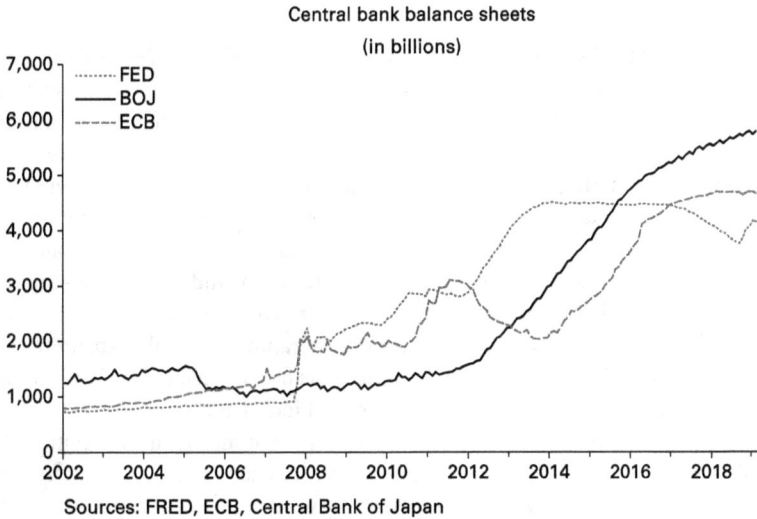

Figure 4.3 Central banks expansion of their balance sheets since the start of the financial crisis.

policies was deployed to get the economy back on track, once interest-rate policy had lost its effectiveness; i.e. the reference interest rate was close to its zero lower-bound. The other main central banks followed suit, and their intervention played a major role in preventing a much deeper recession, as it happened in the 1930s. Nevertheless, as Figure 4.3 shows, the expansion of central banks' balance sheets did not end with the end of the financial crisis; indeed, a new era of central banking started in 2008.

Real GDP normalized 2000–2010 Q1 (2008, Q1 = 100)

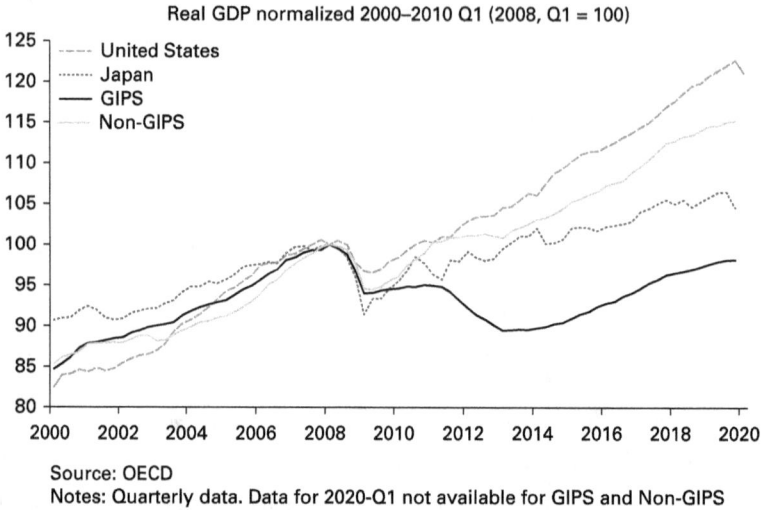

Source: OECD
Notes: Quarterly data. Data for 2020-Q1 not available for GIPS and Non-GIPS

Figure 4.4 The financial crisis in perspective. GIPS: Greece, Italy, Portugal & Spain; Non-GIPS: the (2020) fifteen euro area countries, which are not GIPS.

Other central banks followed suit because by the end of 2008 the crisis had already spread through developed economies, as Figure 4.4 shows. In other words, rephrasing our Lesson #1, the US financial crisis had a major immediate effect across advanced economies. However, the financial crisis was novel in two respects. First, for being a crisis originated in the most advanced economies rather than in emerging ones. Second, because it was the first crisis to spread from an established monetary union – the US – to a recently formed monetary union, the euro area (EA) or eurozone.

As we have seen, macroeconomists who had extensively studied the fiscal–monetary link underestimated the financial–monetary–fiscal connection. Nevertheless, there were already farsighted articles in the academic literature that could explain that link, and which became the theoretical foundation of the new monetary policies,[5] although, in general, these policies preceded their theoretical foundations.

Most 'unconventional' monetary policies are aimed at managing expectations and/ or a disruption in a specific market. For example, in economies where the reference interest rate was close to its zero lower-bound, 'forward guidance' policies attempted to coordinate private expectations on future inflation in order to determine when and how the economy would exit the zero lower-bound. Central banks' asset purchase policies were targeted to specific sectors of the economy that could benefit from monetary injections and where such benefit had social value (e.g. keeping the market active and/or replacing inside money with outside money). There was an interesting

---

[5]   Two key elements of this link are: 1) the role of collateralized credit, since a shock to asset prices can be amplified when assets are also used as collateral; 2) the, already mentioned, change in the relative liquidity of assets vs money (inside vs outside money). Kiyotaki and Moore (1997) pioneered a literature on (1), but their (2019) was also a frontrunner of (2) (the paper was first presented in the Society for Economic Dynamics' 2001 meeting!).

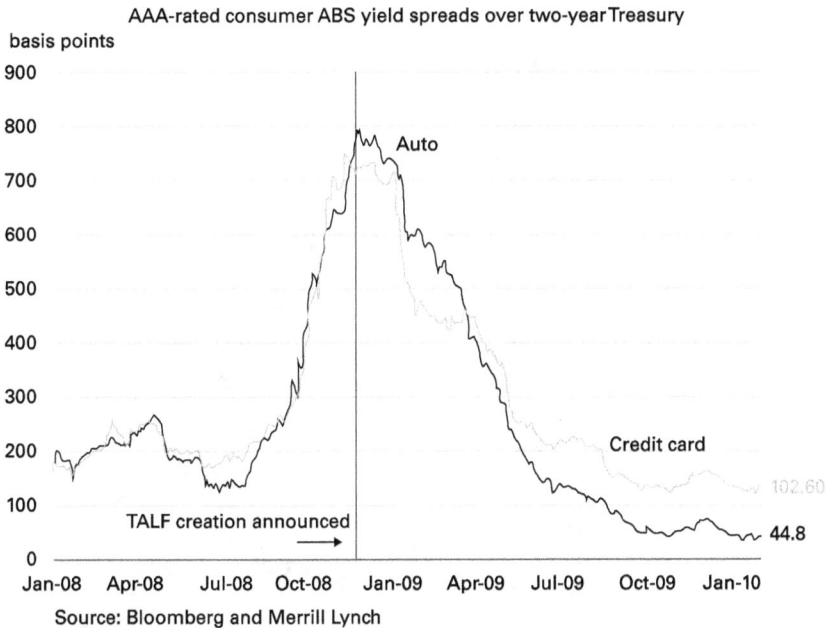

AAA-rated consumer ABS yield spreads over two-year Treasury

Figure 4.5 The collapse of the ABS market in 2007–08.

example of a policy that had both objectives – the 2009 Term Asset-Backed Securities Lending Facility (TALF) – which is illustrative of these new central bank policies.

Beginning in mid-2007, the number of defaults started to rise in the US. Investors began to fear that more defaults were coming and either could not – or did not want to – continue buying asset-backed securities (ABS). The whole ABS market started to collapse at the end of 2007, with yield spreads skyrocketing in 2008 (Figure 4.5). The Fed decided to step in with TALF, which provided buyers of newly generated ABS with a subsidy contingent on ex-post realized losses, with the backing of the US Treasury. Being a subsidy (which eventually amounted to $71.1 billion) to the unpopular crowd of financial intermediaries, it was highly criticized, but at the end TALF fulfilled its objectives at no cost; in fact, ultimately there was a large benefit for taxpayers.[6]

The AAA-ABS collapse, and subsequent recovery with the introduction of TALF (Figure 4.6),[7] is an example of the capacity of a central bank to intervene in a situation where there are multiple equilibria. Acting as lender of last resort, the central bank can move the economy from an inefficient equilibrium to a more efficient one. For example,

---

[6] On 30 September 2010, the Fed announced that more than 60 per cent of the TALF loans had been repaid in full, with interest, ahead of their legal maturity dates. The Fed finally announced that 'as of May 2011, there has not been a single credit loss. Also, as of May 2011, TALF loans have earned $1.2 billion in interest income for the US taxpayer' (Gaetano and Marimon (2021)).

[7] Figure 4.6 (from Gaballo and Marimon 2021) shows, at the micro level of the AAA-Auto ABS, the differential impact of TALF on interest rate spreads, as well as the persistence of this effect after TALF, comparing the behavior of interest rates on new issued AAA-Auto ABS with the interest on Minimal Risk Loans of private banks.

Interest-rate spreads from Libor 1m

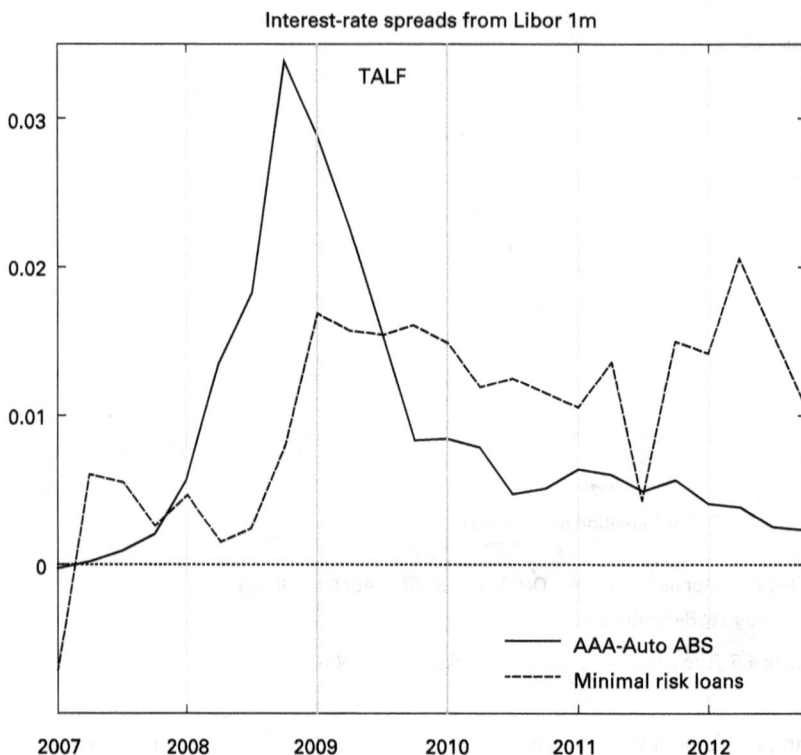

Figure 4.6 The recovery of the AAA-Auto ABS market after TALF. (Newly issued AAA-Auto ABS interest rates vs interest rated on private banks' minimal risk loans.)

the introduction of the FDIC in 1933 helped to prevent bank-run equilibria, where depositors fearing a bankruptcy would recall their deposits provoking the bankruptcy. Asset-runs, during the financial crisis (resulting in fire sales and runs to perceived safer assets), resulted in *self-fulfilling equilibria*; that is, investors *believe* that an asset or a bank is not as safe as it was supposed to be, sell the asset – possibly, forced by regulation – or withdraw their deposits and, if many investors share the same belief, the asset, or the bank, is indeed not as safe as it was supposed to be: thus *beliefs have been self-fulfilled*. The investor had no other rational option than 'to run'.

The case of the AAA-ABS collapse is slightly different, however. In this case, 'to run' meant selling at high interest rates, since default losses were expected to be significant. However, a seller could issue a new AAA-auto-ABS at a lower interest rate and find out that the fear of widespread car loan defaults was unfounded. Nevertheless, given his beliefs, he may never try this, and if it is the same for other sellers, their beliefs are, at the end, self-confirmed (i.e. the AAA-auto-ABS market is in an inefficient self-confirming equilibrium). The TALF intervention broke this doom loop. TALF was also a case of economic policy action being ahead of economic theory, which only came much later (Gaballo and Marimon 2021).

For the record, there is one more element, already noted, that makes TALF specially interesting:

> Unlike our other lending programs, this facility [TALF] combines Federal Reserve liquidity with capital provided by the Treasury, which allows it to accept some credit risk.
>
> Bernanke 2009

However, possibly the best example from the financial and euro crisis of the ability of a central bank to avoid an inefficient self-fulfilling crisis – in particular, a debt crisis – was 'just' an announcement (the 'just' is qualified below):

> within our mandate the ECB is ready to do whatever it takes and, believe me, it will be enough.
>
> Mario Draghi, 26 July 2012[8]

Lesson #4: If a central bank – possibly, in coordination with the fiscal authority – can commit to a 'lender of last resort' policy, it is able to change and coordinate private agents' beliefs and prevent an inefficient equilibrium outcome.

As we have seen, the Fed often acted in explicit coordination with the Treasury. Was there a similar initiative on the fiscal side?

The fiscal side (debt and stimulus packages)

Figures 4.7a and b shows one fiscal counterpart to the monetary response: the increase in sovereign debt between 2009 and 2011, both in the US and the EA (with an important component being the primary deficit), mostly due to the need to cover for the loss of tax revenues, the cost of financing the debt and to finance fiscal stimulus packages. However, Figure 4.7 also shows that – as was the case with central banks' expanded balance sheet (Figure 4.3) – both in the US and the EA, the increase in sovereign debt did not stop, or even slow down, with the end of the financial crisis. On the contrary, the crisis seems to have marked the *start* of a trend, particularly in the US.

With some small (but relevant) differences, monetary responses to the crisis were similar across developed economies. However, fiscal responses – in particular, fiscal stimulus packages – were substantially different. Figure 4.8 shows that while across OECD countries the size of stimulus packages was positively related to the loss of GDP in the crisis, there are important differences. In comparison to other countries, the US – and, to a lesser extent, Germany and Spain – had a relatively generous package. Italy and Japan experienced a similar GDP loss (−6.2 per cent and 6.5 per cent,

---

[8] At the Global Investment Conference at the British Business Embassy: https://www.youtube.com/watch?v=hMBI50FXDps

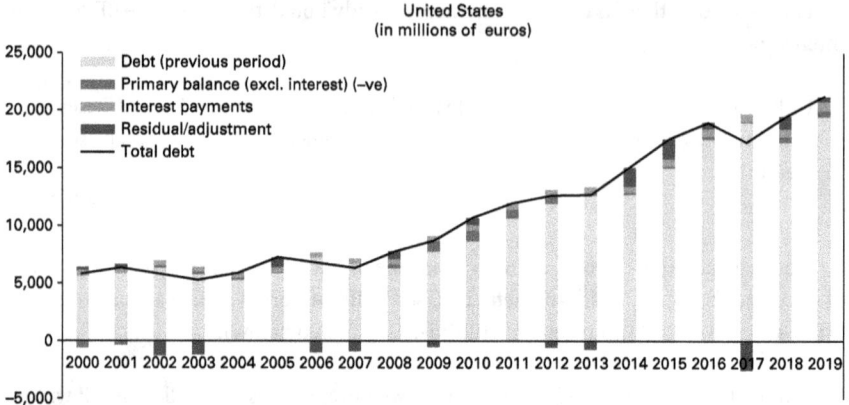

Source: AMECO

Figure 4.7a The evolution of sovereign debt in the twenty-first century: United States.

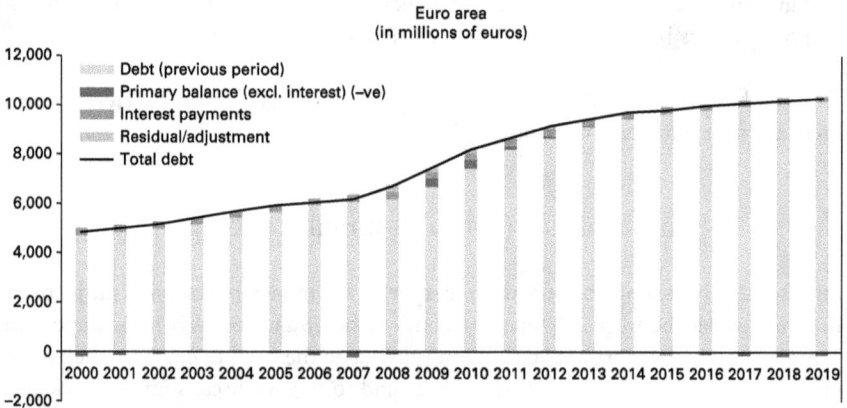

Source: AMECO

Figure 4.7b The evolution of sovereign debt the twenty-first century: euro area.

respectively between 2007 and 2009), but Italy had a negligible stimulus package, while Japan had one of the largest (4.5 per cent of GDP).

One of the major reasons for the relative higher generosity (or stinginess) of different stimulus packages is that different countries have different fiscal capacities; in particular, that countries with higher levels of debt may not be able to afford to be generous. Figure 4.9 vindicates this, if one excludes Japan. However, according to this metric, France, and particularly the UK, did have the fiscal capacity but did not exploit it fully with a larger stimulus package. Japan stands out (and distorts the line in Figure 4.9) with the highest level of debt and, as we have seen, one of the largest stimulus packages.

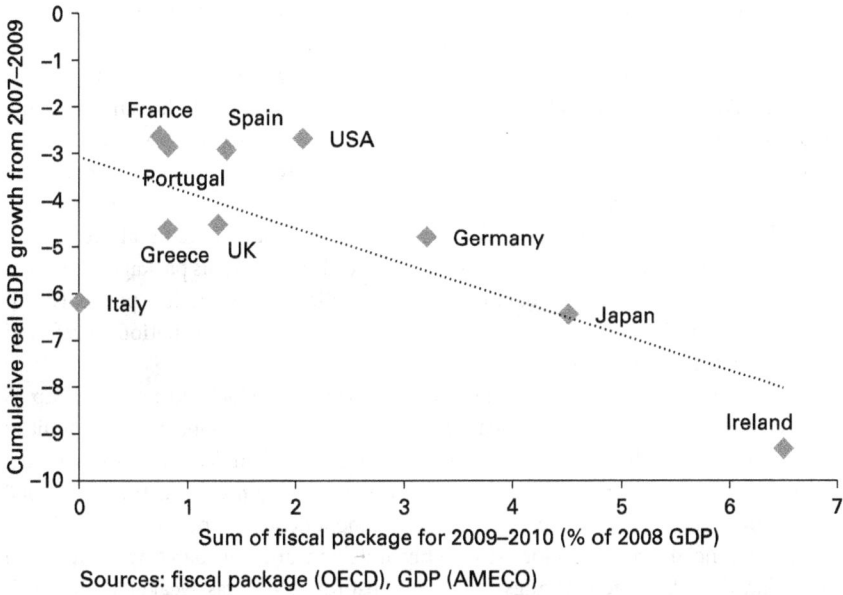

Figure 4.8 Fiscal stimulus relative to loss of GDP.

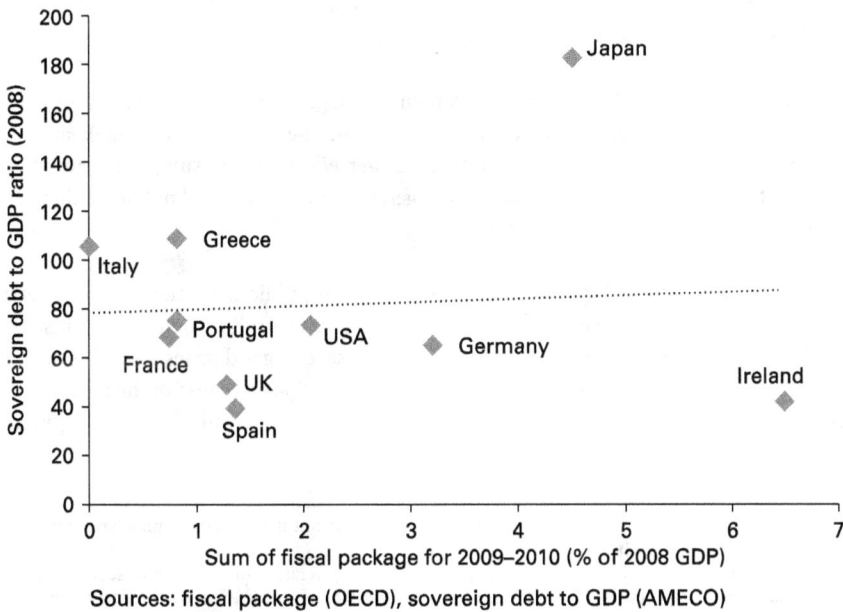

Figure 4.9 Fiscal stimulus vs fiscal capacity (sovereign debt).

The level of sovereign debt only partially reflects a country's fiscal capacity, for two reasons. First, because it is only one of a nation's liabilities: for example, countries with a relatively large social welfare state usually have large additional liabilities (e.g. pensions). Alternatively, asset levels vary between countries. The IMF has an interesting report on this issue (International Monetary Fund 2018). The report shows how Japan's large sovereign debt is almost compensated by its 'sovereign assets', while Spain, and epecially Italy, have a fairly negative liabilities-to-assets balance. Similarly, the IMF research shows that both France and UK do not seem to have large fiscal capacity. In sum, this can explain Japan's capacity to implement a large stimulus package,[9] as well as the US' capacity to increase its debt in the decade following the crisis – particularly if one accounts for the intangible asset of having the dollar as the international preferred 'safe currency' for trade and financial transactions.

Furthermore, there are government implicit liabilities which do not show up as such (i.e. in the IMF government fiscal accounting): these are national private liabilities that eventually may become government liabilities. For example, Spain was a model member of the EA in terms of fulfilling 'the EU government fiscal constraints' in 2008 (sovereign debt to GDP ≤ 60 per cent and government deficit ≤ 3 per cent, in 2008) but the non-financial private sector was highly indebted and the banking sector – in particular, the 'liberalized' savings and loans institutions – was weaker than it was perceived in 2008. Both fault figures being, in part, the legacy of a crashed real estate boom. As a result, Spain swung from a government budget surplus of 2 per cent of GDP in 2007 to a deficit of 11.2 per cent in 2009. A similar reversal was experienced in Ireland as a result of their banking crisis. In effect, banks were bailed out by the government and their plight was the main catalyst behind Ireland's loss of GDP. These two factors, together with their ambitious stimulus package, resulted in the Irish seeing the largest upsurge of sovereign debt in Europe.

> Lesson #5: The effect on growth of stimulus packages was mixed. However, most had two components: 'pain killers' (i.e. to limit the economic damage); and 'recovery pills' (i.e. to create positive multiplier effects on consumption and/or investment). The fact that, for some packages, the second effect did not occur does not exclude the effect of the first.[10]

As we have seen, private liabilities often become public liabilities, which means that both need to be accounted for. In fact, their joint cyclical behaviour must be accounted, since, for example, it is more efficient to save in good times. In this regard, a country's sound fiscal behaviour can be measured by the 'positiveness' of the correlation between the Primary Surplus (PS): Output (Y) minus private (C+I) and public

---

[9] Note that the reference is the October 2018 Fiscal Monitor, but these balances may have not been very different ten years before.

[10] With the financial and euro crises there has been a new generation of studies on fiscal multiplier effects, showing their larger effect in times of crisis, as well as when the effect on the lower groups of the income distribution – with larger marginal propensities to consume – is accounted for; see Marimon and Cooley 2018: Introduction.

Table 4.1 Correlations between primary surplus over GDP and GDP; i.e. Corr(PS/Y, Y).

	Japan	US	UK	Euro area	Non-GIPS	GIPS
1995–2019	0.77	0.52	0.43	0.30	0.44	0.07
2000–2019	0.93	0.55	0.53	0.44	0.66	0.11
	Germany	France	Italy	Spain	Portugal	Greece
1995–2019	0.46	0.40	0.12	0.08	0.01	−0.19
2000–19	0.71	0.50	0.22	0.09	0.00	−0.19

(Yearly data with HP-filtered PS and Y; Data source: AMECO & OECD.)

spending (G).[11] Table 4.1 provides this perspective and reinforces what has been said regarding the fiscal capacity of Japan, the non-GIPS and GIPS of Figure 4.4[12].

> LESSON FOR THE FUTURE #1: Fiscal capacity determines the ability of a government to react in a crisis. It is, in turn, determined by the explicit and implicit assets and liabilities of a country and its cyclical behaviour; a sound fiscal-capacity position must be procyclical.

The role of linkages in crises

Going back to Figure 4.4., a closer look to 'the crisis-cascade year' (Q1 2008–Q1 2009) shows the effect of having strong linkages between advanced economies. But the role of linkages, and interdependence, is pervasive in crises. In fact, Bernanke's 'definition' of a financial crisis as an abrupt increase of the 'cost of credit intermediation', is about the malfunction of a basic link in an advanced economy: financial intermediation. Similarly, the 'benign neglect' of the financial and macroeconomics link kept most of the academic economic profession oblivious of the crisis until it erupted. On the policy side, understanding the link between outside and inside money – and the role that a central bank should play in times of a financial crisis – was crucial in preventing the 2007–09 crisis from becoming a sequel to the Great Depression of the 1930s. In summary:

> LESSON FOR THE FUTURE #2: Linkages are at the root of, and characterize, socio-economic crises.

---

[11] That is, PS= Y– (C+I+G) – i.e. PS is also the current account of the country – and the closer Corr(PS/Y,Y) is to +1, the more the country 'saves in good times and is able to react in bad times' – i.e. the more procyclical the fiscal position of the country is (and countercyclical the corresponding fiscal policy).

[12] Note that a low, or negative, correlation does not necessary mean that a country is not saving enough in good times: it may also mean that it is simply not able to spend in bad times. Fiscal consolidation (austerity) programmes in times of crisis have this effect, although they may be the necessary result of past debt accumulations in good times.

This is because:

1. in the main, links work. As a result, contagion is easy. With contagion, the linked-weak are likely to suffer more (e.g. the rapid internationalization of the financial crisis and its ultimate consequences for GIPS).
2. links do not work properly when subject to shocks (e.g. financial intermediation).
3. links are more important than previously thought (e.g. the financial–macro link).
4. in some cases, however, links are weaker than they should be.

Corrective approaches also differ across this classification, since: for 1) contagion may need to be prevented, but links cannot be destroyed since they must work properly to get out of the crisis (e.g. international trade, value chains, free capital movements); for 2) they need repair, but the repair should not be disruptive for normal times once the shock has passed (a major trade-off for regulation); for 3) policies and institutions must be designed accounting for links, active or inactive, that become relevant in exceptional states of the economy (e.g. when private liabilities become public liabilities and vice-versa); and for 4) to strengthen them (e.g. the Treasury backing the Fed on TALF or Draghi's speech making clear the ECB's commitment with the EA).

Financial-monetary-fiscal linkages: a short tale of two monetary unions

The financial crisis rapidly crossed the Atlantic, but while it was of relatively short duration in the established US monetary union, it lasted for a very long time in the relatively new EA monetary union, eventually becoming the euro debt crisis. The contrast between the situation on either side of the Atlantic reflects, in part, the differences between the two unions.

Both unions can be characterized by having – albeit with different forms or development – the following elements: a single market, as a 'level playing field', with internal free movement of goods, people, etc.; a legal and political structure; and a tripartite union: i) the Monetary Union; ii) the Economic and Fiscal Union; and iii) the Capital and Banking Union. United States has historically followed the sequence (ii) – (i) – (iii), with the last step being done during the last century, starting with the already-mentioned federal deposit insurance (FDIC) in the aftermath of the 1930s crisis. Instead, at the outset of the financial crisis, the European Union only counted with the following elements: for (i) the EA, for (ii) some policy agreements – in particular the Stability and Growth Pact (SGP) – and for (iii) only the free movement of capital and the Basel regulations.

Modern macroeconomic theory defines three basic fiscal-monetary links. First, in a country – as well as in a monetary union – there is unique government budget. Even if there are separate monetary and fiscal authorities – and perhaps even multiple fiscal authorities with specific budgets – ultimately, they all share the same budget. Second, this (national or union) budget is always satisfied in expected present value terms (i.e.

external balances should cancel out in the long run). Third, the current sovereign debt position of a government (i.e. current liabilities minus assets) reflects the past history of accumulated primary deficits, as well as the expected discounted value of future primary surpluses.[13] The third is a corollary of the second and it is also known as the 'fiscal theory of the price level'.[14]

These are basic links over which a more or less complex political-economy structure operates. In the case of the United States, it is relatively simple: the US Department of the Treasury and the Federal Reserve Bank are the institutions responsible for fiscal and monetary policy, respectively.[15] Although the Fed is independent, there is a fluid connection between the two, based on the understanding that they share a common US budget. We have already seen that the FRB needed, and had, the back-up of the Treasury to play the role of 'buyer of last resort' in TALF, but coordination and complementary has been the norm. For example, US Treasury deposits with Federal Reserve banks expanded from an historical average of less than $5 billion to over $50 billion; this not only reflected a change in the Treasury cash management (Santoro 2012), but the start of a 'new era of Treasury intervention'.[16] Finally, states also have a part to play in the integrated budget, but self-imposed 'balanced budget' (or similar) rules, as well as the federal rule prohibiting bailouts to states, severely limits their contribution to the value of US debt.

The European Union is very different. First and foremost, the member states of the euro area are a subset of those that form the EU (out of twenty-seven, there were fifteen in the EA in 2008 and nineteen in 2020). For the euro area, the European Central Bank (ECB), with the European System of Central Banks, is relatively akin to the FRB, with its Federal Reserve System, but there is no euro area (or European Union) Treasury, since fiscal policy is conducted by member states, with their own Treasuries, and the EU has a minimal budget (of the order of 1 per cent of EU GDP). Also, and more importantly, to date the ECB has had no sources of revenue. In other words, the euro area debt position shown in Figure 4.7b reflects member states' historical accumulated primary deficits, as well as the expected discounted value of their future primary surpluses. One can argue that the level of debt in the EA, as shown in Figure 4.7b, is a statistical construct rather than a reflection of (non-existent) 'the EA budget'.[17] While this does not tally with the description of the first link above – i.e. the 'unique budget' – the link is real and one cannot understand the euro crisis, or rather the Global Financial Crisis as it played out in Europe, without accounting for this link. In fact, the EA's fiscal entry rules (i.e. the Maastricht criteria setting a cap for the debt and deficit levels, 60 per cent and 3 per cent of GDP, respectively), as well as the fiscal rules inside

---

[13] To simplify, I am abstracting from the external position (reserves) of a country.

[14] For an account of these links see (Sargent 2012) and (Cochrane 2019).

[15] Ultimately, it is the federal government who is responsible for fiscal policy and, in different forms, both institutions are accountable to Congress and Senate, but the focus here is on the economic architectural design.

[16] What was a radical change in the financial crisis, seems a tiny step seen from the perspective of the COVID-19 crisis: the Treasury deposits in the FR banks reached $1,805 billion on 22 July 2020 (see https://fred.stlouisfed.org/series/WTREGEN).

[17] It is expected that with the 2021–7 EU budget, there will be an EA budget (the BICC) as part of the EU budget; i.e. without revenue sources.

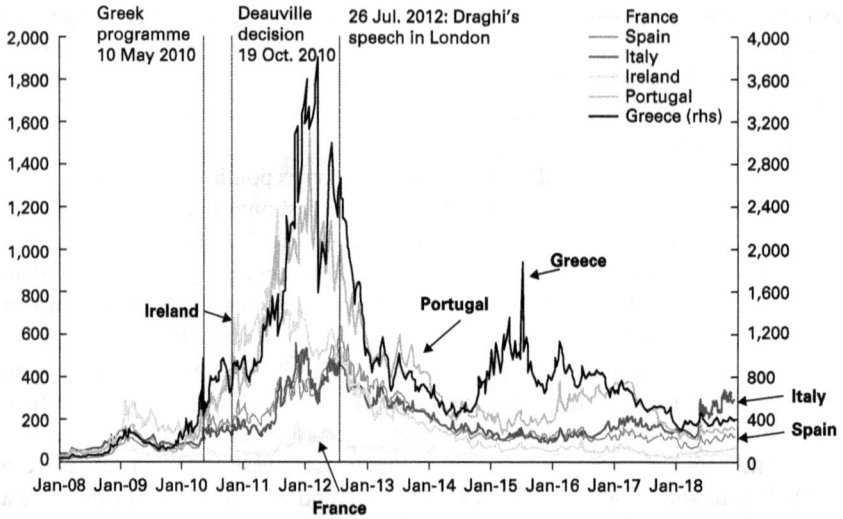

Figure 4.10 Ten-year sovereign spreads of selected euro area countries vis-à-vis the ten-year Bund yield.

the EA (mainly the Stability and Growth Pact), are designed to isolate national fiscal policies within the (implicit) EA budget. If the latter did not exist, and needed to be protected, such rules would be redundant.

Figure 4.10 is possibly the best summary of the euro debt crisis, showing how financial markets – represented by the stressed countries' sovereign debt spreads over the ten-year Bund yield – anticipated and reacted to the main events of the crisis. It is also a summary of how the perception, and political economy, of the implicit euro area budget changed with, and through, the crisis.

To begin with, it shows that the direct immediate effect of the financial crisis on EA debt liabilities was small. The 2009 spreads broke the euro history of full convergence of EA countries' sovereign debts, but seen in perspective the spreads were small. The spread was significant for Ireland's sovereign debt which, as we had already mentioned, was the result of the government's bailout of their banking system, which had defaulted. Nevertheless, since – aside from its excessively leveraged banking system – the Irish economy was relatively sound, it appeared that thanks to the ECB's intervention, things would return to normal and the implicit EA budget would be safe.[18]

However, the 2009 spreads sowed the seeds of uncertainty. First, regarding the state of the EA economies; second, regarding whether the ECB intervention in Ireland was

---

[18] As Jörg Asmussen, Member of the Executive Board of the ECB, said in 2012: 'Before the EU/IMF programme was agreed, the total Eurosystem loan support for Ireland (combining monetary policy operations to all eligible banks and emergency liquidity assistance from the Central Bank of Ireland) amounted to about 100% of Irish GDP.' https://www.ecb.europa.eu/press/key/date/2012/html/sp120412.en.html

proof that it acted, and would act, as 'lender of last resource', or the commitment to the no bailout clause' of the European treaty (TFEU) was, and would be, maintained.[19]

On 6 October 2009, George Papandreou took office as Prime Minister of Greece and soon after declared that Greece, with a yearly deficit of 12.7 per cent, could not meet EA fiscal limits. Furthermore, with a yearly −4.3 per cent GDP growth rate, Greece was in a deep economic crisis, and, with a sovereign debt to GDP ratio already at 126.7 per cent, in dire straits regarding its future. The seeds of uncertainty were being nourished and tested from the outset. ECB action was not enough and, in May 2010, the First Greek Economic Adjustment Programme started, with Greece agreeing to the conditions of the First EU/IMF debt relief programme with a €110 billion loan (41.5 per cent of its GDP). Many economists argued at the time that the Greek debt was unsustainable and, therefore, debt rescheduling was more appropriate than debt relief. In retrospect, they were right, but the issue was whether the infant monetary union could, and was willing to, do it. Debt rescheduling would have been more consistent with the 'no default clause'. However, there were two reasons for not doing it, which in the end prevailed. First, as in any debt rescheduling, lenders needed to be accounted for and, possibly, compensated; the main ones being German banks. Again, in hindsight, it may had been cheaper and may have partially spared Greece from a two-year drop of their income per capita of 7.15 per cent (and an increase of its debt/GDP ratio of 45.4 per cent). However, legally and politically it may have not been easy to implement debt rescheduling. More importantly, there was a second reason: contagion. Would other EA sovereign debts follow?

Ireland and Greece were not the only 'stressed countries' in the EA; spreads were starting to rise in Portugal, Spain and Italy, and not because they had any particular special links to Ireland and Greece. They had their own weaknesses but were subject to the same (implicit) EA budget and, hence, subject to and feeding its increasing uncertainty. The fears of contagion were grounded and, therefore, a need for political action by the EA, but who would take the lead?

There is another idiosyncrasy of the EA: its governing body is the Eurogroup, 'an informal body where the ministers of the euro area member states discuss matters relating to their shared responsibilities related to the euro'.[20] Nevertheless, the 'informal body' - conscious that a 'Greek loan facility' was not going to calm the financial markets and a firewall was needed - acted after an intense weekend of negotiations (7–9 May 2010): the European Financial Stability Facility (EFSF) was created, as a €500 billion euro area rescue fund,[21] which in 2012 became the European Stability Mechanism

---

[19] Article 125 TFEU reads: 'The Union shall not be liable for or assume the commitments of central governments, regional, local or other public authorities, other bodies governed by public law, or public undertakings of any Member State, without prejudice to mutual financial guarantees for the joint execution of a specific project.' Therefore, Art. 125 is usually known as the 'no bailout clause'.

[20] https://www.consilium.europa.eu/en/council-eu/eurogroup/

[21] More precisely, the EFSF was agreed by the Council of the European Union, on 9 May 2010, as a 'special purpose vehicle that the euro area member states would guarantee', to provide financial assistance to euro area countries in difficulties and, in parallel, the Council Regulation (EU) No 407/2010 of May 11 2010 established the European Financial Stabilisation Mechanism (EFSM) for all EU countries. The €500 billion included €60 billion for rapid reaction (corresponding to the EFSM) and the euro area backed €440 billion (of the EFSF); the latter vehicle 'would expire after three years'. See European Stability Mechanism (2019) for a more in-depth account.

(ESM). As Jean-Claude Trichet, then president of the ECB, put it: 'Default is out of the question. It is as simple as that' (6 May 2010).[22]

Unfortunately, neither the president's declaration nor the creation of the €500-billion EFSF resolved the uncertainty surrounding the EA budget. Two equilibrium paths were still possible: the no-default path advocated by Trichet; and the bail-in with private sector involvement (PSI) in partially bearing the cost of the resulting debt restructuring. While the Eurogroup was moving ahead along the first path, on 18 October 2010, Sarkozy and Merkel surprised them and almost everyone else, financial markets included, with a press release from the seaside resort of Deauville in Normandy, endorsing the bail-in & PSI path.[23] Financial markets understood what they said and reacted, further increasing the sovereign spreads already underway – starting with Ireland. Nevertheless, Ireland did not follow the bail-in and PSI path; instead, pressured by the ECB, it accepted the EU/IMF conditions for what became the first EFSF programme; a €85 billion loan, in which Sweden, UK and the IMF also participated.

However, the Irish path did not resolve the uncertainty either, although Portugal followed the same path on 16 May 2011.[24] Greece was already some way ahead of them and, as Figure 4.10 shows, its troubles had *not* been solved with the first debt relief EU/ IMF programme. Months of financial turmoil and (mostly away from public view), preparation and political discussions within the EA resulted in both paths crossing in 2012. The preparation work was to strengthen the EA firewall, transforming the temporary EFSF into a permanent European Stability Mechanism (ESM) – which was launched 8 October 2012 – with more fire power (a combined ceiling of EFSF and ESM of €700 billion; EU Council, 30 March 2012). The main Eurogroup political discussion regarded the second assistance package for Greece, which in the end involved private sector involvement (PSI) in a historic debt restructuring of Greek debt on 9 March 2012.[25] In sum, the promise of a strengthened firewall was not used to deter default – with the soon to be ESM joining the ECB as lenders of last resort – but to orchestrate a 'once-and-for-all' bail-in with PSI.[26] The no-default path crossed the bail-in path; but will it prove to be just 'once-and-for-all'?

This question was heating financial markets in the Spring and early Summer of 2012, until Draghi gave the famous speech noted above on 26 July 2012. But his words

---

[22] https://www.ecb.europa.eu/press/pressconf/2010/html/is100506.en.html

[23] For a more detailed account of the Deauville's shock, see Brunnermeier et al. (2016) and Tooze (2018).

[24] A €78 billion loan, with equal €26 billion contributions from the EFSF, the EFSM and the IMF.

[25] 'Out of a total of €206 billion in bonds eligible for the offer, approximately €199 billion, or 96.9%, were exchanged (…) for a package of new Greek bonds, short-dated EFSF securities and extra securities linked to Greece's GDP growth'; exchanged for write-downs of 53.5% of the principal amount of the existing bonds. In sum, 'the biggest sovereign write-down in history reducing Greece's outstanding debt by about €107 billion' (European Stability Mechanism 2019: 192). Nevertheless, given the drop of GDP, the sovereign debt to GDP ratio was only reduced by 12.5 (from 172.1 in 2011 to 159.6 in 2012).

[26] The period between 2010 and 2012, was also used by German and other banks to reduce their holdings of Greek debt, an important fraction of which went to Cyprus!

were not empty. First, the ECB was ready to lower its interest rates once more (Figure 4.2) and shift from a 'passive' policy of liquidity provision, accommodating banks' demands, to an 'active' policy of using its balance sheet as a policy instrument to provide liquidity and, through the banking system, reinforce its interest rate policy and stabilize the economy (Figure 4.3).[27] Second, preparations for the ESM were being finalized and those for banking union were soon to begin.[28] Draghi's speech is said to have avoided a 'self-fulfilling' debt crisis. It was certainly a key element, but one must also account for the work being done to pave the no-default path.

All in all, the financial crisis started in the mature US fiscal and monetary union, where monetary and fiscal authorities reacted relatively quickly with innovative central bank policies and in coordination when needed. Historical rules preventing states from accumulating high debts guaranteed that the financial and fiscal crisis did not translate into state debt crisis. Nevertheless, US debt started a decade of debt accumulation and the FRB engaging in balance-sheet expansion (backed by the Treasury). The US crisis was short and it did not usher in any institutional changes, just new central bank policies. In contrast, the fiscal rules of the euro area (the Stability and Growth Pact) proved to be unequal to the challenge and the financial crisis rapidly became a debt crisis. The ECB maintained its price stability mandate and, with some delay, applied the new unconventional monetary policies, but there was no Treasury counterpart, thus no fiscal stimulus from either the EU or the EA. Yet, with the euro debt crisis the fledgling monetary union has developed institutionally with the ESM, and important steps have been taken to develop a European Banking Union. Nevertheless, the (tripartite) European Union is far from complete and the GIPS–Non-GIPS divide has widened with the financial and euro crises (Figure 4.4).

LESSON FOR THE FUTURE #3: From a historical perspective, what is most important about a crisis is how a country exits from it.

Given the GIPS–Non-GIPS divide, it has also been said that the euro itself was the cause of the euro debt crisis, and that without the Economic and Monetary Union (EMU) things would had been different. The latter view is an oxymoron and the counterfactual scenarios are neither trivial not necessarily better. The historical roots of the euro area divide are deeper than that.[29]

---

[27] The 2012 Outright Monetary Transactions (OMT) programme was a powerful – but rarely used – tool that opened the door to several programmes that effectively applied the new policy from 2014 onwards, was called the '*combined arms* approach comprising three main elements: the introduction of a negative interest-rate policy (NIRP); a series of targeted long-term refinancing operations (TLTROs); and a large-scale Asset Purchase Programme (APP) encompassing public and private sector securities' (Rostagno et al. 2019:2).

[28] Of the three key elements of the banking union, two would see the light of day in 2014: the Single Resolution Mechanism (SRM) was agreed by the European Council and the Parliament on 20 March and the Single Supervisor Mechanism (SSM) was up and running by November 2014; while the European Deposit Insurance Scheme (EDIS) will be indefinitely delayed.

[29] The same argument has been made by Sandbu (2015) and others.

Epilogue

The final version of this chapter has been written during the first wave of the COVID-19 crisis. It has been often argued that this crisis, being an exogeneous shock affecting all the global economy, has nothing to do with the financial and euro crises of a decade ago. On the one hand, it minimizes the severity of those crises and, on the other hand, being exogenous, no specific sector or country is to blame, which should help the recovery. Nevertheless, I think at least the three MAIN LESSONS apply. Unfortunately, COVID-19 exacerbates the GIPS–Non-GIPS divide: Italy and Spain have been the most COVID-damaged EU countries; how GIPS came out of the euro crisis has made them less resilient to this one, and tourism, one of the most COVID-damaged sectors, represents more than 10 per cent of the GIPS' GDP. Fortunately, the ECB has been an experienced and active player from the start of the crisis and, this time, there will be an EU stimulus package. Hopefully, further institutional EMU development will follow too.

References

Acharya, V.A. and M. Richardson. 2009. *Restoring Financial Stability*. New York: John Wiley & Sons, Inc.

Acharya, V.A., T.F. Cooley, M. Richardson and I. Walter, eds. 2011. *Regulating Wall Street: The Dodd-Frank Act and the New Architecture of Global Finance*. New York: John Wiley & Sons, Inc.

Bernanke, B. 1983. 'Nonmonetary Effects of the Financial Crisis in the Propagation of the Great Depression.' *American Economic Review* 73 (3): 257–76.

Bernanke, B. 1995. 'Inside the Black-Box: The Credit Channel of Monetary-Policy Transmission.' *Journal of Economic Perspectives* 9 (4): 27–48.

Bernanke, B. 2004. *Essays on the Great Depression*. Princeton, NJ: Princeton University Press.

Bernanke, B. 2009. 'The Crisis and the Policy Response.' The Stamp Lecture, London School of Economics.

Bernanke, B. 2013. *The Federal Reserve and the Financial Crisis*. Princeton, NJ: Princeton University Press, and Oxford: Oxford University Press.

Blanchard, O., D. Romer, M. Spence and J. Stiglitz, eds. 2012. *In The Wake of the Crisis: Leading Economists Reassess Economic Policy*. Cambridge, MA: The MIT Press.

Brunnermeier, M.K., H. James and J-P. Landau. 2016. *The Euro and the Battle of Ideas*, Princeton, NJ: Princeton University Press.

Cecchetti, S. and K. Schoenholtz. 2017. 'The Financial Crisis, Ten Years On.' Vox, CEPR Policy Portal (29 August). https://voxeu.org/article/financial-crisis-ten-years

Claessens, S., M.A. Kose, L. Leaven and F. Valencia. 2014. *Financial Crises: Causes, Consequences, and Policy Responses*. Washington, D.C.: International Monetary Fund.

Cochrane, J.H. 2019. 'The Value of Government Debt.' NBER Working Paper 26090.

European Stability Mechanism. 2019. *Safeguarding the Euro in Times of Crisis: The Inside Story of the ESM*. Luxembourg: European Stability Mechanism.

Friedman, M., and A.J. Schwartz. 1963. *A Monetary History of the United States, 1867–1960*. Princeton, NJ: Princeton University Press.

Gaballo, G., and R. Marimon. 2021. 'Breaking the Spell with Credit-Easing: Self-Confirming Credit Crises in Competitive Search Economies.' *Journal of Monetary Economics* (forthcoming).

International Monetary Fund. 2018. *October 2018 Fiscal Monitor.* Washington, D.C.: IMF.

Kiyotaki, N., and J. Moore. 1997. 'Credit Cycles.' *Journal of Political Economy* 105 (2): 1477–1507.

Kiyotaki, N., and J. Moore. 2019. 'Liquidity, Business Cycles, and Monetary Policy.' *Journal of Political Economy* 127 (6): 2926–66.

Lucas, Jr., E. 2003. 'Macroeconomic Priorities', *American Economic Review* 93 (1): 1–14.

Marimon, R., and T. Cooley, eds. 2018. *The EMU after the Euro Crisis: Lessons and Possibilities: Findings and Proposals from the Horizon 2020 ADEMU Project,* e-Book Voxeu: https://voxeu.org/The-emu-after-the-crisis

Rajan, R.G. 2010. *Fault Lines: How the Hidden Fractures Still Threaten the World Economy.* Princeton, NJ: Princeton University Press.

Romer, C.D., and D.H. Romer. 2017. 'New Evidence on the Aftermath of Financial Crises in Advanced Countries.' *American Economic Review* 107 (10): 3072–118.

Rostagno, M., C. Altavila, G. Carboni, W. Lemke, R. Motto, A. Saint Guilhem and J. Yiangou. 2019. 'A Tale of Two Decades: The ECB's Monetary Policy at 20.' ECB, Working Paper Series No 2346.

Sandbu, M. 2015. *Europe's Orphan: The Future of the Euro and the Politics of Debt.* Princeton, NJ: Princeton University Press.

Santoro, P.J. 2012. 'The Evolution of Treasury Cash Management during the Financial Crisis.' *Federal Reserve Bank of New York Current Issues in Economics and Finance* 18 (3): 1–11.

Sargent, T.J. 2012. 'Nobel Lecture: United States Then, Europe Now.' *Journal of Political Economy* 120 (1): 1–40.

Tooze, A. 2018. *Crashed: How a Decade of Financial Crises Changed the World.* New York: Viking.

5

The Wasted Legacy of a Crisis

Pervenche Berès

This chapter looks at the legacy of the Global Financial Crisis from the viewpoint of a Member of the European Parliament who chaired the Economic and monetary Committee (ECON) when the crisis broke out (2004–09) and the Employment and Social Affairs Committee (EMPL) in its aftermath (2009–14). The author was the rapporteur for the Special Committee on the financial, economic and social crisis (2009–11). More often than not, she was also rapporteur on the project to establish a fiscal capacity for the euro area (EA). Most recently, she handled the review of the European Supervisory Authorities (ESAs) as co-rapporteur. Considering this background, the subsequent analysis offers a highly European Union (EU)-oriented perspective.

At the time of writing, the world is facing the COVID-19 pandemic, a crisis of much bigger magnitude than the Global Financial Crisis, although of a very different origin. The current situation does not change the analysis regarding the legacy of the 2008 Crisis, but it does highlight the price being paid today for the unlearned lessons and for the untaken actions following this legacy.

Before discussing the legacy of the Global Financial Crisis, one should remember the shared assumptions ahead of the crisis when everybody, including the IMF, was discussing macroeconomic imbalances in global trade because of the new trend of globalization. But, ultimately, the debate was not so much about the level of indebtedness of the private sector. It ignored the vulnerabilities linked to the opacity and complexity of financial markets. It also disregarded the risks associated with securitization and, more widely, with the financialization of economies. In the United States, Congress discussed subprime as a local constituency issue. Credit Rating Agencies (CRAs) remained silent, not signalling the flaws of the system to the markets.

The general assumption is that it all started in 2008. One could argue that it began on 9 August 2007, when the European Central Bank had to inject €95 billion into the market to avert a liquidity crisis following BNP's decision to stop valuing its UCITS when it realized that it did not understand the amount and the value of the underlying subprime positions. The financial crisis mutated into a solvency crisis on 15 September 2008, with the collapse of Lehman Brothers. In between, governments had been reluctant to jump in, happy to leave the problem to central bankers who thought it was their job and found themselves alone in the driving seat.

Not everyone immediately recognized the depth and the nature of the crisis. Before the ECON committee, ECB president Jean-Claude Trichet refused to qualify the situation as a 'crisis', neither during the exceptional monetary dialogue on 11 September 2007 nor at the ordinary one on 9 October the same year. He assessed the financial turbulences as an 'episode of market correction' in September, adding 'significant' in October. According to him, the sensitivity of the EA economy to bank financing justified the above-mentioned bold and prompt decision on the money market and the different timing of the Bank of England or the FED. Interestingly, he also mentioned during these monetary dialogues the need for full transparency of financial markets as a legacy of the Asian financial crisis.

I recall visiting in April 2008 the main advisor of French president Nicolas Sarkozy for the preparation of the incoming EU presidency starting on 1 July. Based on the important work both achieved[1] and ongoing[2] in the European Parliament, I suggested making the issue of financial market supervision a priority. The proposal, viewed as not looking exciting enough, was discarded. This may be no more than an anecdote, but it shows, as do the other examples below, the somewhat general blindness that reigned at that time.

In its communication on the ten years of the euro[3] published on 7 May 2008, the Commission indeed failed to mention the turmoil in financial markets and, in July 2008, the ECB even decided to increase its rates by a quarter of a point, up to 4.25 per cent.

After the collapse of Lehman Brothers and the fall in car sales in Germany in the first quarter of 2009, European economic leaders explained in March 2009 that the slow-down of the economy was US specific as it was only the American model, relying primarily on capital markets, that was in crisis. They asserted that the EU economy maintained sound fundamentals, also thanks to its automatic stabilizers, and that it was, overall, in much better shape.

This crisis also has an EA-specific dimension; it could be the one with the heaviest legacy. It started at the end of 2009 after Giorgos Papandreou, the incoming Greek prime minister, revealed the real figures of the country's public deficit and debt, opening the EA sovereign debt crisis, even though some actors wanted to see it as a Greek crisis only.

This could be a first legacy of the Global Financial Crisis. Although it might not be specific to this crisis, it played an important role. Indeed, it emphasizes how the fear of self-fulfilling prophecies prevents the first signals of a crisis from being appropriately and taken fully into account.

The analysis of the legacy should explore the main lessons to be drawn from the Global Financial Crisis, look at what has been fixed and outline what is still dysfunctional.

---

[1] European Parliament resolution of 11 July 2007 on financial services policy (2005–10) – White Paper (2006/2270(INI)).

[2] European Parliament resolution of 9 October 2008 with recommendations to the Commission on Lamfalussy follow-up: future structure of supervision (2008/2148(INI)).

[3] Communication from the Commission to the European Parliament, the Council, the European Economic and Social Committee, the Committee of the Regions and the European Central Bank – EMU@10: successes and challenges after 10 years of Economic and Monetary Union {SEC(2008) 553} /* COM/2008/0238 final */

What should be remembered of the Global Financial Crisis?

Such recollections are essential when analysing the legacy of the Global Financial Crisis in order to learn from, and to correct the principal errors made at the time as set out below in more detail.

The Global Financial Crisis started because of the rise of inequality in globalized economies where the outsourcing of jobs decreased the purchasing power of working- and middle-class consumers, pushing an essentially self-regulated financial system to develop subprime lending to sustain the real estate internal demand. For the US, the following graph illustrates this situation:

The share of U.S. pre-tax income accruing to the bottom 50 percent and top one percent of income earners, 1962–2014

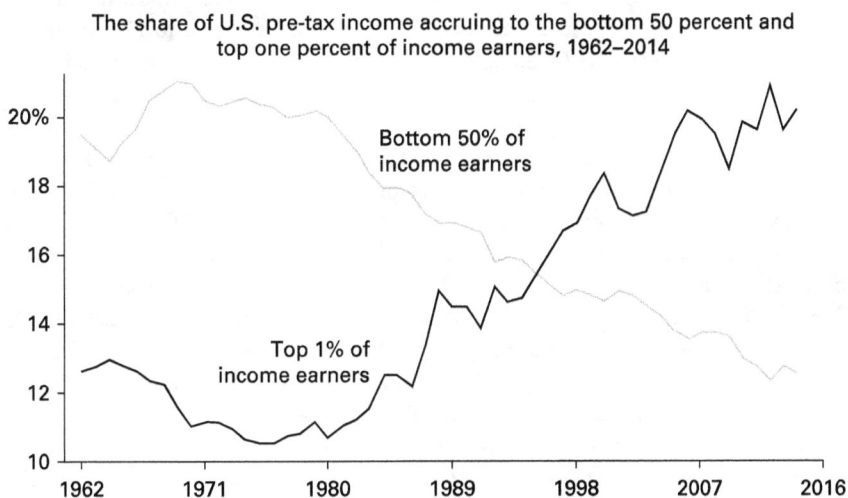

Source: Thomas Piketty, Emmanuel Saez, and Gabriel Zucman, "Distributional National Accounts: Methods and Estimates for the United States," 2016. Cambridge, MA: National Bureau of Economic Research
Note: The unit is the individual adult and incomes within married couples are split equally.

Figure 5.1 A tale of two countries.

It was very much linked to a purely short-term approach of economies in which the remuneration models largely based on stock options and the supremacy of shareholders' rights in the governance structure were detrimental drivers in the conduct of financial markets. In his book published in October 2009, Tommaso Padoa-Schioppa[4] demonstrates how much the bubble that had exploded was 'first financial for sure, but also political, economic, mental and cultural'. It is for him 'the crisis of a system' that got upside down because of 'fundamentalist market ideology, short sight and economic nationalism'.

The CRAs and accounting standards were not giving the right signal to the markets. This means that the thermometers displayed the wrong temperature. The mistakes

---

[4] Tommaso Padoa-Schioppa and Beda Romana, *Contre la courte vue : entretiens sur le Grand Krach*, 2009, Odile Jacob

related to the Global Financial Crisis for which the CRAs are somehow accountable are twofold. First, they are guilty for not disclosing accurate information on the fragility of subprime schemes and secondly they are responsible for waking up suddenly after ten years of silence to differentiate the ratings of the sovereign debt of EA countries.

In the aftermath of the outbreak of the crisis, the willingness to put the whole blame on CRAs to avoid changing the main pieces of the system was strong. Using them as a scapegoat was notably convenient for the EU Commissioner in charge of financial markets. From the beginning of his mandate in 2004, Charlie McCreevy had indeed been advocating for a 'regulatory pause'. Regarding accounting standards, the whole debate about fair value and its short-term bias had been opened ahead of the Global Financial Crisis but was then re-launched. In addition, the banking structure was not robust enough. Bank exposures included high-risk with one third to US originated Mortgage Backed Securities (MBS) and two third to Asset-Backed Commercial Papers (ABCP). The recourse to systematic internalization and securitization was frequent, extensive and not properly supervised.

The importance of macroeconomic imbalances related to financial markets was underestimated, as were the inherent risk of market reactions derived from the extensive interconnectedness between countries' public finances and financial markets. Four significant cases leading to the build-up of systemic risk could, among others, be observed during the Global Financial Crisis. First of course is the collapse of Lehman Brothers, but then there was also the panic following the adoption by Ireland of an unlimited guarantee for bank deposits on 30 September 2008, the impact of CRAs downgrading the Greek sovereign debt starting in December 2009, and the return of speculation on government bonds after the Deauville declaration on 18 October 2010.

Despite calls for banks to fully disclose their losses as early as September 2007 – ironically by the CEO of Deutsche Bank: 'As long as nobody knows where the risks are, people are very reluctant to buy some of these assets because they think it could be toxic'[5] – and to clean up their balance sheets, transparency was obviously very limited in the EU, leading to the poor management of toxic assets and to the massive creation of non-performing loans (NPLs) on top of the credit distribution due to the economic downturn.

The reliance on self-regulation was too great and the deficiencies of the shadow banking system, including those embedded in money market funds, were not properly addressed. This allowed governance misfires at the level of banks and financial markets themselves, but also at the level of national, European and global institutions. The countervailing powers of supervisors were too weak; some of them were 'too close to talk' from the 'too big to fail'; others simply did not exist. This resulted in a paradox for EU financial markets. Before the Global Financial Crisis, integration had progressed in a context dominated by national rules. But after it, a full catalogue of EU regulation accompanied a growing fragmentation. The lack of trust among member states and an ill-designed home-host framework explain this evolution.

---

[5] 'Ackermann puts faith in embracing transparency', *Financial Times*, 5 September 2007, Peter Thal Larsen and Ivar Simensen.

Attempts at fixing the Global Financial Crisis focused obsessively on saving the banking system. Therefore, there was a missed opportunity to adjust the financial system and address the long-term challenges that the developed economies where already facing. In fact, the EU economy, even with its own currency, was strongly dependent upon and interlinked vis-à-vis the US dollar. Since the creation of the euro, no significant progress had been made regarding its external role, including its representation.

The Global Financial Crisis hit the EU and the EA while they were very poorly equipped to face such a crisis. It shed the light on their weaknesses, in particular the failure to complete the Economic and Monetary Union (EMU). It also revealed the conditions under which, following the adoption of the euro, the EU had managed to open its financial markets without remedying shortcomings in its economic governance. This happened despite constant warnings and recommendations aimed at establishing an optimum currency area, the first of these even dating back as far as the Werner Report (1970). The EU and the EA lacked a central fiscal capacity to face a symmetric or an asymmetric shock as well as intervention mechanisms to support a country deprived of market access. Economic governance focused merely on the surveillance of country-by-country fiscal situations. There was no serious consideration of financial positions, no proper assessment of systemic risk, no smart evaluation of externalities. The EU was unable to manage financial markets home-host issues or discrepancies between national insolvency regimes. The sovereign-bank nexus was tight. Even though the EU had adopted an important financial market action plan, no true European bank existed and only a few had an EU dimension.

For the first time since 1976, an EU member state encountering economic challenges had to deal with the involvement of the IMF. It began in Hungary in October 2008. The country was the victim of serious market turbulences and difficulties in refinancing government and external debt after the foreign banks decided to repatriate capital to ensure their solvency at home. The IMF then sealed a deal with Latvia in December 2008 and with Romania in March 2009. All these interventions took place together with the trigger of the balance of payment facility mechanism (TFEU, article 143). They somehow paved the way for what was at the time unthinkable, namely the IMF assisting an EA country, starting with Greece. The legacy of this is quite diverse, to say the least, and came with a political and social cost that was either undervalued or ignored.

The EU lagged behind in the design and implementation of recovery plans after the Global Financial Crisis severely hit its economy because of the Commission and Council's inability to define a clear and joint strategy that could be accepted by member states. In the end, countries like Germany, which had adopted significant national recovery plans and had been careful not to dismantle their enterprises thanks to partial unemployment schemes, were less badly hit and much faster to restart their economy.

Tackling taxation issues need to be undertaken, including tax heavens and the way they helped create bad incentives or favour detrimental practices. During the IMF and World Bank annual meetings in Washington in 2008 that took place in the aftermath of the collapse of Lehman Brothers, it was quite striking to realize that there was no debate about the role of tax heavens in the development of speculative activities that had led to what became the Global Financial Crisis.

The Global Financial Crisis designed a new world equilibrium characterized by a growing role for China and a relatively lighter influence than hitherto for Europe. Not equipped as a sovereign nation, the EU is no longer the world centre even if it remains a major market.[6]

What has been fixed?

Rescuing the financial system was understood as the main priority. Many initiatives were rolled out for this purpose following the collapse of Lehman Brothers and its impact on financial markets. In the EU, the package of measures included special temporary state aids, notably through the recapitalization of banks and even some nationalisations in the United Kingdom.

After these emergency interventions, the EU introduced several legal initiatives following coordinated guidelines that a series of G20 summits partly defined (Washington, November 2008; London, April 2009; Pittsburgh, November 2009; Toronto, April 2010; Seoul, November 2010) together with the work of the Financial Stability Board (FSB), established as such during the first of these summits, and with the Basel Committee on Banking Supervision (BCBS). To strengthen the resilience of the financial system, banks were forced to dramatically increase the quality and quantity of their own funds and to prepare recovery plans. Multiple revisions of the Capital Requirements Directive (CRD) and Capital Requirements Regulation (CRR) as well as of the Banking Recovery and Resolution Directive (BRRD) incorporated such improvements into EU law.

In parallel, the EU passed on useful legislations regarding financial markets such as, in 2011, the Alternative Investment Fund Managers Directive (AIFMD), in 2014 the adoption of the Market Abuse Directive (MAD) and the revision of Markets in financial instruments (MIFID). The European Securities and Markets Authority (ESMA) gained direct monitoring and enforcement powers over CRAs within the EU while EU leaders launched a (still ongoing) debate on whether a European public CRA should be created to issue credit ratings, including on sovereign debt.

On the supervisory side, the European System of Financial Supervision (ESFS) targeted both the macro and the micro levels. On the macro level, the Global Financial Crisis had 'revealed important shortcomings in financial supervision, which has failed to anticipate adverse macro-prudential developments and to prevent the accumulation of excessive risks within the financial system'[7]. The establishment of the European Systemic Risk Board (ESRB) followed the advice of the High-level Group (HLG) on

---

[6]   Share of the world GDP in 2004: EU-28 31.4%, US 28.1%, Japan 10.7%, China 4.5%, Canada 2.3%, other G20 10.9%; in 2014: EU-28 23.8%, US 22.2%, China 13.4%, Japan 5.9%, Brazil 3%, other G20 14.3% (source: Eurostat)

[7]   Regulation (EU) No 1092/2010 24 November 2010 on European Union macro-prudential oversight of the financial system and establishing a European Systemic Risk Board, recital 1.

financial supervision in the EU, which delivered its recommendations on 25 February 2009. The report, named after former managing director of the IMF and governor of Banque de France and chairman of the HLG, Jacques de Larosière, also guided the reshuffle of the micro-prudential level, though at the price of epic fights reflecting the strict understanding member states had of their sovereignty, vested national interests and power games between national competent authorities. The discussions ended up in the transformation of the three Committees into three Authorities, the ESAs. The Committee of European Banking Supervisors (CEBS) became European Banking Authority (EBA). The Committee of European Securities Regulators (CESR) became ESMA. And the Committee of European Insurance and Occupational Pensions Supervisors (CEIOPS) became European Insurance and Occupational Pensions Authority (EIOPA).

In the wake of the Global Financial Crisis, the European sovereign debt crisis pushed the creation of the banking union, an essential forward-looking move towards EA integration. The June 2012 European Council decided to anchor it to three pillars: the Single Supervisory Mechanism (SSM), the Single Resolution Board (SRB) and the European deposit guarantee scheme. In April 2014, only the first two pillars were successfully introduced.

On the monetary side, the ECB has been acting as a major federal institution for the betterment of the EA. Overcoming some legal constraints, it finally purchased sovereign bonds on a massive scale, either to preserve the euro while facing adverse financial and macroeconomic developments or to insure stability price as it had defined it. The words uttered in a speech in London in 2012 by its president, Mario Draghi, will for many years mark the role that central bank played during the period: 'Within our mandate, the ECB is ready to do whatever it takes to preserve the euro. And believe me, it will be enough.'[8]

Since May 2010, the ECB has put in place successive, innovative, accommodative monetary programmes: the Securities Market Programme (SMP), Emergency Liquidity Assistance (ELA), Long-term Refinancing operations (LTRO), Outright Monetary Transactions (OMT) programme... and finally in 2015 quantitative easing (QE). These non-conventional policies have caused controversy but they also illustrate a situation where the ECB was the main pilot on the EA plane.

The difficulties encountered in setting up the proper economic governance and its consequences on the economy could well be the worst legacy of the Global Financial Crisis for the EU and the EA, even beyond its social and potential political impacts. Several initiatives have addressed the governance puzzle. However, none of them questioned the core logic of the Stability and Growth Pact.

At the end of 2010, EU leaders decided to put in place the European Stability Mechanism (ESM), with a view to fixing the situation of Greece, which could no longer access the market to finance its sovereign debt. The ESM could enter in function based on a borrowing capacity on the market guaranteed by member states' budgets, but only after the adoption of the Treaty on Stability, Coordination and Governance (TSCG),

---

[8]   https://www.ecb.europa.eu/press/key/date/2012/html/sp120726.en.html

which introduced a framework of strong conditionality in the EMU. This move has reinforced inter-governmental monitoring of the euro and added new stringent constraints on public finances. However, some member states still consider it as the biggest step towards solidarity among EA countries.

The fiscal rules themselves were adapted to the new situation with the adoption of the 6 pack and 2 pack in 2011 and 2013. The adjustments introduced into the EU legal framework some of the concepts put forward by the TSCG. These macro-economic aggregates, such as the output gap, the structural deficit and potential growth looked academically relevant. But they soon appeared to be quite difficult to use in practice. Medium-term budgetary objectives were prescribed, with the unusual situation that the fiscal trajectory of a member state moving from the corrective to the preventive arm of the Stability and Growth Pact finds itself in a more demanding situation. The Macroeconomic Imbalance Procedure (MIP) was also implemented, following an important battle to include social indicators in the scoreboard. Here, one should admit that the debate was in fact biased from the start, since the parameters were set to accommodate the only country in excessive surplus. In the end, the MIP turned out to be far less forceful than expected.

Finally, the 'European semester' was created as an economic and fiscal cycle to compensate for the weaknesses of the economic coordination among member states. It defines a framework that starts with an 'annual growth survey', since renamed 'annual sustainable growth survey', which aims to set out the general economic and social priorities for the EU as a reference for the country-specific recommendations that are to a large degree based on the evaluation of national reform programmes and stability/convergence programmes. Nonetheless, this process has not led to a proper debate on the macro situation of the EA economy. It fails to determine the right aggregate fiscal stance for the area even if a yearly recommendation for the EA is produced.

The debate between rules and policies invariably reached a deadlock, because changing the rules had been impossible, so making the rules more 'sophisticated' turned out to be next best thing. This approach proved counter-productive, however: the rules actually became more complex, more opaque and less democratic. The medicine may well be killing the patient.

In the end, during the period 2014–19, when the Commission and member states were busy dealing with the Greek situation, every initiative fell short, except the communication on flexibility,[9] which helps alleviate (under certain circumstances) the fiscal rules hindering investment.

Without revisiting every single event around this time, including the Deauville summit or the telling Cypriot and Irish cases, let us look at the Greek crisis and at the way it was handled.

Greece, which represents 2 per cent of the EA's GDP, could have triggered the 'butterfly effect'. Having made a lot of money out of the country, Goldman Sachs helped it falsify its data. Eurostat in 2004 already flagged up made-up figures. But the reform

---

[9] http://ec.europa.eu/economy_finance/economic_governance/sgp/pdf/2015-01-13_
communication_sgp_flexibility_guidelines_en.pdf

in March 2009 failed to reinforce properly Eurostat, partly because countries like France or Germany refused onsite and offsite inspections.

Greece entered in recession when it was deprived of market access after the downgrade of its sovereign debt. The situation was worrying for many parties, including for foreign banks. It escalated into an open conflict among EA member states, however: was it a Greek problem only or a collective issue? Some member states seriously considered letting Greece leave the EA. Fortunately, a 'Grexit' was avoided because the argument that it would be detrimental not only for the country, but also for the EA as a whole, prevailed. But it resulted in the intervention of the 'Troika' (European Commission, ECB, IMF) and in the Commission's creation of the Task Force for Greece (TFGR) to coordinate the delivery of three assistance programmes in the country, which imposed harsh austerity measures that would prove to bring devastating social costs.

What has not been fixed?

It goes without saying that this Global Financial Crisis wreaked havoc on the financial markets, but it had economic and social root causes that have not yet been fully addressed or corrected. It was both urgent and necessary to rescue banks and save the global financial system after the collapse of Lehman Brothers. But retrospectively, this could be a missed opportunity to define new collective preferences. During the Global Financial Crisis, financial markets were badly affected because of economic and social developments following the financialization of the economy and the overconfidence in self-regulation. In return, the Global Financial Crisis would go on to have a huge economic and social impact. As in the 1929 crisis, the upstream and downstream sides of social inequality were neglected; the valuable work of people like Tony Atkinson[10] in this regard was ignored. Finance ministers, central bankers and regulators at different levels of governance were called to the rescue. However, no other relevant stakeholders were asked to join in and address the economic and social elements of the crisis. A joint meeting of the IMF and the ILO took place in Oslo on 13 September 2010 as an attempt to take a wider approach, but this is the only event of this kind along the Global Financial Crisis years.

The state of the play was aggravated in the EU when, following the triggering of the ESM, the Troika intervened in some member states (Greece, Ireland, Portugal and Cyprus) on the basis of largely secret negotiations of memoranda of understanding, with very little consideration given in the making-up of fiscal packages either for social dialogue or for the social fallout. It ended up with the condemnation by the Council of Europe in October 2012. Two months later, the International Labour Organization (ILO) also denounced the weakening of freedom of association and collective bargaining, contrary to the principles laid out in its conventions 87 and 98.

---

[10] Tony Atkinson. 2016. 'Inequality: What Can Be Done About It?', Social Europe. Accessed 7 December 2017. https://www.socialeurope.eu/inequality-can-done

In a landmark resolution, the European Parliament stated the following:

> ... recovery from the financial, economic and social crisis and an exit from the sovereign debt crisis will require a long-term process which must be well designed and ensure balanced and sustainable development; acknowledges that compromises may have to be made between growth, fairness and financial stability and that such compromises must be the subject of political decision making; asks the Commission to present financial development proposals that take these aims into account, particularly with regard to the EU 2020 strategy, and to explain the types of compromise on which political choices may have to be made; hopes that this will provide a basis on which the Union can facilitate debate and permit policy comparisons, following consultation with all parties that have a stake in financial-market reform (banks, investors, savers and the social partners)[11].

But such a holistic approach never saw the light of day. José Manuel Barroso, then president of the Commission, was too preoccupied to be invited to the negotiation tables. Initiatives undertaken by the EU presidency, starting with the Euro summit in Paris on 12 October 2008, indeed put him in a secondary position. He was also busy protecting his financial markets commissioner, who was in the hot seat. In short, he was above all eager to make sure that member states followed his proposals. Therefore, he never dared to fully encourage EU members to reflect on a broader *post*-crisis picture. In addition, he may well have been unsure himself of the need to do so.

The EU emergency banking package reforms adopted in the wake of the Global Financial Crisis overlooked the issues of long-term investment and sustainable development. These challenges were not a real priority during the recovery phase, although the objectives had been on the table since the European Council meeting in Gothenburg in June 2001. The suite of more than forty pieces of financial services legislation adopted during Barroso's second presidency (2009–14), and proposed by Commissioner Michel Barnier, illustrates this perfectly. Indeed, it only opened the door for an initiative on long-term investment in March 2014.[12] The hard truth is that shifting towards this paradigm would have involved revisiting most of the previously enforced regulations and directives. The political will to do so was obviously not there.

In addition, for the EU and the EA, long-standing areas of disagreement were not addressed ahead of the Global Financial Crisis. They therefore prevented raising the appropriate questions and answers that would have constituted a useful legacy of the Global Financial Crisis and helped the EA be ready for the next one. Somehow, one of the reasons why the EA was badly equipped to face the Global Financial Crisis resides in unresolved historical political strife. The inability to bridge ideological divides led most of the time to decision-making being 'too little too late', which widened the political gap and weakened the effect of measures. All in all, in addition to the unsolved

[11]	European Parliament resolution of 20 October 2010 on the financial, economic and social crisis: recommendations concerning measures and initiatives to be taken (mid-term report) (2009/2182(INI)), paragraph 120.
[12]	Communication on long-term financing of the European economy, 27 March 2014, COM/2014/0168

issues around inequality, this generated a very high political cost, nurturing scepticism and populism while creating a vicious circle that made it even more difficult politically to move ahead.

Rules – not policies – remain the fundamental drivers underpinning the economic governance of the EA. This gets in the way of holding a consistent European economic debate before member states define their own fiscal trajectory. Discussions around the aggregate fiscal stance, fiscal multipliers and spill-overs cannot take place. The European semester still looks like an exam of each member state situation by the Commission on a isolated basis rather than integrating it in a global approach.

After the Global Financial Crisis, the EU and the EA in particular went through a recovery phase for which it was nearly impossible to define a common strategy. Each member state adopted its own plan. A quick decision was then made to restore fiscal rules, resulting in the sub-optimal situation shown below.

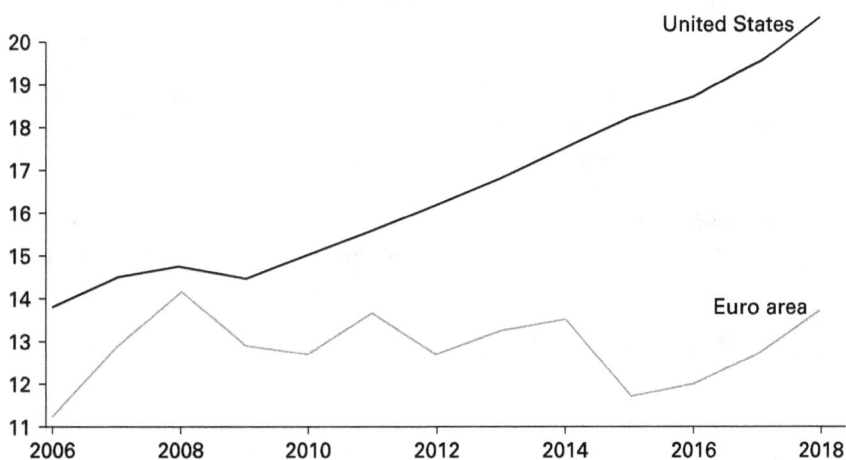

Source: World Bank

Figure 5.2 GDP (current US$) United States, euro area.

Out of this broad picture, three critical points emerge as follows.

First, inside the EU and particularly within the EA, the Stability and Growth Pact was never put aside. Some member states were eager to restore the full implementation of Pact's rules as soon as possible in an environment of acute mutual distrust. This materialized in the reforms described above. Nevertheless, the lack of tools available to tackle the Global Financial Crisis obliged political leaders to consider the issue of an uncompleted economic and monetary Union. The debate on the need to equip the EA with a fiscal capacity that the European Parliament had already called for in 1998[13] was therefore revived. The question of the adequacy of the Stability and Growth Pact given the EU's economic situation was also reopened.

---

[13] Resolution on the adjustment mechanism in cases of asymmetric shocks, Official Journal C 098, 09/04/1999 P. 0171. Sitting on Thursday 17 December 1998.

Herman von Rompuy ran the first test. Even before taking up his role as president of the European Union, he had planned to organize a special summit dedicated to the governance of the EMU. He convened the meeting on 11 February 2010. But developments in Greece turned the agenda on its head. The topic somehow came back on the table on 25 March 2010 at an EA heads of state or government summit that established a working group under the leadership of von Rompuy. Member states decided to send their finance ministers as their representatives. But on which long-term vision could these people agree on when they had a gun pointed at their head, considering the unhealthy games financial markets were playing around sovereign debt?

I was convinced that a committee, like the one set-up by Jacques Delors in 1988, would be a much better way to think about the new stage of the EMU. Therefore in the draft first crisis report presented to the European Parliament, I had proposed 'to contribute to the debate open by the constitution of a working group on economic governance, chaired by Herman von Rompuy, to create inside the European Parliament a wise persons group of independent persons with a multidisciplinary experience'.[14] After being consulted, Tommaso Padoa-Shioppa had agreed to chair it. But before the idea was discussed within the decision-making body of the Parliament, general secretary of the Commission, Catherine Day, convinced the main political group leaders that such a process would be too slow and that the Commission was already about to put the necessary proposals on the table.

It took heads of state or governments much more time than expected to reach an agreement on what was strictly required by the circumstances. They thought they did not have time for the broader picture. In the end, advancing through a working group may have saved some time.

Later, the European Council re-launched the negotiations twice. First, the Four Presidents' Report published on 5 December 2012 proposed in stage 3, i.e. after 2014, 'establishing a well-defined and limited fiscal capacity to improve the absorption of country-specific economic shocks, through an insurance system set up at the central level' after 'ensuring fiscal sustainability and breaking the link between banks and sovereigns' in stage 1 and 'completing the integrated financial framework and promoting sound structural policies' in stage 2. But given the inability to find an agreement in June 2013, the project was postponed until after the September 2013 German general election; the new government did not take office until 17 December, however. This clearly did not allow any proper discussion at the European Council just three days later. It was then argued, perhaps by member states most opposed to the initiative, that any implementation waits for the European Parliament election in May 2014 and for the installation of the next Commission. The Five Presidents' Report published on 1 July 2015 represented another attempt at effecting change. But the European Council never really opened the core debate. In parallel the European Parliament was trying to act. I wrote a report with CDU MEP Reimer Böge[15] in which

---

[14] Draft report of 6 May 2010 on the financial, economic and social crisis: recommendations concerning measures and initiatives to be taken (mid-term report) (2009/2182(INI)), paragraph 153.
[15] European Parliament resolution of 16 February 2017 on budgetary capacity for the euro area (2015/2344(INI))

we proposed a fiscal capacity for convergence and stabilization within the EA. On 31 May 2018 the Commission finally came up with a modest proposal: a regulation on the establishment of a European Investment Stabilization Function,[16] for which it was impossible to find a majority, even in the European Parliament.

The whole economic governance structure was not reformed to the level required. The necessary overhaul would have involved the creation of an EA fiscal capacity. Such a tool would have been able to absorb symmetric and asymmetric shocks and a European unemployment benefit scheme (EUBS) would have performed as an automatic stabilizer.

The reform of the Stability and Growth Pact to allow a proper aggregate fiscal stance and ensure an adequate level of investment was never agreed. The debate was very divisive: one side thought the economic outlook of the EA was gloomy because the rules were not appropriate to the situation, while the other believed that prospects were poor because of those rules had been badly implemented! On top of that, these discussions fuelled a high level of mistrust between creditors and debtors' countries. Even with clear and reliable figures produced by the Macroeconomic Imbalance Procedure (MIP), convincing countries with fiscal space to increase their spending proved nearly impossible.

This refusal by member states to debate any real macro-economic change left the ECB quite alone on the front line to implement 'whatever it takes'. The policy mix was less than ideal to say the least. The lack of proper EA fiscal policy and tools challenged monetary policy. ECB president Mario Draghi outlined these stakes in many of his speeches and interventions.[17] But for the time being, heads of state or government never translated these calls into concrete actions. This taboo would be overcome only with the following crisis, because of COVID-19's economic impact, and the proposal by German Chancellor Angela Merkel and French President Emmanuel Macron for an €500 billion recovery fund that will be decided by the European Council for finally €390 billion.

Second, following the proposal by then newly elected French President François Hollande in June 2012 to boost investment in the EA, the 2014 Juncker plan and the 2019 Invest EU program could be considered as the recognition of the investment gap in the EU.

These investment plans represent significant progress since the failure to implement Jacques Delors' 1994 white paper on 'Growth, competitiveness and employment'. This programme would have favoured investments in large, Europe-wide infrastructures in transport, energy, telecommunications and the environment. But finance ministers rejected it because they refused to use resort to Union bonds.

Since then, the critical situation in the EU regarding the lack of public and private investment – one that was aggravated by the Global Financial Crisis – finally meant the Juncker plan, which is based on bonds to finance projects, got the green light. But this is only one step in the right direction: no way has yet been found to remove the gridlock

---

[16] COM(2018) 387 final
[17] See notably his farewell remarks, 28 October 2019, but also his answers to my questions during Monetary dialogues, 23 March 2015 or 21 June 2016.

when it comes to directly financing member states, before the COVID-19 crisis, through solidarity bonds, to mutualize debt or, as described earlier, to draw the needed lessons from the flaws of the Stability and Growth Pact.

And third, in the EU, economic and social divergences between member states pre-existed the crisis inside and outside the EA. The Global Financial Crisis has exacerbated them. They have not been addressed – anything but, in fact – which could create an unsustainable situation in the long run. This should encourage every European decision-maker to: i) revisit the performance of the cohesion policy as a tool for convergence inside the Union; ii) question the impact of the pro-cyclical measures taken during the crisis, notably for EA countries; and iii) reflect on the capacity of an asymmetric strategy to overcome the negative fallout of excessive divergences.

In his time as Commission president, Jacques Delors thought that the structural funds should be adapted to the challenge of the introduction of the euro. Such adaptation never happened; non-EA countries against it too, feared that it would lead to a reduced share in the structural funds they receive. The Global Financial Crisis shone a very bright light on this challenge, but its end did not coincide with a significant reform of EU cohesion policy.

The financial, economic and social crisis special committee raised the issue in the European Parliament. However, member states, guided obviously by the logical of financial return, refused to open the debate. The cohesion policy had not narrowed the divergences enough before the crisis. Correcting it became even more necessary after the Global Financial Crisis. But reforming an existing policy based on national vested interests is a very delicate task.

The debate on divergences between the core and the periphery and on the effects of polarization is almost forbidden inside the EA. Indeed, countries that benefit the most from the internal market or from the single currency refuse any analysis of fiscal multipliers or any assessment of the dynamics at stake that makes one plus one greater than two within a currency union. These member states only wish to refer to the responsibility of others by focusing squarely on national structural reforms.

Even on this narrow front, a debate on the nature of the structural reforms to be implemented has been raging. Conservatives advocated for Troika-like reforms, i.e. fiscal measures that decrease public spending through labour market and pension reforms. Progressives have been trying to move the discussions to the definition of more sustainable reforms. Commissioner László Andor introduced the useful concept of social investment in this regard.

But instead of redesigning a fully efficient cohesion policy, the debate shifted to the promotion of contracts established per member state aimed at supporting each of them based on the implementation of co-defined structural reforms. This approach is contrary to the spirit of the cohesion funds, which were initially disbursed to help divergent countries or regions to catch up. Taxation regimes exacerbated the divergences. But, as in most EU fields governed by the rule of unanimity, it is very difficult to modify.

After the adoption of the euro, the Lamfalussy process had created the conditions inside the EU for the rise of a financial services wholesale internal market. The Global Financial Crisis hit the EU at the stage of a market's development where the appetite for a wide opening is very high and strong arguments are made to oppose any regulation or supervision in parallel. Since the Global Financial Crisis, some progress has been made in this area. But very little has been done on shadow banking. The painful reform of Money Market Funds (MMF) in the EU appears to be a weak compromise, despite the G20 strong commitment (Seoul, November 2010).

Besides, the EU never properly handled the question of the architecture of the banking sector. Proposals addressed only one side of the coin, whereas a broad approach would have enabled the EU to find the right equilibrium needed to neutralize all national vested interests. More precisely, the focus on banks considered 'too big to fail' did not allow any serious scrutiny of the building-up of systemic risk in smaller financial institutions. In other words, proportionality in supervision cannot only be a matter of size.

As regards the banking union, the lack of a European deposit guarantee scheme creates secondary undesirable effects. It also hinders any move towards a more consistent banking architecture in the EU. Such a structure is also made hard to achieve because of no substantial progress in the harmonization of bankruptcy regimes across member states. Besides, there lies a paradox: the ones who most oppose the availability of such a tool are also the ones who consider that any cross-border banking consolidation is impossible in its absence. Here, the bargaining ground is between risk reduction and risk sharing, with the rating of the sovereign debt feeding into the discussion as a newcomer. The outcome of the review of the ESAs, initiated when the Commission put on the table a useful package of proposals towards more integration, as a corollary requirement of the willingness to build a Capital Markets Union (CMU), illustrates the little progress possible. In a nutshell, the vast majority of member states – which did chose to ignore the Global Financial Crisis's legacy for banks but were willing to have a CMU based on vested interests – fiercely opposed the reform by only supporting 'Members States driven' supervisory authorities.

Another facet of the Global Financial Crisis's legacy is that the banking sector has been restored. Nevertheless, one could raise questions about the efficiency of structures and processes used by banks in the financing of the economy. The Juncker plan has demonstrated that private investment was not restarting fast enough. It has also inaugurated a new era where the European Investment Bank (EIB), National Promotional Banks and Institutions (NPBIs) and development banks play a more prominent role.

Finally, obstacles to learning real lessons from the Global Financial Crisis came from the resistance of market players, which had to be rescued by public authorities when they found themselves in emergency situations, but countered any attempt to effect change globally afterwards. Governments unable to overcome their long-lasting divide described throughout this chapter tended to support them in doing so, maybe waiting for the next crisis. The truth is that the panic made governments step in, but once the political impulse faded away, so did the reforms that could have corrected the original flaws. The guilty had been saved, at only little cost to themselves. Soon enough, the momentum had gone.

The Commission had initially been set up to build the internal market. On economic policies, the Treaty on the Functioning of the European Union foresees that 'Member

States shall regard their economic policies as a matter of common concern and shall coordinate them within the Council'[18] while economic policies remained of national competences. In this context, no crisis management tools existed before the Global Financial Crisis. They were built in the heat of the moment, favouring hybrid solutions and a rise of inter-governmental oversight, and difficult to reverse.

Those who, at the height of the Global Financial Crisis, advocated for IMF support to cope with the fiscal situation in some member states finally abandoned the idea of IMF intervention in the EA. However, their hidden agenda is to recreate an equivalent body inside the EU, but outside the Commission. That is what is at stake in the unfinished debate about the future of the ESM and, as requested by the European Parliament and foreseen by the Five Presidents' Report, about its integration into the EU legal framework.

The Global Financial Crisis opened some crucial issues that could feed into the next crisis because, more than a decade after the crash, adequate answers still have not been found. The crisis arose out of short-termism. Its legacy may well be short-sightedness. The architect could only do a modest amount of redesigning after the fireman had put out the flames.

[18] Article 121.

Part Two

National Experiences

6

The Financial Crisis, National Policy Responses and the Rise of Conservative Nationalism

Dorothee Bohle

It may be ruled out that immediate economic crises of themselves produce fundamental historical events; they can simply create a terrain more favourable to the dissemination of certain modes of thought, and certain ways of posing and resolving questions involving the entire subsequent development of national life.

Antonio Gramsci, *Prison Notebooks*

Introduction

In the decade since the outbreak of the Global Financial Crisis, European societies have struggled to find answers to two major conflicts: first, how to distribute the costs of the financial crisis while restoring growth; and second, how to reconcile national political and economic preferences with requirements stemming from international markets, institutions and actors. European societies have found four answers. The first attests to the resilience of the pre-crisis neoliberal and pro-integrationist policy consensus, and is supported by mainstream political forces from the conservative, liberal and sometimes left spectrum. The second answer, promoted by right-wing nationalist forces, pushes for selectively restoring national sovereignty and heeds particularistic economic interests without, however, breaking with the distributional priorities and the competitiveness agenda of neoliberalism. The third, nationalist left-wing, answer seeks a decisive break with the distributive priorities of neoliberalism by promoting a return of the state able to provide social cohesion within the national society, and opts for a modification of international integration so as to increase the room for manoeuvre for domestic policies. Finally, a fourth, pro-integration, answer from the left seeks to combine a pro-social, anti-neoliberal agenda with a strong commitment to international integration.

These answers have not been distributed equally. Existing literature has established a surprising resilience of neoliberalism, despite the heavy social costs that it entailed, and even though neoliberalism was at the origin of the Global Financial Crisis (e.g. Crouch 2011; Schmidt and Thatcher 2013). Over time, however, right-wing nationalism has become a successful challenger in Europe as elsewhere, as witnessed among others by the pursuit of such policies under Viktor Orbán in Hungary, Donald Trump in the US, Boris Johnson in the UK or Jair Bolsonaro in Brazil. In contrast, both left integrationist and left nationalist answers have so far been comparatively weak.

This chapter seeks to explain the different capacity of right-wing versus left-wing nationalist answers to challenge the pre-crisis neoliberal and integrationist consensus. To this end, it compares two cases that have challenged mainstream neoliberalism: Hungary and Greece. The second Hungarian Orbán government (2010–14) successfully implemented right-wing nationalist responses. In contrast, the Syriza government's (2015–19) attempt to implement a radical left alternative in Greece was short-lived. What explains the differences?

I argue that for an answer to be successful, it must be both politically and economically viable. Politically, any answer must resonate with public sentiments, and economically, it must garner the support of powerful economic actors and be reasonably successful in its economic outcomes. Further, political and economic viability is also determined by the constraints stemming from international actors and markets. My argument is that these conditions have discriminated against left-wing solutions, while rewarding national right-wing answers to the crisis.

The chapter is structured as follows. The next section conceptualizes the four responses and maps them in the European peripheral countries that were hardest hit by the crisis and had to turn to the IMF/EU for a bailout. The third section introduces my explanatory framework and argument. The fourth section provides a structured comparison between the successful right wing nationalist challenge to mainstream neoliberalism under the second Fidesz government and the failed left-nationalist challenge of the Syriza government.[1] It identifies two factors that explain the different outcome: the role of international markets and actors; and the different economic models. The conclusion summarizes the findings and outlines the further research agenda.

Policy responses to the Global Financial Crisis

The crisis that started in 2008 and returned to Europe in 2010 was primarily a financial crisis, caused by an 'implosion in interbank credit' (Tooze 2018: 8), in the wake of which banks and, alongside them, states got into serious trouble. To be sure, countries differed in what exactly triggered their perilous situation in which they found themselves. Some countries were vulnerable to an external financing gap because they had high public debt – Greece being the prime example, but this was the case in Hungary too – some had hugely overleveraged banking sectors – Ireland or Iceland –

---

[1]   Although both governments were coalition governments – Fidesz has formed a political alliance with the Christian Democratic People's party KPDN, and Syriza a coalition with the national conservative Independent Greeks (ANEL) – Fidesz and Syriza are the dominant partners, and have been responsible for economic policies. In the paper I therefore will use – somewhat incorrectly – Fidesz/Syriza government, dropping the smaller coalition partners.

and in others, banks were vulnerable because of their links to foreign countries – such as the Cypriot banks' exposure to Greek government debt. However, almost all crisis-ridden European economies had to cope with the fall-out from liquidity or solvency crises in their banking sector, resulting in a 'weakening economy, and overburdened fiscal authorities' (Schelkle 2017: 159).

These developments confronted European societies with tough questions, around which political conflict arose. The first of these concerned substantive policy and distributive questions. How should banks be stabilized and who would pay for it? How urgent a task was fiscal consolidation and how should it be achieved? How could vulnerable members of society be protected from the fall-out of the crisis, and how could growth be restored? A second set of conflicts centred on how to reconcile national political and economic preferences with requirements stemming from the international markets, institutions and actors. Especially at the height of, and the immediate years after, the crisis, international requirements seemed to put unduly restrictive conditions on domestic policy choices. Should these restrictions be accepted, or should policy-makers try to carve out increased domestic policy space?

Conceptualizing responses

This chapter identifies four answers to the questions above that are structured along two dimensions. The first is a social-economic left-right dimension. Commonly, the literature understands this as opposing state intervention and free markets. However, it is not very plausible and even not very correct to argue that state intervention is exclusively left-wing. As Polanyi (2001 [1944]: 147) famously noted, 'laissez-faire was planned, while planning was not'. More recently, scholars have shown that even the supposedly market fundamentalist neoliberalism 'primarily reregulates and institutes an alternative set of infrastructural arrangements', rather than doing away with state intervention altogether (Mirowski 2013: 16; Gamble 1994; Slobodian 2018). I therefore follow a different approach in defining the left-right axis by focussing on the substantive *ends* towards which state policies in general, and state intervention in particular, are geared. Building on Bobbio (1996) and his application by Jahn (2011), I argue that leftist policies are those that ultimately aim at greater equality among citizens (and residents) of a country, whereas right-wing policies exhibit greater tolerance for inequality, which they find legitimate. This tolerance can be justified on conservative or liberal grounds. Conservatives endorse what they see as given inequalities and hierarchies and expect that if individuals take the place in society that is 'naturally theirs', harmony will ensue. As the comparative literature on welfare states has convincingly argued, conservatives endorse state intervention that protects against the vagaries of markets, but state intervention is aimed at maintaining status differences among members of society (Esping-Andersen 1990). Liberals, on the other hand, see inequality to a large part stemming from individual capabilities and industriousness. They thus see as the main task of the state to 'free' individuals and enterprises from the impediments that prevent them from deploying their capabilities and industriousness. Protection of property rights, individual freedoms and the liberalization and privatization of economic resources are thus cornerstones of liberalism. Even liberals, however, are not opposed to public social policies. These take the form of means-tested programmes, with the aim of assuring that the poorest are not fully left behind.

The second dimension is the position on international integration, pitting pro-integration against national sovereignty. In the literature on party positions, this conflict line is variously known as 'integration-demarcation' (e.g. Kriesi et al. 2008), or 'transnational' conflict (e.g. Hooghe and Marks 2018). It is seen as a reaction against globalization, European integration and immigration and is often conceptualized as a cultural rather than socio-economic conflict, where political parties exploit the cultural anxieties of heterogeneous groups of those who have lost out due to globalization and integration. (but see Manow 2018). However, for my purpose, this integration/sovereignty dimension has a clear socio-economic content. It concerns the fact whether governments try to push back against the constraints that international markets and organizations exert on their domestic social and economic policy choices, or whether they accommodate these constraints.

Based on these two dimensions, four ideal typical responses can be identified (Figure 6.1). Two of those are left wing answers to the crisis. As discussed above, I follow Bobbio (1996) in defining the left as being more concerned with reducing inequalities than the political right. This refers in particular to social inequalities, which, the left believes, can be significantly reduced. After the Global Financial Crisis, the left was confronted with the following set of questions: How to protect the most vulnerable of the society against the fall-out from the crisis, especially high unemployment, underwater mortgages or overindebtedness? How to distribute the costs of bank bailouts and how to service public debt in such a way that this does not

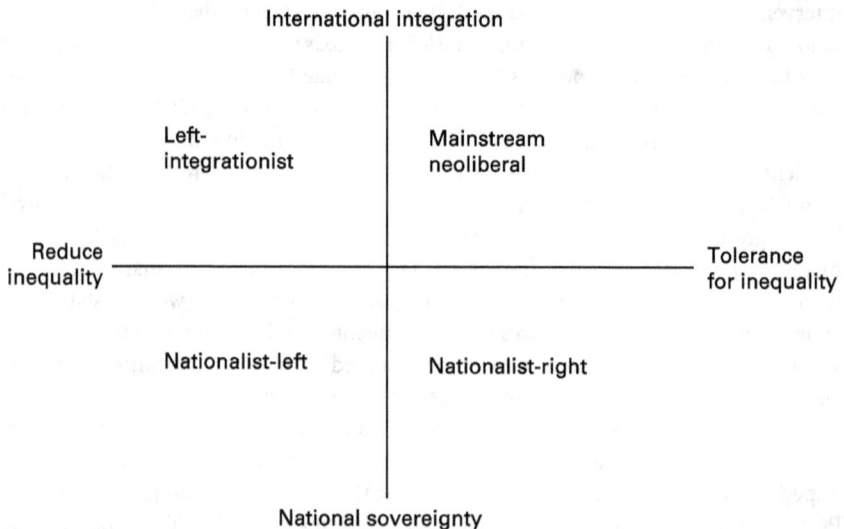

Figure 6.1 Policy responses to the crisis.

undermine social cohesion? How to reduce overall long-term inequalities, some of which had been triggering the crisis to begin with? Finally, how to restore growth while securing equality? Left-wing policy packages include a mixture of policies that protect (weaker) members of society by decommodifying their income streams and compensating for loss of income in case of unemployment, old age and sickness (Esping Andersen 1990), enforcing social rights such as the right to work and to affordable healthcare, education and housing, and seeking to tackle inequality of opportunities by investing in public childcare and education. In terms of growth policies, left-wing answers should prioritize public investment over supply-side policies.

Left-wing answers can be divided by their integrationist or nationalist outlook. Left-wing integrationists try to combine their agenda with the requirements of international organizations and markets, while left-wing nationalists seek a modification of international conditions to increase the room for manoeuvre for domestic policies. The latter see the EU's economic governance in particular as a hindrance to implementing left-wing policies.

On the right, two answers can be distinguished as well. The first attests to the resilience of the pre-crisis neoliberal and pro-integrationist policy consensus. To be sure, there have been ample debates about whether neoliberalism is a useful concept at all (e.g. Boas and Gans-Morse 2009). Yet, if applied with greater precision, the concept certainly stands for crucial policy responses to the Global Financial Crisis. One way of specifying the concept is to look at how neoliberals themselves have identified it. In 2014, the London-based Adam Smith Institute, a think tank founded in 1977, which having spent decades rolling its eyes at any mention of the term neoliberal, . . . rather surprisingly declared . . . that it had decided to assume full and unapologetic ownership of the moniker' (Peck and Theodore 2019: 252). This is how one of the Institute's members sees neoliberalism: 'We promote low, simple taxes because we want economic growth and to give people more power over their money. . . We promote competition in healthcare, education, utilities and other public services. . . We promote globalization. . .because we want to raise the living standards around the world through trade and investment' (Bowman 2016, 1–2; quoted in Peck and Theodore 2019: 252). In another surprising reversal, three IMF economists reflect on debates within the Fund about whether their own 'neoliberal agenda' might have been less successful than intended. These authors refer to 'policies that foster increased domestic competition through deregulation and opening their economies to foreign capital' as neoliberal (Ostry et al. 2016: 39). While they hail the results of free trade, foreign direct investment (FDI) and privatization, they find that capital account liberalization and fiscal consolidation have had adverse effects, leading to increased inequality, which in turn hurts growth.

As noted above, it would be wrong to equate these policies with free market fundamentalism. At the core of neoliberalism is a redefinition of state activities with the aim of protecting private property and markets. This is best achieved through constitutionalizing the neoliberal order at the international rather than national level (Slobodian 2018). Especially in Europe with its territorial political fragmentation, democratic policy-making can easily encroach on private capital rights, resulting in economic fragmentation. International institutions thus act as a control on national governments. The statist underwriting of markets and private property also clearly came to the fore during the Global Financial Crisis. As Tooze (2018: 10) writes: 'In fact, neoliberalism's regime of restraint and discipline operated under a proviso. In the event of a major financial crisis that threatened 'systemic' interests, it turned out that we lived in an age not of limited, but of big government, of massive executive action.'

To sum up, neoliberalism is thus concerned with empowering private capital and private initiative through privatization, deregulation and international integration with the aim of fostering competitiveness and growth. The state is not absent: on the one hand, it creates and secures the 'encasement' (Slobodian 2018) by international and more generally non-majoritarian institutions that removes economic policy making from the (short-term) political arena. On the other hand, in hard times, it acts as the saviour of systemically important corporations and private property.

A second right-wing response to the crisis is nationalist. It is characterized by two distinct features. First, right-wing nationalists push for restoring a degree of national sovereignty, which has a political and an economic dimension. Politically, it questions the legitimacy of international obligations and their repercussions on domestic policies and politics. This goes hand in hand with a redefinition of democracy as expressing in an unmediated way the 'will of the people'. In its most radical form, it holds that 'there must not and cannot be any check on the will of the Nation' (Ost 2018). Economically, restoring national sovereignty manifests itself in an economic nationalist agenda, which *selectively* pushes back against globalization and regional integration of trade, finance and/or labour markets. Contemporary economic nationalism does not endorse full autarchy, as was the case in the 1930s. Rather it assumes a defensive protectionist stance, promising to shield declining economic sectors and social strata threatened by a perceived status loss from effects of international integration, while embedding this in a nationalistic competitiveness ideology (Becker 2015a; Manow 2018).

Right-wing nationalism is not a wholesale rejection of neoliberalism. Rather, it combines neoliberal, unorthodox statist and nationalist conservative policies (Becker 2015a). As is the case with neoliberalism, the corporate sector is seen as the motor of growth, and right-wing nationalists typically embrace the private appropriation of economic resources and an agenda of competitiveness and deregulation. It is, however, more selective in picking and choosing which corporations should underpin economic growth, and uses state resources, macroeconomic, labour market and/or monetary policies to foster these corporations. Instead of markets, it is the state that picks winners and punishes losers, hence the significance of unorthodox economic policies. In terms of social policies, right-wing nationalists also embrace austerity and the restructuring of the welfare state. Social policies are, however, embedded in a nationalist conservative ideology. They thus reflect conservative value judgements differentiating between 'deserving' and 'undeserving' welfare beneficiaries. Welfare chauvinism, which excludes non-nationals from benefits, generous family polices geared towards raising fertility, or harsh workfarist policies punishing and disciplining the unemployed are examples of nationalist conservative social policies. It is the *combination* of neoliberal, heterodox and conservative policy elements that is hallmark of the right-wing nationalist answer.

Mapping the responses

Figure 6.2 below takes a closer look at the responses in European peripheral countries, which have been hardest hit by the crisis. These are the countries that had to ask for an international bailout. I focus on these peripheral countries, because here the post-crisis conflict lines and the trade-offs involved in the choices have been particularly sharp, threatening at times to tear the societies apart. While the social costs of the crisis and disenchantment with the pre-crisis growth model have been very high and consequently demands for putting the costs of adjustment on those perceived as responsible for the crisis have been strong, governments had at the same time very narrow policy space to embrace these demands. Furthermore, while the dependency on markets and international conditionality favours mainstream neoliberal policies, it also provides fertile ground for a nationalist backlash. In this sense peripheral cases are paradigmatic cases, as they show generalizable trade-offs and choices in sharp relief.

Figure 6.2 shows some puzzling features. In Europe's periphery, neoliberalism has been very resilient. Indeed, many countries have continuously pursued neoliberal responses despite the depth of the crisis. Thus, in a number of European countries, there have been few debates about socializing the costs of bank bailouts, and austerity

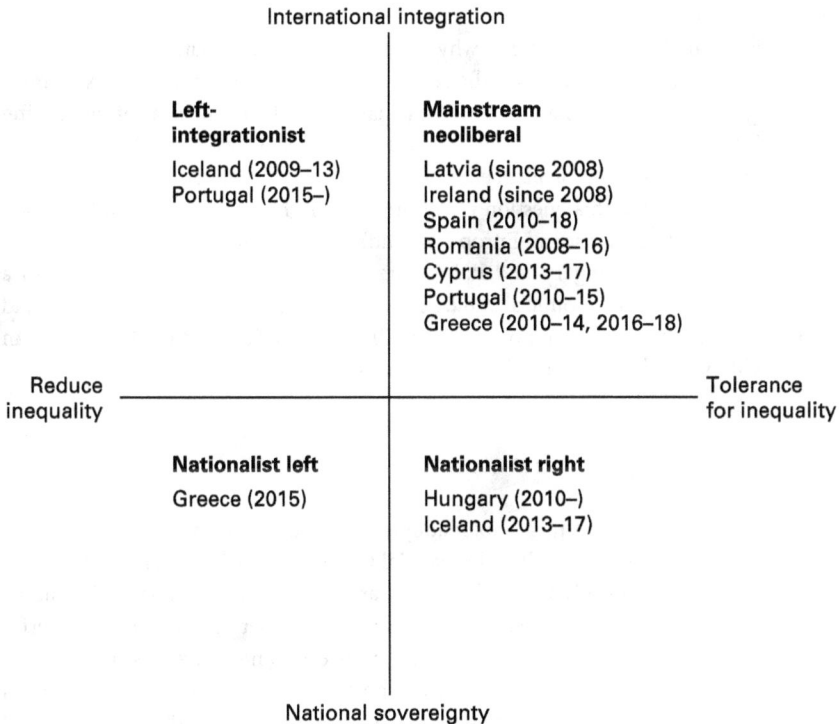

International integration

Left-integrationist
Iceland (2009–13)
Portugal (2015–)

Mainstream neoliberal
Latvia (since 2008)
Ireland (since 2008)
Spain (2010–18)
Romania (2008–16)
Cyprus (2013–17)
Portugal (2010–15)
Greece (2010–14, 2016–18)

Reduce inequality — Tolerance for inequality

Nationalist left
Greece (2015)

Nationalist right
Hungary (2010–)
Iceland (2013–17)

National sovereignty

Figure 6.2 Cases and their distribution on the response matrix.

and restoring national competitiveness have been the ways for ensuring post-crisis recovery. While banks were bailed out, public sector workers faced wage cuts, and welfare states were retrenched. In these countries, governments have also stayed committed to European integration, despite the fact that European socio-economic governance has taken a coercive turn in the aftermath of the financial crisis.

This is at odds with earlier experiences after great crises. Thus, historically, major economic crises have also always been turning points for mainstream policies and policies. Crises were moments for critical choices, when established policies collapsed and alternatives were tested (e.g. Gourevitch 1986; Blyth 2002). The Great Depression sounded the death knell for economic liberalism. The victorious policy alternative, Keynesianism, saw itself discredited half a century later, when the end of Fordism undermined its foundations and brought a new version of economic liberalism – neoliberalism – to the fore. In this respect, the resilience of mainstream policies in so many European (peripheral) countries is puzzling.

Second, what seems particularly puzzling is the relative weakness of left-wing answers to the crisis, be they nationalist or integrationist. Historical patterns certainly suggest that left-wing forces can offer convincing and popular answers in the wake of a major economic crisis. This was the case after the Great Depression, when Social Democracy emerged as strong contenders to liberal, conservative and radical right political forces (e.g. Luebbert 1991). It was also the case after the Latin American debt crisis of the 1980s, which – albeit with a delay – unleashed a wave of 'pink populism' (e.g. Roberts 2017).

Closely related, a third puzzle is why a durable policy alternative to mainstream neoliberalism has only emerged on the south-eastern quadrant of the matrix, namely the Hungarian right-wing nationalist. What has allowed the survival of right-wing nationalism here, while all other alternatives have been short-lived? Why has (the Hungarian) right-wing nationalism emerged as the main challenger to the mainstream answer? The answer to this question is important, as right-wing nationalist forces are clearly on the rise. In peripheral Europe, Poland's PiS government promotes a similar economic agenda as Hungary, and Italy's Forza Italia has been campaigning with a right-wing nationalist economic agenda. In core countries, Britain's Conservatives and the US Republicans have both moved in that direction. Understanding the Hungarian case thus allows to draw some wider implications.

The argument in brief

To understand the outcome, this chapter adopts a political economy approach. It argues that for a policy answer to the Global Financial Crisis to be successful, it must be both politically and economically viable. Politically, any answer must resonate with public sentiments. To be economically viable, an answer must garner the support of powerful economic actors and be reasonably successful in its economic outcomes. This implies that not anything goes. Policy responses must be able to generate growth, and as such are constrained by the underlying national growth regime. Further, political and economic viability is also determined by the constraints stemming from international actors and the international economy. My argument is that these conditions make it more difficult to implement left-wing policies, while rewarding mainstream neoliberal or nationalist right-wing answers to the crisis. To put it differently: in Europe (and beyond) the cards are stacked against a left-wing political answer.

Why would this be the case? This chapter is embedded in a larger critical juncture argument. This argument identifies the Global Financial Crisis as such a critical juncture, during which international organizations and market actors set new constraints for governments. For Europe, two choices proved to be most consequential: the first concerns the mode of crisis response, characterized by Adam Tooze (2018: e-book location 326) as 'denial, lack of initiative and coordination'. To put it differently, European policy-makers underestimated and misinterpreted persistently how the crisis would hit European economies, and once the effects could no longer be ignored, there was little coordination. And even if coordination were forthcoming, it was too little and too late. The second consequential choice for Europe was the understanding of the financial crisis as a sovereign debt crisis, which put austerity and structural reforms at the core of adjustment policies. European policy-makers had little understanding of the financial origins of the crisis. Instead they fell back on the familiar terrain of fiscal consolidation and competitiveness, with dire consequences for countries particularly hard hit by the crisis.[2]

Unequal adjustment, which pushed the costs of adaptation largely on the more vulnerable countries, reinforced the political woes of left-wing political forces, which had already been weakened before the Global Financial Crisis. Thus, Europe's neoliberal turn since the 1980s has by and large wiped out the traditional social democratic left. Many centrist labour parties have bought into the ideology of the third way, accepting the superiority of markets over states, of social investment over traditional redistribution, and, in some cases 'privatized Keynesianism' over public Keynesianism (Crouch 2011). In the light of the crisis, centrist labour parties thus had lost much of their credibility. They were seen as the problem, rather than the solution. In addition, more radical left-wing forces were delegitimized with the collapse of communism. Finally, two and a half decades of neoliberalism have also chipped away at once powerful collective organizations such as trade unions (Baccaro and Howell 2017). In contrast to the mainstream neoliberal and right-wing nationalist answers to the crisis, left-wing political forces would therefore have to reinvent themselves and their programs.

In contrast to the left, in many European countries, nationalist right-wing challengers did not have to invent themselves from scratch. As discussed above, transnational integration of trade, investment, capital flows and labour mobility had already led to the emergence of a new cleavage, pitting the cosmopolitans against those who had lost out due to globalization, and the rise of right-wing nationalist challenger parties who sought to restore national sovereignty.

The focus on austerity and competitiveness in the wake of the crisis makes redistributive policies very difficult. This is reinforced by the 'disciplining effect' of

---

[2] This is not the place to re-iterate the origin of Europe's crisis management and its obsession with fiscal rather than financial policies. For insightful accounts, see (for example) Tooze (2018), Matthijs and McNamara (2015), Eichengreen (2015), Schelkle (2017), Sandbu (2015) and Blyth (2013).

international market forces. The most likely policy option therefore is neoliberalism. Whether the neoliberal policy programme can prevail even in light of a deep crisis, depends however on whether it is a feasible economic project, which allows comparatively fast recovery. It is therefore easier to implement in countries that had developed a growth model prior to the crisis that was compatible with neoliberalism. The comparative political economy literature identifies two such growth models in Europe's periphery: FDI-led growth, where export competitiveness is fostered by foreign firms; and 'lean' models, which rely on macroeconomic orthodoxy and strictly limit state intervention to foster adjustment (Bohle and Regan 2021; Bohle and Jacoby 2017). In contrast, in countries that had (credit-based) demand-led growth models prior to the crisis, adjustment is more difficult.

The framing of the crisis as sovereign debt crisis, however, is also conducive to the rise of nationalist policy solutions, as it pits debtors against creditor countries, allowing them to frame economic conflicts in nationalist terms (e.g. Kriesi and Pappas 2015: 8; Streeck 2014). Whether or not a nationalist answer emerges depends on prior cleavages and political entrepreneurship. Whether it prevails depends on whether it resonates with voters, and is economically viable. Here my contention is that it is easier for right-wing than for left-wing nationalists answers to win out. This is because right-wing nationalists have no issue with combining nationalism with austerity and competitiveness. Further, in contrast to traditional or radical left-wing forces, national conservatives also have their 'international enablers' (Johnson and Barnes 2015). This is partly the flipside of the fact that these political forces selectively embrace economic neoliberalism.

Finally, there is also a temporal dimension. Over time, the likelihood that governments join the nationalist conservative camp increases, as continuous mainstream neoliberalism is only viable in few cases, and left-wing alternatives not feasible. Figure 6.3 below summarizes the detailed argument.

The next section will apply this framework to analyse the different outcomes of right-wing and left-wing nationalist answers to the crisis in Greece and Hungary.

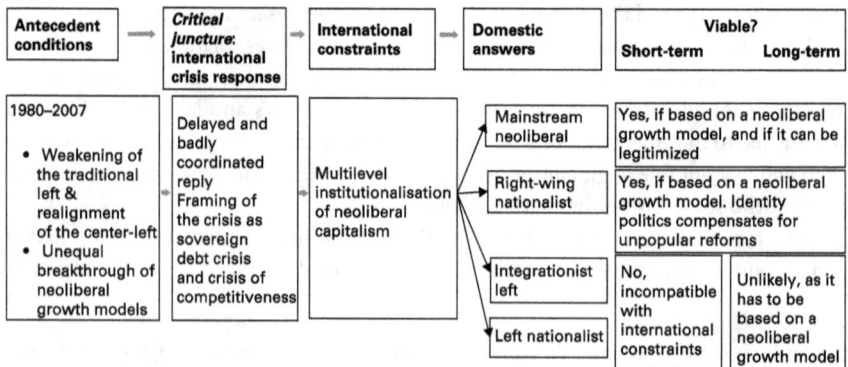

Antecedent conditions	Critical juncture: international crisis response	International constraints	Domestic answers	Viable?	
				Short-term	**Long-term**
1980–2007 • Weakening of the traditional left & realignment of the center-left • Unequal breakthrough of neoliberal growth models	Delayed and badly coordinated reply Framing of the crisis as sovereign debt crisis and crisis of competitiveness	Multilevel institutionalisation of neoliberal capitalism	Mainstream neoliberal	Yes, if based on a neoliberal growth model, and if it can be legitimized	
			Right-wing nationalist	Yes, if based on a neoliberal growth model. Identity politics compensates for unpopular reforms	
			Integrationist left	No, incompatible with international constraints	Unlikely, as it has to be based on a neoliberal growth model
			Left nationalist		

Figure 6.3 Summary of the argument.

Why did the right-wing nationalist answer to the crisis succeed while left-wing nationalist answer failed? The second Fidesz government (2010–14) and the Syriza government (2015–19) compared

Two revolts in the name of national sovereignty

The first European country to endorse a right-wing nationalist answer to the Global Financial Crisis was Hungary, under the second Fidesz government (2010–14). Fidesz was propelled to power after Hungary, as the first European country, had to turn to the IMF and EU for a bailout in November 2008. The IMF-supported programme had two key objectives: fiscal consolidation; and the stabilization of the financial sector. Political scandals of the then governing socialist party and unpopular austerity paved the way for a landslide Fidesz victory in May 2010.

The Greek crisis hit the headlines in 2009, when a newly elected socialist government revealed the true scale of the country's fiscal deficit. In May of the following year, it became the first country in the eurozone to request a bailout. In the end, Greece underwent two bailout programmes, five years of deep austerity and four governments before the new left-wing party, Syriza, won a landslide victory and formed a coalition government with the nationalist-right wing Independent Greeks. The coalition was tied together by strong anti-bailout and anti-establishment sentiments.

The two countries share several similarities. To be sure, Greece's external vulnerabilities were much higher than Hungary's, but both cases had developed unsustainable twin deficits of high budget deficits and current accounts, and their debt-to-GDP ratio was very high in comparison to their regional peers and judged unsustainable by the EU and international financial organizations (IFOs). In addition to public debt, they had also rapidly built up private debt prior to the crisis. Both countries were therefore very vulnerable to the freezing of external lending.

The two nationalist political camps came to power by campaigning to end austerity and to alter the conditions of their international integration, although both parties shied away from advocating a full-fledged break with the EU and IFOs. Thus, Fidesz' main wrath was directed against international banks and the IMF, while initially being somewhat less confrontational vis-à-vis the EU. Syriza's main aim was to alter the conditions of its bailout, but it did not want the country to leave the eurozone. Both governments staged a revolt against the conditionality and policy advice of the EU and IFOs and both governments justified this in term of restoring national sovereignty (e.g. Johnson and Barnes 2015, Dendrinou and Varvitsioti 2019).

At the core of the Hungarian revolt were three policies: reducing the influence of foreign banks and currencies; undermining the independence of the central bank; and rejecting the terms of the IMF agreement and ultimately the IMF (Johnson and Barnes 2015). Foreign banks were targeted as they had extended foreign currency loans and unfair interest rate policies to large parts of the population, exposing them to significant risks (Bohle 2014). The government imposed a high levy on the financial sector in 2010. It allowed mortgage holders to exchange their foreign currency debt into forint at preferential exchange rate for those who could repay their debt in one stroke, and introduced an exchange rate protection mechanism. In 2014, finally, the government forced almost all debtors to swap their forex loans into local currency at the then current rate. Banks were also forced to pay significant compensation to indebted households for unfair lending practices. These (and other) measures pushed the banks into loss-making territory, which led some of the foreign banks to leave Hungary (Bohle 2014, 2018; Bohle and Greskovits 2019; Johnson and Barnes 2015).

The government also actively undermined the independence of the central bank, whose governor had been appointed by the previous socialist-liberal coalition. It cut his salary by 75 per cent and ruled that all members of the Monetary Council be appointed by Parliament. In 2011 Parliament passed a controversial Central Bank Law, which sought to alter the distribution of power between the executive and legislative. The government also sought to merge the central bank and the supervisory authority. Due to international pressure and an EU infringement procedure, it eventually had to back track on some of the most controversial legislative proposals. However, attacks on the central bank continued, and in March 2013 the government appointed a close Orbán ally as new governor (Johnson and Barnes 2015).

With these and other measures, the government provoked strong conflicts with and an increasing estrangement from the EU, and an outright rupture with the IMF. Initially, when coming to power, the government had sought to negotiate a new standby loan with the IMF. At the same time, however, it contested the terms of the loan. It sought to get concessions on the deficit target of below 3 per cent for 2011, as it had promised its voters to end austerity. It was therefore not ready to compromise on the bank levy and other sectoral taxes. To achieve better terms, party officials at one point even compared Hungary to Greece, floating the possibility that Hungary might default on its loans (Bryant 2010a and b). The negotiations between IMF and the government broke down in Summer 2010, and were resumed only in Winter 2011, when the plunging currency and the downgrading of its sovereign bonds brought the government back to the negotiation table. The relations remained however frosty, culminating in the government's decision to pay back its IMF loans early and close its Budapest office in August 2013.[3]

At the core of Syriza's revolt was its electoral pledge 'to end austerity, repeal the memoranda programme, abolish the Troika and negotiate a new deal with the international creditors' (Koliastasis 2015: 363). When the government came to power, the future of the second bailout programme somewhat hung in the air. The previous conservative government had failed to complete its last bailout review. Instead, in December 2014 the eurozone finance ministers granted a two-month extension period of the programme. When the new government came to power, it was assumed that the country would run out of money by the end of February 2015. Despite wanting to negotiate a new deal, the government therefore reluctantly agreed on an extension of the programme. It however entered in fierce conflicts with the creditors about the terms of the extensions and the concrete reforms. While creditors pushed for further pension cuts, sales tax hikes and high primary surplus, these conditions deemed unacceptable to the government. The latter was however entirely unwilling or unable to

[3] E.g. https://uk.reuters.com/article/uk-hungary-imf-repaid/hungary-repays-2008-imf-loan-in-full-government-idUKBRE97B07720130812

come up with concrete reform proposals that would satisfy its creditors. The government also wanted the creditors to recognize the 'humanitarian catastrophe' that five years of austerity had wrought on Greek society and sought to renegotiate parts of the debt.

The conflict came to a head in June 2015, when in light of what seemed to the Syriza team ever changing and wholly unacceptable conditions from its creditors, the government held a referendum to decide on the bailout extension deal. For the Eurogroup, this and the fact that the government was supporting a 'no' vote was a clear signal that the deal they had proposed was dead. The second bailout would therefore be terminated. As is well known, the paradoxical outcome of Syriza's first six months in government was that while trying to pursue their electoral pledge, they ended up with a new bailout programme the terms of which were far worse than the one it sought to repeal. In doing so, they also brought the economy and the banking sector close to a collapse, defaulted on their IMF loan and faced the spectre of being kicked out (or leaving) the eurozone. Against this background, despite a landslide victory of the 'no' vote, the government agreed to a new bailout programme 'which included all the painful measures that had led to the impasse in negotiations and subsequent referendum' (Dendrinou and Varvitsioti 2019, e-book location 268; see also Tooze 2018: e-book locations 519–36).

These early experiences of both governments in their relations with the EU, IMF and international markets were consequential for the further trajectory in economic policies. In both countries, the initial government period was characterized by a lot of trial and error and both had to backtrack on some of their promises. Further, in electoral terms, both governments had a strong mandate to pursue their policies. In both countries, governments bolstered their legitimacy with a discourse of victimization which strongly resonated with broad segments of society (for Greece, see Lialiouti and Bithymitris 2017; Knight 2013). However, Hungarian policy-makers came out of the initial period feeling more confident. They had learned that even if they had to backtrack somewhat, they were still able to get their main policy priorities through. The Syriza government, in contrast, learned the hard way that it was impossible to defy the conditions of their creditors. Thus, while Orbán started to push through his nationalist-right wing policies ever more assertively, Syriza resigned to implement further neoliberal reforms. What accounts for these differences?

Explaining the differences

There are two broad sets of factors that explain for the differences in outcome. The first and most obvious are the different external constraints stemming from Greece's EMU membership versus Hungary's status as an EMU outsider. Second, the two countries' growth models differed, making adjustment a much easier task in Hungary than in Greece.

EMU insider versus outsider

How did EMU membership matter? While libraries have by now been written about how EMU membership has affected Greece before and after the euro crisis, comparisons of the effects of external assistance on policies and outcomes inside and outside of the eurozone in the wake of the crisis have been scarce. One exception is Mabbett and Schelkle (2015), who, comparing Latvia, Hungary and Greece, find that EMU membership mattered in three ways. First, the two countries outside of the eurozone were much earlier hit by the Global Financial Crisis than Greece. This is because eurozone members, no matter their financial vulnerability, were initially shielded from its impact due to the ECB's provision of liquidity and collateral policy (Gabor 2012). By contrast, in Hungary and Latvia, governments and banks experienced liquidity problems early on, which is why they needed to turn to the IMF and EU for a bailout. The fact that Greece was initially shielded from the effects of the Global Financial Crisis, however, also meant that its imbalances could accumulate for yet another year, making them even more unsustainable.

Second, for countries outside of the eurozone, the bailout was combined with an international cooperative effort to stabilize the countries' – mostly foreign-owned – banking systems. This is the contrary of what happened inside the eurozone. Here, the ECB's decision to start its exit strategy from its liquidity support in 2009 and the discussion of a new regime concerning lower-rated sovereign debt led to a withdrawal of foreign banks from Greek debt and increasing market pressure, which ultimately forced the country into the first bailout.

Third, the withdrawal of foreign banks from Greek debt also led to adverse consequences of the second bailout, which incorporated a considerable debt write-down. The private sector involvement in the debt write-down affected almost exclusively the domestic banks, who by now held most of Greek's sovereign debt. As a consequence, much of the debt write-down was spent on recapitalizing the banks. That is, Greece was affected by the now well-known pattern of a sovereign-bank 'doom loop' (De Grauwe 2012: 117, quoted in Mabbett and Schelkle).

But there is more to how EMU membership mattered. The eurozone crisis also opened stark distributional and political struggles within and between countries, and conflicts within and between international institutions. These conflicts have been much less severe in the case of EMU outsiders. EMU insiders dealt with a variety of different actors, from nation states to the Troika to the Eurogroup, for whom nothing less than the future of the eurozone was at stake. These actors had different views on what the eurozone is about, who should bear the costs of adjustment in crisis, how to make the zone safe against future crises and how to play the multiple levels of the europolity.

This is not the place to detail the eminently political character of the negotiations between Greece and its creditors, which were mostly absent in the interaction of Hungary and the IMF.[4] Suffice it to say that Greece got an unnecessarily tough deal for four reasons. First, there was the unwillingness of major actors to acknowledge the financial origin of the crisis, as well as the fact that the Greek government was insolvent. Most of the adjustment focussed on the fiscal aspects of the crisis, thus reinforcing the country's downward spiral (e.g. Sandbu 2015; Matthijs and McNamara 2015). Second,

---

[4] For insightful accounts, see for example Dendrinou and Varvitsioti 2019, Varoufakis 2017, Tooze 2018 and Lütz et al. 2019.

crisis management involved different institutions, all of which had their own special interests. The Troika was made of the ECB, the European Commission and the IMF, each of which at times fought for their own vision of what had to be done (Lütz et al. 2019). The outcome was often devastating for Greece (Dendrinou and Varvitsioti 2019: e-book location 172). Third, within the Eurogroup's very diverse membership, there was little sympathy with Syriza's requests to renegotiate the deal, and arguably, the Greek finance minister undermined even the little solidarity that would have been forthcoming. Finally, there was a clash of political cultures. The Greek negotiators came as outsiders, with little understanding of the functioning of EU institutions (in particular the Eurogroup), and their behaviour was often seen as arrogant, incompetent and at the wrong end of the political spectrum (Dendrinou and Varvitsioti 2019). In contrast, in the Hungarian case, the EU thought it had little stake. It left negotiations to the IMF, which had a long track record of dealing with more or less willing debtors. Hungary also relied much less on the solidarity of other EU members, although it benefited from other sovereigns bailing out its (foreign-owned) banks.

To sum up, in the face of a major financial crisis and panic, stabilization was both economically and politically much easier outside EMU than inside it. After stabilization, the next major issue was how to restore growth.

FDI-led growth versus clientelistic decline

Hungary and Greece are both late industrializers: their industries developed behind protective walls, were highly regulated and not competitive internationally. They also share a legacy of dictatorship. After the fall of their respective authoritarian governments, both countries had to master the double transition from dictatorship to democracy, and from being a small closed economy to one open to world markets and the EU. Here, the similarities end. After the fall of Communism, Hungary rapidly opened its economy to Foreign Direct Investment (FDI).[5] Foreign investment rapidly became the most dynamic part of the Hungarian economy. As early as the mid 1990s, these companies accounted for half of all investments, 40 per cent of the value added in industry, and 70 per cent of the country's exports and foreign companies' significance have still increased (Bohle and Regan 2021). FDI in manufacturing is concentrated in complex industries, and the most important foreign companies are closely integrated with German supply chains, mostly in the automobile sector. Hungary is an attractive location for FDI as it has a legacy of manufacturing industry, a comparatively cheap and skilled labour force, low corporate taxation and a state that is willing to offer a battery of investment incentives to keep Hungary's locational advantages.

Hungary's FDI-led growth had two specific consequences for Fidesz' right-wing nationalist agenda. First, the country could rely on Germany's recovery for its own, and export its way out of the crisis. While the Hungarian growth performance after the crisis lagged behind its equally FDI-led regional peers, it did experience a moderate recovery in 2010 and 2011 driven by exports, and from 2013, gross fixed-capital formation turned positive (European Commission 2015: 3). This contrasts with the

---

[5]   This section is based on Bohle and Greskovits 2012, 2018, and Bohle and Regan 2021.

austerity-inflicted continuous decline of the Greek economy. Second, FDI-led growth produced specific opportunity structures for right wing nationalist policies. The dominance of FDI in the economy made foreign capital a natural scapegoat for the crisis. This is particularly the case as not only manufacturing, but also finance and other services, were controlled by FDI. Fidesz' 'financial nationalism' (Johnson and Barnes 2015) therefore resonated with large shares of the population. Moreover, domestic entrepreneurs felt marginalized in an economy in which foreign companies occupied the commanding heights. Fidesz' policies of nurturing the domestic bourgeoisie while punishing foreign firms in the service sectors addressed some of these grievances.

At the same time, it is important to note the selective nature of Fidesz' economic nationalism. Central to Hungary's right-wing nationalism was a distinction between 'good' and 'bad' FDI. While foreign firms in the service sectors experienced special sectoral taxes and partial re-nationalization, continuity prevailed in government policies towards the foreign-owned manufacturing sector. Here investment promotion has remained a central pillar. The government generously provided cash subsidies and tax incentives to attract new manufacturing FDI, and designed a new policy instrument ('strategic partnerships' with foreign investors) which aims to promote investment, employment and education, and foster stronger ties to domestic suppliers. Moreover, some of the government's neoliberal economic policies benefited both domestic and foreign companies. Fidesz' radical overhaul of the labour law in 2012, which led to a 'large-scale flexibilization' of it and a significant downgrading of labour rights, is a case in point (European Trade Union Institute 2012).

Finally, FDI-led growth also mattered politically. Transnational business alliances have been backed and reinforced by transnational political alliances. Hungary's strong links with the south-Germany-based car industry was cemented by Fidesz' strong links to Bavaria's ruling party, the conservative Christian Democratic Union (CSU). This right-wing alliance travelled to the very heart of the European Parliament's political power centre, with CSU politician Manfred Weber serving as a leader of the European People's Party.

The Greek economy is starkly different to its Hungarian counterpart. Its defining feature is pervasive state control, clientelism and familialism, which was already built in the country's industrialization history, and was extended considerably as a reaction to the crisis of the 1970s (e.g. Mouzelis 1986; Featherstone 2005; Pappas 2009; Trantidis 2016; Liagouras 2019). State control gave political parties extensive resources for particularistic allocations to political supporters, allowing for the stabilization of the two main parties after the dictatorship. Politicians could also hold to power due to their close ties to a handful of wealthy families and 'by rewarding a small number of professional associations and public sector unions that support the status quo' (Eleftheriadis 2014: 140).

Inevitably, however, favouritism and clientelism undermined the economic resources of the Greek economy. Even before the Global Financial Crisis, the country had undergone recurrent fiscal crises resulting from inflation and over indebtedness. The costs of stabilization typically were distributed in such a way that public company and central government employees, government bondholders and importers counted as the winners, whereas small and medium enterprises, private sector workers and some exporters lost out (Tranditis 2016: 116; Pagoulatos 2003: 150–78). This way, the public sector increasingly encroached on the private economy, exacerbating the economic malaise of the country. Pervasive clientelism and state control had thus resulted in the Greek economy being 'the most protected and monopoly ridden economy in the euro area' prior to the crisis (Ioannides and Pissarides 2015: 350).

What is more, the country's most successful export sectors, shipping and tourism, are not conducive to becoming the country's growth engine. Greece's shipping industry, by far the most competitive sector of the economy, is also the most disconnected from the domestic economy. Not only is its aversion to paying taxes notorious (Liagouras 2019: 11), but in addition, most of its operation is situated in the 'no-man's-land of global product, capital and labor markets', and as such it has 'very little interest in the reform of the Greek state' and contributes very little to the Greek economy (ibid; see also Bergin 2015). The second important export sector, tourism, is mostly made up of micro-enterprises and the self-employed, who more often than not operate in a grey zone of tax evasion, illegal construction and non-payment of social security contributions (ibid: 1125). It is also hard to see how these micro-entities could coordinate to upgrade the sector. Growth in Greece before the crisis had therefore been mostly fuelled by transfers and cheap credits, something that was of short supply once the crisis hit.

Adjustment to the EU's post-crisis competitiveness agenda was therefore a much more difficult task than in Hungary, as it meant overthrowing the very economic model the country had relied upon since democratization. Moreover, the previous Troika-administered adjustment programmes had partly reinforced the skewed structures of the Greek economy (Pelagides and Metsopoulos 2016: 155–95; Rettman 2012). Pursuing a left-wing agenda was even more of a Herculean task against the background of massive tax evasion, high inequality and an abundance of particularistic interests. It is therefore perhaps not all too surprising that Syriza's record in implementing left-wing policies was rather dismal. The promises to tackle the country's oligarchs and their massive tax evasion went nowhere. Instead, one of the first laws passed after Syriza came to power was to remove a cap on a budget law allowing Greeks with overdue tax bills to pay them off over a protracted period. This benefited the very rich, too. The government also caved in to the pressure of the wealthy shipowners, who threatened to leave the country if their tax burden increased (Dendrinou and Varvitsioti 2019: e-book location 201; Bergin 2015; ship2shore 105).

More surprising is arguably Syriza's meagre track record on improving the country's 'humanitarian crisis'. While its failure to spare pensioners further cuts in pensions is explained by the demands of creditors, it is less clear why legislation to provide immediate relieve to poorer social strata 'amounted to a mere 0.06 percent of GDP in 2015' (Matsaganis 2019: 91).

Conclusions and outlook

The aim of this chapter was to explain the different capacity of right-wing versus left-wing nationalist answers to challenge the pre-financial crisis neoliberal and integrationist consensus. It compared two cases that have challenged mainstream neoliberalism from a nationalist perspective: Hungary and Greece. While the second Hungarian Orbán government (2010–14) successfully implemented right-wing nationalist responses, Greece's Syriza government's (2015-19) attempt to implement a radical left alternative was short lived.

The argument of the chapter can be summarized as follows: while both countries staged a revolt against the conditions of their bailout and the subsequent constraints stemming from this, Fidesz was successful because the country's growth model made adjustment comparatively easy; it could implement its agenda *with* the consent of some of its powerful economic elites; and constraints from IFOs and the EU were relatively mild. In contrast, as an EMU member Syriza faced harsh and very politicized external constraints, Greece's economic model was dysfunctional and would need a wholesale overhaul against the entrenched interests of powerful economic elites. This was an endeavour in which Syriza ultimately failed.

In some sense, then, the different outcome is overdetermined. In order to tease out whether my hypothesis – that in contemporary Europe, the cards are stacked against left-wing policy solutions – holds true more generally, further cases such as failure of the main-stream left answer in Iceland under Jóhanna Sigurðardóttir (2009–13), and the record of the incumbent Portuguese government under Antonio Costo should provide answers. Iceland shares with Hungary less constraining international conditions and easier sources of growth after the crisis. While Portugal is a member of the eurozone, the left-wing government came to power after the hardest tasks of adjustment were accomplished and growth restored.

Do success and failure of policy packages implemented half a decade ago still matter? I think they do. Thus, Fidesz' formula of combining selective neoliberalism with nationalist policies is being carefully observed by other countries, while the failure of Syriza is a blow for other left-wing forces. Moreover, as right-wing nationalism has received a second lease of life with the refugee crisis, it is likely to be here to stay. Further, the way how countries came out of the last economic crisis is likely to have a bearing on how they can and will cope with the fall-out of the COVID-19 crisis.

References

Baccaro, Lucio, and Chris Howell. 2017. *Trajectories of Neoliberal Transformation: European Industrial Relations Since the 1970s*. Cambridge, UK, New York, Port Melbourne: Cambridge University Press.

Becker, Joachim. 2015a. 'Editorial: Konturen Einer Wirtschaftspolitischen Heterodoxie von Rechts.' *Kurswechsel* 30 (3): 60–9.

Becker, Joachim. 2015b. 'Der Selektive Wirtschaftsnationalismus Der Fidesz Regierung.' *Kurswechsel* 30 (3): 70–4.

Bergin, Tom. 2015. 'The Great Greek Shipping Myth.' Reuters. 25 November 2015. http://www.reuters.com/investigates/special-report/eurozone-greece-shipping/

Blyth, Mark. 2002. *Great Transformations: Economic Ideas and Institutional Change in the Twentieth Century*. Cambridge: Cambridge University Press.

Blyth, Mark. 2013. *Austerity: The History of a Dangerous Idea*. Oxford and New York: Oxford University Press.

Boas, Taylor C., and Jordan Gans-Morse. 2009. 'Neoliberalism: From New Liberal Philosophy to Anti-Liberal Slogan.' *Studies in Comparative International Development* 44 (2): 137–61.

Bobbio, Norberto. 1996. *Left and Right: The Significance of a Political Distinction*. Oxford: Polity Press.

Bohle, Dorothee. 2014. 'Post-Socialist Housing Meets Transnational Finance: Foreign Banks, Mortgage Lending, and the Privatization of Welfare in Hungary and Estonia.' *Review of International Political Economy* 21 (4): 913–48.

Bohle, Dorothee. 2018. 'Mortgaging Europe's Periphery.' *Studies in Comparative International Development* 53 (2): 196–217.

Bohle, Dorothee, and Béla Greskovits. 2012. *Capitalist Diversity on Europe's Periphery*. Ithaca, NY: Cornell University Press.

Bohle, Dorothee, and Béla Greskovits. 2019. 'Politicising Embedded Neoliberalism: Continuity and Change in Hungary's Development Model.' *West European Politics*, 42 (5): 1069–93.

Bohle, Dorothee, and Wade Jacoby. 2017. 'Lean, Special, or Consensual? Vulnerability and External Buffering in the Small States of East-Central Europe.' *Comparative Politics* 49 (2): 191–212.

Bohle, Dorothee, and Aidan Regan. 2021. 'Business Power, Quiet Politics and State Elites: Explaining the Continuity of FDI-Led Growth in Ireland and Hungary.' *Politics and Society* 49 (1).

Bowman, Sam. 2016. 'Coming out as Neoliberals.' Adam Smith Institute. Accessed 27 August 2019. https://www.adamsmith.org/blog/coming-out-as-neoliberals

Bryant, Chis. 2010a. 'Hungary's Leaders Count Cost of Loose Talk.' *Financial Times*. 7 June 2010. https://www.ft.com/content/16fcaa48-7256-11df-9f82-00144feabdc0

Bryant, Chris. 2010b. 'Hungary IMF Talks Suspended.' *Financial Times*. 18 July 2010. https://www.ft.com/content/4d442bb8-9267-11df-9142-00144feab49a

Crouch, Colin. 2011. *The Strange Non-Death of Neo-Liberalism*. Cambridge, UK and Malden, MA: Polity Press.

De Grauwe, Paul. 2012. *Economics of Monetary Union*. Oxford: Oxford University Press.

Dendrinou, Viktoria, and Eleni Varvitsioti. 2019. *The Last Bluff: How Greece came face-to-face with Financial Catastrophe & the Secret Plan for its Euro Exit*. Athens: Papadopoulos Publishing.

Eichengreen, Barry. 2015. *Hall of Mirrors: The Great Depression, The Great Recession, and the Uses-and Misuses-of History*. New York: Oxford University Press.

Eleftheriadis, Pavlos. 2014. 'Misrule of the Few: How the Oligarchs Ruined Greece.' *Foreign Affairs* 93 (6): 139–46.

Esping-Andersen, Gosta. 1990. *The Three Worlds of Welfare Capitalism*. Cambridge: Polity Press.

European Commission. 2015. 'Macroeconomic Imbalances Country Report – Hungary 2015.' European Economy Occasional Papers 220. European Commission. https://ec.europa.eu/economy_finance/publications/occasional_paper/2015/op220_en.htm

European Trade Union Institute. 2012. 'Labour Reforms in Hungary.' Accessed 27 August 2019. https://www.etui.org/ReformsWatch/Hungary/Labour-reforms-in-Hungary-background-summary

Featherstone, Kevin. 2005. 'Introduction: "Modernisation" and the Structural Constraints of Greek Politics.' *West European Politics* 28 (2): 223–41.

Gabor, Daniela. 2012. 'The Power of Collateral: The ECB and Bank Funding Strategies in Crisis.' https://papers.ssrn.com/sol3/papers.cfm?abstract_id=2062315

Gamble, Andrew. 1994. *The Free Economy and the Strong State: The Politics of Thatcherism.* London: Macmillan.

Gramsci, Antonio. 1971. *Selections from the Prison Notebooks.* New York: International Publishers.

Gourevitch, Peter Alexis. 1986. *Politics in Hard Times: Comparative Responses to International Economic Crises.* Ithaca: Cornell University Press.

Hooghe, Liesbet, and Gary Marks. 2018. 'Cleavage Theory Meets Europe's Crises: Lipset, Rokkan, and the Transnational Cleavage.' *Journal of European Public Policy* 25 (1): 109–35.

Ioannides, Yannis M., and Christopher A. Pissarides. 2015. 'Is the Greek Crisis One of Supply or Demand?' *Brookings Papers on Economic Activity*, 349–83.

Jahn, Detlef. 2011. 'Conceptualizing Left and Right in Comparative Politics: Towards a Deductive Approach.' *Party Politics* 17 (6): 745–65.

Johnson, Juliet, and Andrew Barnes. 2015. 'Financial Nationalism and Its International Enablers: The Hungarian Experience.' *Review of International Political Economy* 22 (3): 535–69.

Knight, Daniel M. 2013. 'The Greek Economic Crisis as Trope.' *Focaal* 2013 (65): 147–59.

Koliastasis, Panos. 2015. 'The Greek Parliamentary Elections of 25 January, 2015.' *Representation* 51 (3): 359–72.

Kriesi, Hanspeter, Edgar Grande, Romain Lachat, Martin Dolezal, Simon Bornschier and Timotheos Frey. 2008. *West European Politics in the Age of Globalization.* Cambridge: Cambridge University Press.

Kriesi, Hanspeter, and Pappas, Takis S. 2015. 'Populism in Europe During Crisis: An Introduction.' In Hanspeter Kriesi and Takis S. Pappas (eds.), *European Populism in the Shadow of the Great Recession.* Colchester: ECPR Press.

Liagouras, George. 2019. 'On the Social Origins of Economic Divergence: Familism, Business and State in Greece.' *West European Politics*, 42 (5): 1115–39.

Lialiouti, Zinovia, and Giorgos Bithymitris. 2017. 'A Nation under Attack: Perceptions of Enmity and Victimhood in the Context of the Greek Crisis.' *National Identities* 19 (1): 53–71.

Luebbert, Gregory M. 1991. *Liberalism, Fascism, or Social Democracy: Social Classes and the Political Origins of Regimes in Interwar Europe: Social Classes and the Political Origins of Regimes in Interwar Europe.* Oxford: Oxford University Press.

Lütz, Susanne, Sven Hilgers and Sebastian Schneider. 2019. 'Accountants, Europeanists and Monetary Guardians: Bureaucratic Cultures and Conflicts in IMF-EU Lending Programs.' *Review of International Political Economy* 26 (6): 1187–210.

Mabbett, Deborah, and Waltraud Schelkle. 2015. 'What Difference Does Euro Membership Make to Stabilization? The Political Economy of International Monetary Systems Revisited.' *Review of International Political Economy* 22 (3): 508–34.

Manow, Philip. 2018. *Die Politische Ökonomie des Populismus.* Berlin: Suhrkamp.

Matthijs, Matthias, and Kathleen McNamara. 2015. 'The Euro Crisis' Theory Effect: Northern Saints, Southern Sinners, and the Demise of the Eurobond.' *Journal of European Integration* 37 (2): 229–45.

Matsaganis, Manos. 2019. 'Greece: The Crisis, Austerity, and the Transformation of Welfare.' In Stefán Ólafsson; Daly, Mary: Kangass, Olli, and Palme, Joakim (eds.), *Welfare and the Great Recession: A Comparative Study*, 83–97. Oxford: Oxford University Press.

Mirowski, Philip. 2014. *Never Let a Serious Crisis Go to Waste: How Neoliberalism Survived the Financial Meltdown*. London: Verso.

Mouzelis, Nicos P. 1986. *Politics in the Semi-Periphery : Early Parliamentarism and Late Industrialisation in the Balkans and Latin America*. London: Macmillan.

Ost, David, David. 2018. 'The Attack on Democracy in Poland and the Response of the Left,' 19 July 2018. https://www.thenation.com/article/attack-democracy-poland-response-left/

Ostry, Jonathan, Prakash Loungani and Davide Furceri. 2016. 'Neoliberalism: Oversold?' *Finance and Development* 53 (2): 38–41.

Pagoulatos, George. 2003. *Greece's New Political Economy: State, Finance, and Growth from Postwar to EMU*. Basingstoke and New York: Palgrave Macmillan.

Pappas, Takis. 1999. *Making Party Democracy in Greece*. Berlin: Springer.

Pappas, Takis S. 2009. 'Patrons against Partisans: The Politics of Patronage in Mass Ideological Parties.' *Party Politics* 15 (3): 315–34.

Peck, Jamie, and Nik Theodore. 2019. 'Still Neoliberalism?' *South Atlantic Quarterly* 118 (2): 245–65.

Pelagides, Theodoros K., and Michales Metsopoulos. 2016. *Who's to Blame for Greece? Austerity in Charge of Saving a Broken Economy*. Basingstoke and New York: Palgrave Macmillan.

Polanyi, Karl. 2001 [1944]. *The Great Transformation: The Political and Economic Origins of Our Time*. Boston, MA: Beacon Press.

Rettman, Andrew. 2012. 'No EU Austerity for Greek Super-Rich.' EUobserver. 27 June 2012. https://euobserver.com/justice/116777

Roberts, Kenneth M. 2017. 'State of the Field: Party Politics in Hard Times: Comparative Perspectives on the European and Latin American Economic Crises.' *European Journal of Political Research* 56 (2): 218–33.

Sandbu, Martin E. 2015. *Europe's Orphan the Future of the Euro and the Politics of Debt*. Princeton, NJ: Princeton University Press.

Schelkle, Waltraud. 2017. *The Political Economy of Monetary Solidarity: Understanding the Euro Experiment*. Oxford and New York: Oxford University Press.

Schmidt, Vivien A., and Mark Thatcher. 2013. *Resilient Liberalism in Europe's Political Economy*. Cambridge and New York: Cambridge University Press.

Ship2shore 2015: 'Torrid August Ahead: Greek Shipowners to Escape Syriza and Go towards Tax Havens? – Ship2Shore.' 2015. Ship2shore: Online Magazine of Maritime and Transport Economics. 3 August 2015. http://www.ship2shore.it/en/shipping/torrid-august-ahead-greek-shipowners-to-escape-syriza-and-go-towards-tax-havens_58602.htm

Slobodian, Quinn. 2018. *Globalists: The End of Empire and the Birth of Neoliberalism*. Cambridge, MA: Harvard University Press.

Streeck, Wolfgang. 2014. *Buying Time: The Delayed Crisis of Democratic Capitalism*. Brooklyn, NY: Verso.

Tooze, Adam. y. *Crashed: How a Decade of Financial Crises Changed the World*. ebook: Penguin.

Trantidis, Aris. 2016. *Clientelism and Economic Policy: Greece and the Crisis*. London and New York: Routledge.

Varoufakis, Yanis. 2017. *Adults in the Room: My Battle with the European and American Deep Establishment*. New York: Farrar, Straus and Giroux.

7

Financial Crisis Management: Unanswered Key Questions

Patrick Honohan

More than a decade after the dramatic weeks during which the foundations of the global financial system seemed to be threatened, and as the global economy entered an even deeper downturn resulting from pandemic, there were still large differences between scholars as to how such financial crises should be managed. That is not to say that scholars and policy-makers have been inactive. There have been significant institutional changes: the European Central Bank (ECB) has been charged with the supervision of the major banks in the euro area and has established the Single Supervisory Mechanism (SSM), with over a thousand staff newly recruited for its Frankfurt headquarters. The Bank of England has re-acquired responsibility for bank supervision from the ill-fated Financial Supervisory Authority (FSA). An extensive reorganization of supervisory powers and responsibilities has also been implemented in the United States.

There have also been numerous changes in regulatory rules for banks since the Global Financial Crisis broke. Identifying inadequate capital and (less plausibly) inadequate liquid reserves as key contributors to the banking collapses, international policy-makers established new standards requiring much more equity capital especially in systemically important banks, supplemented in times of boom. Liquidity regulation, previously not subject to hard and fast rules, has been tightened considerably. The international regulatory community hopes that the extra capital will be enough, though a recent survey shows that the average academic expert believes minimum capital standards should have been set even higher (Ambrocio et al. 2019).

Prevention is one thing; crisis management is another. Here too, legislators and regulators have not been idle. The topic of bank resolution has entered centre stage with elaborate decisions on the degree to which a bank must have funded itself through means that can be bailed-in in the event of failure. In practice this means that, in addition to capital, banks are having to issue debt that can be cancelled or converted to equity if the bank is failing or likely to fail. Banks are being required to draw up and refine 'living wills' designed to facilitate the orderly restructuring of a failing institution in such a way that essential services are maintained. European legislation (including the Bank Recovery and Resolution Directive BRRD of 2014) has created a resolution authority, the Single Resolution Board (SRB), to ensure that this planning is adequately implemented and to take decisions around the resolution of failing banks in the euro area.

Despite all of this activity, bank failures have continued – and will continue – to occur. While that is the price society has to pay if the benefits of financial intermediation, access to credit and maturity transformation are to be protected, it is far from clear that an adequate framework for the management and resolution of bank failure is fully functional. Although the bail-in tool of the new European resolution framework has been in place since the beginning of 2016, the first steps in its implementation have been somewhat faltering, suggesting that the concept of bail-in is not fully bedded down. In June 2017 the SSM declared a fairly large Spanish bank – Banco Popular Español, the sixth largest bank in Spain, with total liabilities of about 15 per cent of GDP – to be 'failing or likely to fail'. (Popular had been granted a moderate amount of emergency liquidity in the previous days.) This decision triggered a judgement call by the SRB as to whether, if the bank could not be recapitalized with private funds, it should be liquidated or put into the new resolution procedures. The SRB decided on resolution. Fortunately a private sector buyer (Santander) was at hand, willing to acquire the assets and liabilities after subordinated debt (which had been trading at a deep discount relative to par in the previous days) was written down to zero. Despite some legal challenges, the resolution went smoothly.

The failure of two smaller Italian banks just a few weeks later was dealt with in a different manner which, though compliant with the new legislation, certainly seemed at variance with the new mantra of bail-in. Thus, the SRB decided that resolution of the two failing Italian banks[1] was not warranted in the public interest. Yet, the Italian government was allowed to use public funds to grant state-aid to facilitate the winding down of the two banks to mitigate regional economic effects of the winding down in Italy. These two cases raised doubts in the mind of many observers as to whether bail-in would in fact be applied to future resolution cases.

In addition, some cases of 'precautionary recapitalization' with government funds were authorized, in accordance with provisions of the European legislation. A bank that needs such an injection is evidently close to being considered 'failing or likely to fail', the latter status precluding government assistance without substantial bail-in of other creditors. Several sizable banks have gone down this route.[2]

Looking back

This uncertainty is less surprising when considered against the background of the astonishing degree of flip-flopping exhibited in crisis management in the earlier years

---

[1] Banca Popolare di Vicenza and Veneto Banca.
[2] Piraeus Bank and the National Bank of Greece were the first of these cases in 2015, followed by Monte dei Paschi di Siena in 2017 and Norddeutsche Landesbank Girocentrale in 2019. A principle applied to these cases was that government funds might be provided for a precautionary recapitalization if the bank was projected to remain adequately capitalized in the base case of an asset-quality review, but undercapitalized in a stress case.

of the crisis. And while the extent of regulatory and legislative reforms that have been agreed internationally and in Europe might suggest that there has been convergence in expert and official opinion, a closer look reveals that influential voices remain sharply divided on some of the most fundamental questions. Of these, let me focus on just two: first, bail-in or bailout; second, the degree to which the central bank should be ready to provide emergency liquidity assistance (ELA) to weak banks.

Should Lehman Brothers have been rescued with some form of Fed assistance that weekend? Despite their disagreements, Bernanke (2015) and Geithner (2014, 2019) (on the one hand) and Ball (2018) (on the other) seem to agree that this would have been desirable. They differ only in their assessment of the existence of a legal route to achieving this. Yet subsequent legislation has not opened the door more widely to such action. Indeed, there were worries that the Dodd-Frank legislation removed bailout powers which proved essential to stabilising the financial markets after Lehman – and which did so without imposing ex post taxpayer costs. (The Federal Reserve's active use, in the early 2020 pandemic crisis, of its newly constrained emergency lending powers suggests that these worries were overdone.) And in Europe, following costly bank bailouts in half of the member states, the BRRD legislation tightly constrains the degree to which bailout can now occur.

And then there is the question of hard money and an alleged dominance of the price stability mandate over a financial stability and growth mandate. One pound sterling was at €1.50 at the outset of the crisis in mid-2007; by the end of 2008, it had fallen to €1.02. The UK authorities clearly accepted much more currency depreciation and acceleration of inflation as a cushion to the financial and macroeconomic pressures. Eurozone countries more severely affected by the crisis than was Britain hung onto the single currency – though, as we read from Varoufakis' memoir (Varoufakis 2017), some came close to abandoning it.

Public authorities in countries that bailed out bank creditors and adhered to a relatively tight monetary stance were subject to criticism, with some alleging that this policy reflected at best a disregard for progressive distributional considerations and at worst capture of the policy-makers by investor interests. Defenders of the stance pointed to the likely consequences for unemployment and household income declines of a disorderly collapse of the functioning of banks and financial markets.

The highly contrasting cases of Cyprus, Iceland and Ireland help to illustrate how the issues can play out. The pre-crisis flaws of each of the three national systems were rather similar. All three were enthusiastic participants in the global surge in financialization from the mid-1990s. The banks in each country had easy access to funding in the world's capital markets; poorly managed and weakly supervised, their total assets grew exponentially, with the lending at home fuelling a property price and construction bubble, especially in Ireland, and the lending abroad often buccaneering and reckless. (There were also, of course, important differences.)

Let us recall how these countries differed in management of the crisis. Iceland and Ireland are generally taken as the two polar cases on the matter of bail-in. Iceland did not even honour the standing deposit insurance promises made to depositors in Icelandic bank branches in the Netherlands and the UK. In contrast, at the height of the crisis, Ireland provided and honoured the most comprehensive guarantee of bank liabilities. Furthermore, the Icelandic krona collapsed, while Ireland maintained the euro. The third case, Cyprus – also an euro area country – was one which the international financial institutions prevailed upon to bail in bank creditors (at home, but not at foreign branch offices). This case happened much later than the other two, and lessons had been learnt. Indeed, the Cyprus case was a precursor to the BRRD.

So how did these contrasting approaches to crisis management work out for the three countries involved?

Ireland

The Irish downturn was well under way by mid-2008. In real (CPI-adjusted) terms, Dublin house prices had already peaked in 2006. Irish banks, with their large property-related exposure, especially to property developer loans, began to seem vulnerable long before the Lehman Brothers bankruptcy. There was a sequence of liquidity and stock market scares during 2007 and 2008. The international funders on whom they had been relying progressively withdrew. As they ran out of collateral eligible for borrowing at the European Central Bank, the Irish banks found themselves in September 2008 on the brink of failure.

The initial policy response was coloured by official misinterpretation of the emerging situation. Government ministers were advised that the crisis was simply a side-effect of the global meltdown. The underlying quality of the banks' balance sheet was overestimated. Nevertheless, the national central bank was initially averse to using provision of ELA on a large scale to meet the outflows.[3]

Against this background, and realizing that no pan-European solution was in the offing, the Irish government improvised a blanket guarantee of the banks' liabilities on 30 September 2008. A guarantee from an AAA-rated government would, it was assumed, surely enable the banks to retain and recover international funding. Formalized through primary legislation, the guarantee covered old debt and even some of the banks' subordinated debt. It provided temporary relief, but the unperceived damage that had been done to the banks' balance sheets by their extravagant lending into an unsustainable property boom would need far deeper financial support.[4]

With the economy now hit by the global economic downturn on top of the collapse in construction and a contraction of consumer spending, job losses multiplied during 2009. Tax revenue, which had been so strong in the boom, slumped. This meant that, despite austerity measures, the budget deficit was sure to balloon. The Government's AAA credit rating could not be retained for long, and its financial margin for manoeuvre became increasingly constrained.

The second element in the Irish government's approach to crisis management was to carve out the most evidently toxic parts of the banks' portfolio. The huge and hitherto

---

[3]   As is now known, in the following weeks ELA was provided on a very large scale to failing banks in the UK and Belgium, for example.

[4]   The net cost to the Irish government of meeting the bank losses came to about a quarter of Ireland's GDP in 2011. Most of this came from the failure of the third largest bank, Anglo Irish Bank. Further details on the Irish case can be found in Honohan (2019), on which this account draws.

unrecognized losses on the largest property-related bank loans were crystallized when the Irish government's asset management company NAMA bought them (compulsorily) from the banks, starting in mid-2010. Reflecting the sense that market prices for property were artificially distressed, NAMA bought at higher 'long-term economic value' prices, using a valuation procedure tightly controlled by the EU Commission (which was concerned to avoid the provision of state-aid to the banks). Nevertheless, these prices meant that almost all shareholder value in the banks was wiped out. This alarmed investors not only about the banks but about the creditworthiness of the Irish government, since the latter had guaranteed to cover losses not met by shareholder funds.

Although the government continued to guarantee new bank debt issuance, the banking system faced a cliff-edge of maturities as the initial two-year guarantee period expired. As a result, the banking system began to rely heavily on ELA. With the rest of its accounts also badly out of balance now that the boom had ended, the government was facing prohibitive interest costs on its borrowing. Under the circumstances, the only safe course for the government was to seek the assistance of the so-called EU-IMF Troika to provide financial support while it proved its determination to restore balance to the public finances.

The scale of this official borrowing was very large relative to Ireland's IMF quota, triggering heavy interest surcharges which were also applied (at first) by the European lenders. At these dangerously high interest rates, the sustainability of the government's debt profile looked uncertain. And, even though the large and still uncertain banking losses had been a major factor in weakening market confidence in Ireland, the official lenders refused either to countenance a bail-in of the unguaranteed senior creditors of the failed banks or to absorb some of the risks by directly recapitalizing the other banks. Later, though, the interest rates on the European loans to Ireland were lowered and their maturity extended. Furthermore, the liquidation of the failed banks was carried out in a way that enabled the net financial cost to be financed at low interest for a long term: the associated debt (large though it is) amounts to only about one-sixth of Irish government debt, and has been financed at low interest. The loan losses – more than two thirds of GDP – were not all absorbed by the government, which ultimately will end up with just about a third of the total, more than a half having been taken by shareholders, and about one-sixth by subordinated debt holders (Figure 7.1).

The economic and fiscal projections made at the time the programme of assistance was negotiated proved to be sufficiently accurate for market confidence to be gradually restored. Aggregate economic recovery was under way by mid-2012. Unemployment, which had soared from below 5 per cent in 2007 to 16 per cent five years later (despite emigration), began to fall steadily, almost getting back to 5 per cent by 2018.

Scars remain: there are still tens of thousands of unresolved non-performing household mortgage loans. Aggregate real household spending only regained its pre-crisis level in 2016 (despite population growth), while government real current public spending remained below the peak after a decade. Likewise, it was 2018 before the total numbers at work matched the previous peak.

Ireland's crisis management was thus characterized by (i) no bail-in and (ii) extensive use (after an initial hesitation) of emergency liquidity from the central bank.

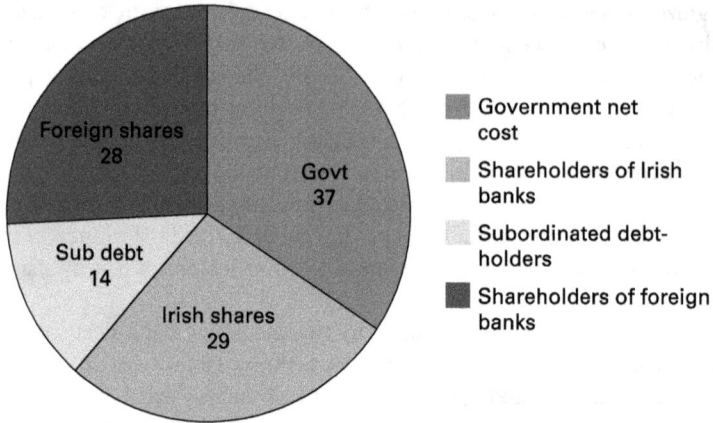

Source: Author's calculations

Figure 7.1 Ireland: How the bank losses were divided (€bn).

The willingness to socialize banking losses was at first home-grown and reflected a perception that bailing in creditors would result in wider credibility damage to Ireland, dependent as it was on continued flows of debt and foreign direct investment (FDI) flows from the rest of the world. The legislative framework for bank resolution was also undeveloped in 2008, making it difficult to distinguish between bank deposits and other bank debt in a bail-in. Later, as the public finances came under stress, bail-in would have been endorsed by the Irish government, but was effectively vetoed by the Troika. The government assured the solvency of the banks by injecting promissory notes. Within the euro area, provision of ELA was a national responsibility, permitted to the extent that it did not 'interfere with the objectives and tasks' of the system (Article 14.4 of the Statute of the ECB).

Iceland

When their banks also lost access to funding in September 2008, the Icelandic authorities' initial reaction, like that of the Irish, was to try to keep the banks afloat. Over previous months the Icelandic central bank had buttressed them already with extensive liquidity loans secured only on bonds issued by the banks themselves. To that extent, the initial liquidity policy response of the monetary authorities to the emerging crisis was more accommodating than that in Ireland. But much of the banks' debt was denominated in foreign currency, which could not be produced in unlimited amounts by the national central bank.

In fact, the banks were too big for Iceland to protect all of their creditors. Advised by J.P. Morgan, who wisely warned against drawing the government any further into a banking mess that they could not pay for, the Icelanders decided to isolate the depositors of the on-shore branches of the banks, and let the rest be worked out over time.

Emergency legislation was introduced to give priority to depositors over other claims (including bonds), and to transfer the deposits and most of the assets booked in onshore branches of the banks into new banks that became the nucleus of a new, much smaller, banking system.[5] Capital controls were introduced to prevent international movements of funds (other than those needed for current imports). In order to provide the financing needed to protect the economy from shrinking even further, Iceland had immediate recourse to the IMF, which (along with four Nordic governments), provided substantial financing.

The Icelandic government still had to inject funds amounting to about 44 per cent of Iceland's GDP into the new banks to keep them afloat. But, partly because of better than expected recoveries on defaulted loans and partly because of the various substantial exit taxes and contributions eventually paid by foreign holders of Icelandic assets subject to exchange control, the Government recovered all of this outlay.

All in all, the ultimate net losses to creditors of the failed banks amounted to about 200 per cent of Iceland's GDP in 2010. In addition to these creditor losses, a 'stability contribution' (in effect an exit tax) of almost a fifth of GDP was paid in 2015–16 by the creditors of the failed banks as part of a deal that freed them from the capital controls that had prevented them from repatriating the amounts recovered.[6] By the time it was negotiated, most of the original holders of these claims had long since sold out to hedge funds at a steep discount. Prevailing attitudes at home and abroad had shifted decisively in the direction of imposing loss-sharing on such creditors in order to protect the public finances. It was this stability contribution that more than offset the net outlays that had been made by the Icelandic authorities to cover the deposits of the protected local depositors in the bank failures.

In Iceland, then, bank resolution was dealt with in a manner which ensured that bank creditors absorbed most of the losses. Admittedly, Iceland suffered reputational damage from what were in some cases arbitrary and retrospective actions against the foreign creditors of the failed banks.

Cyprus

Seemingly less affected at the outset of the Global Financial Crisis than either Iceland or Ireland, Cyprus only began to face evident difficulties in 2011 in the shadow of the deepening Greek economic slump and debt restructuring. The degree to which the economy had been relying on FDI, on a continuing fiscal deficit and (albeit on a lesser

---

[5] Iceland's membership of the European Economic Area made such distinctions somewhat unusual and there were legal challenges, though the relevant international court judged in favour of Iceland in this point. Further detail on the Iceland case can be found in Benediktsdóttir et al. (2017), Jónsson and Sigurgeirsson (2016) and Honohan (2020).

[6] The scale of the international indebtedness which was thus resolved sent some observers back to the old 'transfer problem' analysed by Keynes and Ohlin in the context of the German reparations post-World War I (for a comprehensive account, see for example Brakman and van Marrewijk 1998). Absent the stability contribution, freeing the capital controls would have certainly had a strong effect on the international value of the Icelandic krona.

scale than the other two countries discussed here) on a credit-fuelled construction boom became impossible to ignore.[7]

Like that in Ireland and Iceland, the Cyprus banking system was overscaled, in this case reflecting its use as a safe haven by overseas depositors, including many from Russia and Ukraine. During 2012, the condition of the two main banks (Laiki Bank and Bank of Cyprus) began to give considerable cause for concern. For one thing, the Greek debt restructuring undermined their financial position because, responding to distress-level yields, both of them had piled into Greek government debt shortly before the sovereign debt restructuring, and had then suffered severe losses. (Greek banks had also been hit by the restructuring of their own sovereign's debt. Provision had been made in the IMF-EU financial support package for recapitalization of the Greek banks, but not of those in Cyprus.) In addition, the souring property market and growing awareness that substantial loan losses were in prospect (including for Laiki Bank's sizable portfolio of corporate loans to Greek entities) resulted in an accelerating outflow of deposits, which were financed through ELA from the Central Bank of Cyprus.[8]

By the time the Cypriot government had finally agreed to an IMF-EU programme of assistance, recapitalization of the banks loomed large in the financing needs. The scale of prospective losses, as estimated by independent consultants, at upwards of one-half of GDP, was beyond the capacity of the Cyprus government. Accordingly, it became evident that some form of depositor 'haircut' or levy would be needed.

In February 2013, at one of the late-night meetings of the Eurogroup (the finance ministers of the euro area countries), that characterized top-level political decision-making during the euro area crisis, agreement was reached on a 'horizontal' levy, to be taken on all bank deposits in Cyprus (including those of under €100,000), with the proceeds to be applied to recapitalization of the two big banks. However, market and political reaction to this proposal was immediately and uniformly hostile, as it was seen as undermining the EU-wide deposit insurance system. The Cypriot parliament rejected the proposal and it was replaced by a bail-in of uninsured deposits only (at a much higher percentage rate: about 95 per cent for one of the banks and almost 50 per cent for the other). Bailed-in depositors in Bank of Cyprus received equity in the restructured bank. Laiki was liquidated, following transfers of its assets and liabilities, mainly to Bank of Cyprus.[9]

Following the bail-in, officials were nervous about further deposit outflows and, even though Cyprus remained in the euro area, they imposed administrative restrictions of cash withdrawals and transfers. These applied to the entire banking system even though most of the other banks were not considered to be undercapitalized. The restrictions were not fully removed for over two years.

---

[7] A further contributing factor was a July 2011 explosion at the country's largest power station. Other aspects of the Cyprus case are described in greater detail in Orphanides (2014) and Demetriades (2017). See also Honohan (2020).

[8] ELA amounted at its peak to almost two-thirds of the GDP of Cyprus; in Ireland, ELA had peaked at almost 50 per cent of GDP.

[9] In a curious contrast to the Iceland case, and somewhat controversially, the branches of Laiki Bank in Greece were sold to Piraeus Bank just before the bail-in, exempting the depositors at those branches from bail-in and potentially increasing the percentage bail-in on depositors at the Cypriot branches.

Contrasting macro paths

The banking losses were only a part of the problem. In all three countries, large and painful macroeconomic adjustments were necessary to bring the economies back into a degree of balance. Here too there were big differences between the routes followed, especially as between the euro area countries and Iceland.

In addition to the sizable difference in the direct fiscal cost of bank bailouts, the macroeconomic adjustment of the Icelandic economy to the shock followed quite a different path to that of Ireland. This partly reflected the sharp devaluation of the Icelandic krona which had the effect of lowering Icelandic real wages (Figure 7.2). Although other factors also contributed to the vigorous tourism boom which got under way around 2011, and boosted the economic recovery, the sharp improvement in price and wage competitiveness certainly speeded Iceland's return to full employment (see Figures 7.3 and 7.4).

In this respect, Ireland followed a different path. It is true that there were nominal wage cuts for public servants, but overall, Ireland's real wage rates rose at first, as prices fell sharply in 2008–09 and remained below their 2008 peak for a decade; presumably this will have delayed the employment recovery in Ireland.

At the time of the bail-in and IMF programme, the macroeconomic prospects of Cyprus were considered poor, with the IMF forecasting a cumulative decline in real GDP of 15 per cent between 2011 and 2014 and no recovery to the 2011 peak within a decade. It was thought that, having either been burned by the depositor bail-in or seen

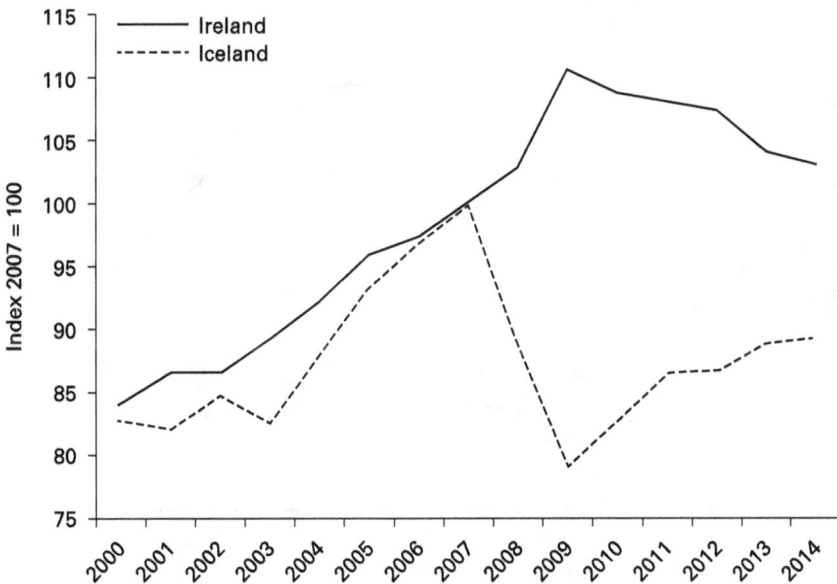

Figure 7.2 Real wages in Iceland and Ireland 2000–14. (Annual average, national currency units, index: 2007=100.)

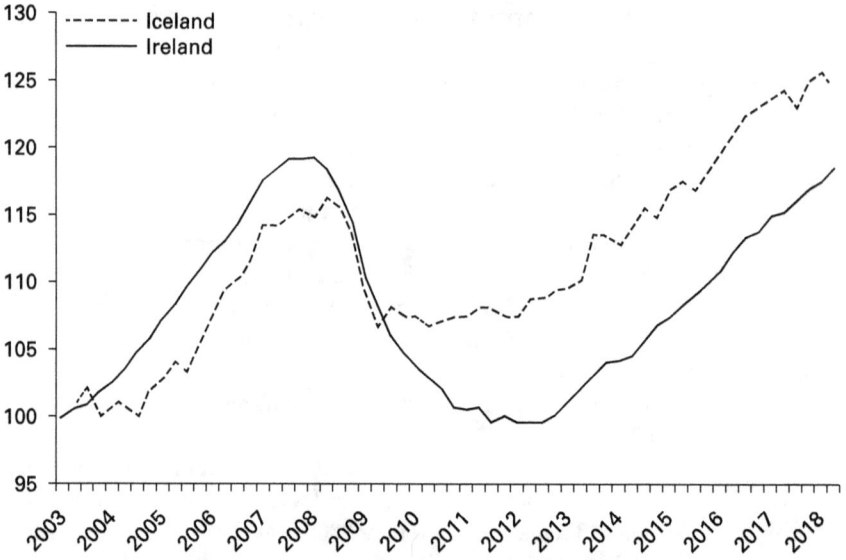

Figure 7.3 Total employment in Iceland and Ireland 2003–18. (Quarterly, seasonally adjusted, index 2003Q1=100.)

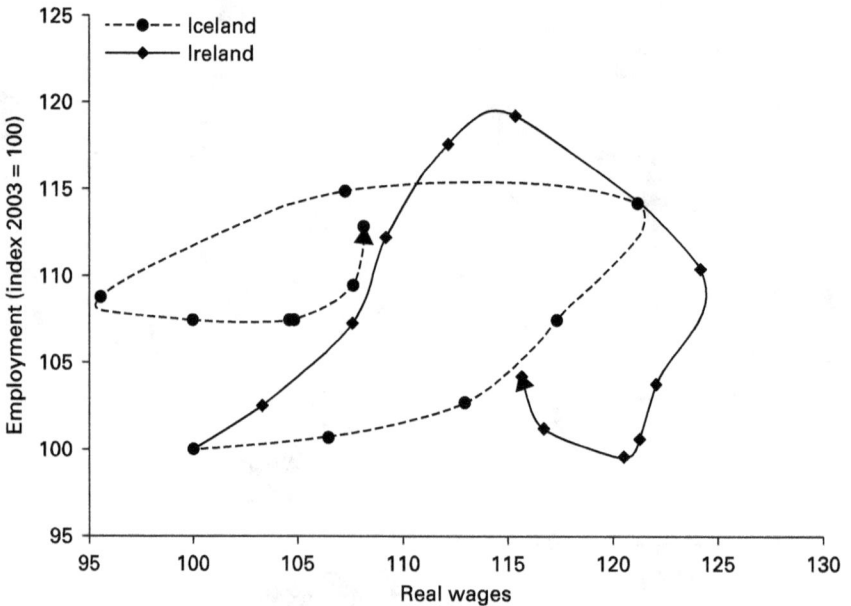

Figure 7.4 Real wages and employment in the boom, bust and early recovery: Iceland and Ireland 2003–14.

others burned, foreign investors would look elsewhere. However, this does not appear to have happened and the economy rebounded well. Once again, as in Iceland, the economy was not as devastated by a bank bail-in as had been foretold by many.

Discussion

The comparison is, of course, no more than suggestive. For one thing, Cyprus, Iceland and Ireland are very different economies. This is evident whether one looks at size (population, GDP), industrial structure, or the nature and depth of the connections with global value chains in manufacturing and services, for example. Arguably the collateral damage risks to the Icelandic economy from bailing in foreign creditors were considerably lower than those facing Ireland. Cyprus remains dependent on foreign investors, but, although non-residents bore the brunt of the bail-ins, the rest of non-resident activities were not impeded.

Nevertheless, the suggestion the comparison makes is that the choice between bail-in and bailout may not be as decisive as it is often made out to be. Iceland dealt nimbly but aggressively with tough creditors, ultimately recovering sizable sums, at a reputational cost that may not have been too severe. Ireland made a different initial choice on bailout and but ultimately managed to turn around an unpromising situation so that its employment recovery was not far behind that of Iceland, and the net banking addition to government debt contributed less than is often alleged to the total amount of fiscal austerity needed to put the public finances back on track.

The optimal choice between bail-in and bailout is surely context-specific. It would have been disastrous for Iceland to attempt the latter route: they would have ended up with greater disruption to economic functioning and likely a bigger indebtedness. And Ireland, deeply embedded in globalization, and relying heavily on certainty of contracts, would have had much to lose from high-handed treatment of guaranteed creditors.

The damage caused to Cyprus' reputation and credibility was likely limited by the fact that the bail-in was at the behest of the international official lenders, and not a home-grown policy.

Adherence to the euro meant that real wages adjusted much more slowly in Ireland, presumably delaying the employment recovery. The Global Financial Crisis shock was outside of the design tolerance of the euro system, and it took some time for ad hoc mechanisms to be put in place to ensure its survival and the recovery of affected countries like Ireland.

The choice between bail-in and bailout was fraught back in 2008. The more recent experience in Spain and Italy suggest that this is still the case. It is unclear whether there is sufficiently broad political acceptance today of the concept of bail-in to make resolution of a major bank with extensive bail-in of creditors trouble-free. And, despite all the preparatory work on living wills, there are sizable questions about the extent to which resolution authorities are really prepared for the smooth resolution of a large bank without considerable disruption to essential financial services (Bank of England 2018).

References

Ambrocio, Gene, Iftekhar Hasan, Esa Jokivuolle and Kim Ristolainen. 2019. 'Expert Survey on Bank Capital Requirements: Preliminary results.' Voxeu.org. 25 April 2019. https://voxeu.org/content/expert-survey-bank-capital-requirements-preliminary-results

Ball, Laurence. 2018. *The Fed and Lehman Brothers: Setting the Record Straight on a Financial Disaster*. Cambridge and New York: Cambridge University Press.

Benediktsdóttir, Sigríður, Gauti B. Eggertsson and Eggert Þórarinsson. 2017. 'The Rise, Fall, and Resurrection of Iceland: A Post-Mortem Analysis of the 2008 Financial Crisis.' *Brookings Papers on Economic Activity* Fall, pp. 191–308.

Bernanke, Ben S. 2015. *The Courage to Act: A Memoir of a Crisis and Its Aftermath*. New York: W.W. Norton.

Brakman, Steven, and Charles van Marrewijk. 1998. *The Economics of International Transfers*. Cambridge and New York: Cambridge University Press.

Demetriades, Panicos. 2017. *A Diary of the Euro Crisis in Cyprus: Lessons for Bank Recovery and Resolution*. Basingstoke: Palgrave Macmillan.

Geithner, Timothy F. 2014. *Stress Test: Reflections on Financial Crises*. New York: Crown.

Geithner, Timothy F. 2019. 'The Early Phases of the Financial Crisis: Reflections on the Lender of Last Resort.' *Journal of Financial Crises*. 1 (1).

Honohan, Patrick. 2019. *Currency, Credit and Crisis: Central Banking in Ireland and Europe*. Cambridge: Cambridge University Press.

Honohan, Patrick. 2020. 'Crisis-driven Capital Controls in Europe, 2008–17.' Independent Evaluation Office Paper BP/20-02/10. Washington, D.C.: International Monetary Fund.

Independent Evaluation Office. 2018. *Evaluation of the Bank of England's Resolution Arrangements*. London: Bank of England. https://www.bankofengland.co.uk/-/media/boe/files/independent-evaluation-office/2018/ieo-report-resolution-june-2018

Jónsson, Ásgeir, and Hersir Sigurgeirsson. 2016. *The Icelandic Financial Crisis: A Study into the World's Smallest Currency Area and its Recovery from Total Banking Collapse*. London: Palgrave Macmillan.

Orphanides, Athanasios. 2014. 'What Happened in Cyprus? The Economic Consequences of the Last Communist Government in Europe.' LSE Financial Markets Group Special Paper 232. London: London School of Economics.

Varoufakis, Yanis. 2017. *Adults In The Room: My Battle with Europe's Deep Establishment*. London: Bodley Head.

8

SEB and the Financial Crisis in the Baltics

Magnus Agustsson and Kārlis Danēvičs

This chapter consists of two parts. The first part, written by Magnus Agustsson, Chief Risk Officer of the SEB Group (Skandinaviska Enskilda Banken AB), deals with its management of the crisis; while the second part, written by Kārlis Danēvičs, Head of Credits in SEB Group's Latvian operations during the Baltic crisis, is an eyewitness account from Riga of the Great Baltic Depression. These complementary sections reflect the varied and unique experiences and impacts of the Global Financial Crisis on both sides of the Baltic Sea. The chapter concludes with a summary by Magnus Agustsson.

SEB's management of the Baltic crisis

Introduction: credit and risk management in SEB

SEB was founded in 1856 and has thus been through several crises that have shaped its risk culture. The most formative for the bank was the Swedish financial crisis in the early 1990s. Five key lessons were learned as a result of this crisis and subsequently formed the basis of SEB's approach to credit and risk management.

First, the importance of supporting our customers. Early detection of credit problems and cooperation with customers is a cornerstone of building trust in long-term relationships and is also a better alternative than bankruptcy when it comes to final loan recoveries. Second, workouts and restructurings take a long time. Third, debt-servicing capacity should be the decisive factor in credit decisions, as opposed to asset-based lending. Fourth, extension of credit must be based on fundamental credit risk analysis, as opposed to name lending. And fifth, SEB, together with other banks, have a central role in society and in a crisis, this social role is put to the test.

During the Swedish financial crisis, one method to manage seized assets was developed and generally used by the banks. Separate divisions were created to manage the assets, and properties taken over were transferred to separate real estate holding companies.[1] By keeping and managing the properties instead of selling them, a price floor was established in the market, and this allowed for the protection of collateral values. The lessons from the Swedish financial crisis proved to be critical for SEB when managing the challenges faced in the three Baltic countries in the aftermath of the Global Financial Crisis.

SEB in the Baltic countries

In 1998, SEB acquired three Baltic banks as part of the bank's strategy of international expansion. By 2001, all three banks had been technically consolidated. The pace of credit growth was exceptionally strong over the following years, with an annual growth rate of around 30 per cent, supported by rapid underlying Baltic economic growth, high demand for credit and an internal business model that at the time rewarded loan growth and market share.

Many Nordic banks entered the Baltic markets around the same time, a result of strong belief in the region's growth potential after the collapse of the Soviet Union as well as prospects of entering the euro area. With a long pent-up credit demand, the Baltic domestic banking systems were highly underbanked. Since the domestic deposit base was vastly insufficient to cover the domestic credit demand, the growth strategy of foreign banks necessitated reliance on intercompany funding. This funding could only be provided in foreign currency and, given the authorities' strong commitment to the fixed-currency regimes aiming to join the euro, the public did not mind holding foreign currency loans. The international banks had to accept foreign currency lending as an integral part of their growth strategies, since the alternative would have been to accept huge foreign-exchange risk in their own balance sheets. This expansion of credit added inflationary pressure on the three small economies, which contributed to their eventual overheating.

In February 2006, SEB was the first bank to question the sustainability of the macroeconomic situation in the Baltic economies. SEB's management decided to take a series of actions to restrict lending growth in the region by implementing stricter policies for the Baltic banks. The growth rate levelled off in Latvia and Estonia at the end of 2007, and a few quarters later in Lithuania. The credit growth in 2008 was mainly due to a weakening Swedish krona. Unfortunately, SEB's restrictive lending policies did not result in markets cooling down, as other banks took the opportunity to expand their market shares during 2007–08. While SEB's total lending volume grew up to the financial crisis, none of its Baltic operations gained market share from 2006 onwards. In fact, market shares declined, with the most notable example being Latvia where the market share declined from 27 per cent in 2006 to 14 per cent in 2008.

In 2009, SEB had 2.2 million private customers and 156,000 corporate customers in the Baltic countries; together, they generated 11 per cent of SEB's overall operating

---

[1]   SEB established the Diligentia Division in 1992, managing non-performing loans as well as properties and mortgages that were repossessed. The Division comprised Diligentia Finance, Diligentia Invest and Diligentia Fastigheter (Properties) units. Day-to-day management and operation of properties were handled by the subsidiaries Arsenalen and Garnisonen.

income. The Baltics' credit portfolio amounted to SEK 156 billion (SEK 194 billion in 2008), or 9 per cent (10 per cent) of SEB's total credit portfolio. The largest sub-segments of the Baltic portfolio were the corporate segment and the household sector, representing 37 per cent and 40 per cent, respectively. Property management accounted for 19 per cent. Latvia had the highest share of foreign currency lending at 87 per cent, followed by Estonia at 76 per cent and Lithuania at 68 per cent.

The Baltic crisis

When the Global Financial Crisis hit in 2008, the impact on the overheated Baltic economies was exceptionally severe. GDP contracted by double digits during 2009–10, unemployment rates increased sharply, and property market valuations deteriorated.

At an early stage, SEB expressed a strong commitment to stay in the Baltic countries, accept its social responsibility and support core customers in order to protect long-term relationships and also to preserve collateral values. A new vision was established: 'To build the most trusted bank for the post-crisis world.' The strategies applied to fulfil the vision differed somewhat between sectors, depending on their needs. In the following section, the main strategies that were used during the Baltic crisis are presented.

Corporate workout

In 2007, in anticipation of a deterioration of the economic outlook and increased credit loss expectations in the Baltics, a new organization called Global Special Credits Management (Global SCM) was established. The organization's primary purpose was to coordinate the existing divisional workout units and provide specialist expertise on workout and restructuring in the Nordic and Baltic markets, Poland and Russia. At the onset of the Global Financial Crisis, SEB applied hands-on crisis management. The bank was divided into 'green' and 'red' teams, where the 'green' team continued to run the business as usual while the 'red' team handled the crisis.

In 2009, SEB had 259 full-time employees dedicated to workout activities, of which 150 were allocated to the Baltic countries. The SCM workout unit in the Baltics soon faced challenges in the form of local business practices and procedures. There was a lack of banking experience and knowledge, but instead an excessive focus on asset-based rather than cashflow-based lending practices.

Language barriers constituted an operational risk factor, in particular in the retail banking branch network. Cultural differences had a significant impact on how corporate governance, credit and business practices had been implemented. Incentive programmes had historically been biased towards increased market share, thereby contributing most likely to an erosion in credit quality. As the crisis erupted, workload increased rapidly and required additional workout resources. A key challenge was to find qualified workout specialists, with relevant restructuring and credit experience. Global SCM had a strong mandate from top management and was able to internally recruit experienced specialists instead of using external consultants, which in hindsight proved to be an important factor to successful restructurings, especially in the Baltic region.

The local legal systems in the Baltic countries were overburdened and relatively untested in bankruptcy and insolvency cases, leading to delays in processing and legal uncertainty. In addition, there was a clear risk of low morale and mental fatigue among both employees and customers. There was a sense of resignation, meaning that an increasing number of customers risked becoming indifferent to participating in restructuring efforts. SEB recognized the importance of engaging constructively as far as possible with customers who had the potential to survive through sound restructuring principles, clear communication and effective monitoring.

The sector where SEB experienced the worst bankruptcy rates was real estate development. In 2009, the real estate development portfolio contained exposure of SEK 10 billion (of which Lithuania accounted for 6 billion). The bank took over title to a large number of properties from bankrupt real estate companies during the crisis. In October 2008, SEB's Board of Directors decided to gather these titles in real-estate holding companies in each of the respective countries. Instead of abandoning the properties in non-functioning markets, the bank assessed their future value and sold them to the three newly established real estate holding companies, owned by SEB, for a total sum of EUR 376 million. More than 5,000 properties – ranging from high-quality buildings to ramshackle houses, half-finished projects and undeveloped land – were placed into these holding companies. The through-the-cycle evaluation model that was developed for this purpose was key to this process.

As the market recovered, the properties were gradually sold off. In September 2018 – ten years after the crisis started – the last property was divested, and the holding companies were closed down. This strategy limited the bank's credit losses in the sector, but also contributed to the re-establishment of well-functioning real estate markets in the three countries.

Leasing transportation was another segment severely hit by the crisis. SEB's leasing transportation portfolios in the Baltic countries totalled SEK 19.3 billion or 90,975 units (cars, trucks, trailers, buses and rail wagons) in 2009. Out of this cars, trucks and trailers accounted for 86 per cent of the exposure at risk, or just below 85,000 units. Around 30 per cent of the portfolio was estimated to be repossessed.

SEB established distribution capacity for repossessed vehicles, both through domestic and international sales channels, in order to avoid warehousing vehicles whose re-marketing value would decline over time. In 2010, 94 per cent of all leased assets were performing or had been successfully restructured. One challenge was that leasing documentation practices deviated substantially from the Nordic and Anglo-Saxon banking practice, with increased credit, legal and operational risk implications. For example, immature legal frameworks resulted in difficult and time-consuming repossession of assets.

Workout for private customers: 'Keeping families in their homes'

There are several reasons why a different strategy was needed in the private segment compared to the corporate segment. First, the social effects should not be underestimated, as families would have nowhere to live if homes were foreclosed. Second, the strategy was challenging for management, with many small properties demanding cumbersome administration. Third, there were market effects – a systematic outflow onto the market would exacerbate the crisis and risk depleting collateral values. And fourth, there were legal issues – insolvency legislation was non-existent up until the crisis.

Taking all these factors into account, SEB made a strategic decision at an early stage to allow private individuals to remain in their homes as far as possible – at least if the customers cooperated with the bank and did their best to service their debt. The programme was called 'keeping families in their homes'.

It aimed to support households that had taken out a loan to buy a home that they lived in. Second and buy-to-let homes were not included. Restructuring solutions included changing the payment schedule, as well as grace periods and a prolongation of loan repayment terms. The most common restructuring tool turned out to be a grace period on principal for between six and eighteen months, with a gradual step-up in amortizations. Early and active involvement by the SEB branch offices was important. A detailed process to communicate and cooperate with clients was set up and implemented, including a first contact after a three-day payment delay. Key to a successful outcome was that customers were willing to communicate and cooperate.

The same approach was applied in all three Baltic countries. However, in the wake of the Global Financial Crisis, SEB experienced the largest number of private customers having problems to service debt in Latvia, due to the country's extremely sharp macroeconomic deterioration. With unemployment quickly surging to 20 per cent, unemployment benefits being depleted, salaries being reduced by up to 25 per cent (depending on sector) and a housing market that practically stopped functioning, private individuals struggled.

At the same time, SME bankruptcy rates skyrocketed. SEB's market share in Latvian mortgages was 15 per cent at the time (in a market where 90 per cent of homes are owner-occupied) and overdue household loans increased rapidly. As it turned out later, 90 per cent of all restructuring decisions in the Latvian retail unit were applied to private customers, primarily household mortgage borrowers.

From SEB's perspective, the social commitment to the families was important. There were also other benefits to that approach, one example being that families staying in their homes took care of maintenance and heating, preserving the value of the bank's collateral. Had the bank chosen the route of aggressive enforcement of private properties, losses would have occurred instantly, pledged properties would not have been maintained and the debt servicing could have been lost. Payday lenders were a serious issue for SEB – the temptation to borrow often led to restructurings that were unnecessary. The risk of eroding payment discipline was debated within the bank but in principle it did not materialize, although there were cases of abuse. For example, a large number of people left the country during this period and thus refused to service their debts.

In 2010, SEB supported more than 5,000 Latvian families via this programme. In the aftermath of the crisis, SEB concluded that 80 per cent of its non-performing exposure to private customers recovered, and that only 20 per cent of the collateral had been foreclosed. SEB also took an active role in developing the legal framework together with the World Bank and the International Monetary Fund, notably Latvia's current three-year period of debt forgiveness.

Financial impact

The level of past due loans served as a leading indicator of problem loans, increasing dramatically during 2008–10 and peaking at 13.4 per cent of the lending portfolio. Non-performing loans peaked at SEK 18 billion in 2009, corresponding to a non-performing loan ratio of 14.2 per cent. SEB used a conservative provisioning policy and total reserves increased from SEK 4 billion to SEK 12 billion during the course of the Baltic crisis.

Despite this, the SEB Group continued to record positive operating result every quarter. A large share of the reserves was gradually recovered and total credit losses during the period 2008–11 were around SEK 10.7 billion, which can be compared with the Swedish FSA's original estimate of SEK 22 billion and analysts' consensus estimates of SEK 32 billion.

Learnings from the crisis

There are several things that proved to be important for managing the crisis. The 'tone from the top' was to do the right thing, and the top management's message was not only simple and clear, but communicated repeatedly. Extensive SEB programmes were put in place during the crisis to educate all the employees of the Baltic banks in order to build up the risk culture. There was 100 per cent attention and involvement from top management down to specific product specialists, enabling early detection of problems and strong hands-on crisis management. The continued support to core customers and long-term relationships, in other words, social responsibility, and a caring, professional approach towards clients built up trust. And finally, capitalization, with an increased capital buffer through rights issue and cancellation of dividends, calmed the markets but its purpose was to be able to support SEB's customers.

There were, however, some challenges, in particular the integration of the Baltic subsidiary banks; cultural barriers and communication problems; the interconnectivity of global financial systems; and the fact that institutions in the financial system, central banks and regulators, did not (with hindsight) have a deep enough understanding of the individual banks, resulting in the publication of stress tests and statements that paradoxically increased risks in the system.

A key learning from the Baltic financial crisis is the importance of integration of business and risk cultures. In hindsight, it is clear that SEB did not have a common risk tolerance or view on risk-taking across the group following the acquisitions of the Baltic banks. It is also evident how important it is to be on the ground to really understand cultural differences. In the aftermath of the immediate crisis, SEB seconded senior managers to various functions in the three countries, including Credits, Risk, and heads of key business areas, in order to fully align the credit policies and risk management framework between the Group and the Baltic banks. As a result, the Baltic banks were later integrated into the bank and since then constitute a division.

The corporate culture of social responsibility and experience of crisis management proved to be of key importance in managing the crisis. Top management's ethical approach to focus on long-term relationships and benefits for society fostered trust in those countries, and employees are proud of working for SEB. The approach has contributed to the strong brand position locally. SEB was named the best employer in Lithuania and the second most customer-oriented company in Estonia across all industries already in 2010, and market shares have increased since the crisis (Latvia is now back at around 20 per cent) – without relaxing credit policies.

SEB's franchise in the Baltic region emerged stronger from the crisis. The Bank's conservative and relationship-oriented stance, combined with a strong balance sheet, provides resilience and flexibility – even in times of crisis.

The Great Baltic Depression: an eyewitness report from Riga, Latvia[2]

During 2008–09, all the three Baltic countries experienced an extremely deep financial and economic crisis, one comparable to a total collapse of an entire country, and something that is rarely seen outside war zones. People in Western Europe typically find it hard to believe many of the facts and accounts that have emerged, reflecting the very different historical experiences and realities of different parts of Europe.

The Baltic economic miracle that took place after the EU accession later turned out to have been a mirage. After the brutal and economically painful fifty years of Soviet occupation, there was a belief that the people living in Baltic countries had almost a 'God-given right' to average EU standards of living. The starting point was that as pre-occupation standards of living were no worse in the Baltic countries than in Scandinavian countries, there must be convergence of living standards. Inflow of EU funds turned out to be one of the longer-lasting drivers of growth, but lack of understanding of the functioning and need for governance of a Western market economy led to lax borrowing. There was a shortage of equity in the economy to start with, and weak government policies made the situation even worse. Current account deficits approached 15–20 per cent during 2005–08 (almost 25 per cent in Latvia), mostly financed by cheap borrowing from abroad and mostly invested in segments that did not boost international competitiveness of the countries, such as real estate and consumption.

At the beginning of 2007, a prominent economist at Stockholm School of Economics in Riga, Morten Hansen, wrote an article that was widely debated. He claimed that Latvia, with its current account deficit combined with huge wage growth, was losing

---

[2]   This text describes Kārlis Danēvičs' personal experiences and opinions and should not be interpreted as being SEB's views.

competitiveness so fast that it might lead to a devaluation. Nobody seemed to listen to Morten; in fact, he ended up being rebuked by the Governor of the Central Bank and even questioned by the secret police for undermining the credibility of the economy. However, the government made some last-minute adjustments and announced an anti-inflation plan. It was too little and too late.

Latvia's economy just need a spark to implode. As for many other countries, that spark turned out to be the sub-prime crisis and Lehman Brothers' collapse. In the inevitable crash that followed, the decline in Latvian GDP was close to 20 per cent. Latvia even set a once-in-a-century record, with a GDP decline in construction and retail segments of approximately 30 per cent. The Latvian situation was even worse than for the other Baltic countries, which can be explained by three main factors.

First, the second-largest locally owned bank, Parex, needed a bailout and was therefore taken over by the government. A lot of lending had been done outside Latvia and in the highly cyclical real-estate segment. Parex had attracted wholesale short-term funding from international investors in order to finance long-term lending, especially in real estate. When the crisis came, international investors left Parex without funding, while there were large volumes of outstanding loans to severely affected sectors.

Second, Riga is the largest city in the Baltics, and therefore of interest to speculative investors from the East (Riga has a large Russian-speaking population), and that created a property bubble that was unlike that in any other European city. From their peak, property prices declined 75–80 per cent. Remembering the time before the crisis, being a very conservative person (and a friend of Morten), I estimated that real estate prices were overvalued by 40 per cent – and no one believed it.

And third, the government leading Latvia during the boom years neglected signs of overheating, with one prime minister afterwards proudly calling his reign 'the fat years'. He has been blamed for being short-sighted, and some have gone as far as suggesting that there might have been a deliberate plan to crash Latvia into the wall in order to drive it away from the Western sphere of influence.

A major international crisis, combined with local economic imbalances and weak governance, made a deep crisis inevitable. The GDP industry mix, with a large share of contributions from retail sales and construction, also contributed to the development of the crisis.

The road to recovery – that proved to be miraculously fast – was rather orthodox. The IMF bailout programme was adopted by a technocratic government led by the now well-known Valdis Dombrovskis. The measures demanded a lot of blood, sweat and tears from fellow Latvians, going through tough salary cuts and a so-called internal devaluation, and also required the remodelling of laws and insolvency procedures. It is also important to bear in mind that a crucial aspect was the strengthening of the financial sector that Sweden contributed to, making injections of capital, liquidity and 'competency and oversight' experience into the two largest remaining banks. Whenever one felt harshly criticized for being a banker in those days and thus being partly responsible for the crisis, the come-back was the following: '... yes, but imagine if all the banks would have been locally owned as Parex and had needed a bailout.' It could have been much worse.

During the first round of discussions with the IMF, it was difficult to agree anything unless Latvians agreed to devalue their currency. I vividly remember being shocked that the IMF did not understand that 'this time it is different'. Usually, those are the most expensive words ever to be said – however, during the crisis it was important to understand that Latvia *did* differ in some aspects.

Latvia is a young country and has only a few things to be proud of (apart from excellent architecture, opera and classical musicians). As some joked at that time: Latvia has a national flag, an anthem and even more importantly a national currency, which is a clear link to our notion of the pre-occupation Latvian paradise. Even the design of the coins and notes was a testimony to the Latvia that existed before the occupation. And the national currency (the Lat) was strong back then, before the war. We went as far as joking with the IMF that in Latvia, there is an eleventh commandment – *Thou shalt not devalue.*

Salaries had been increasing by up to 30 per cent per annum and the requested cuts therefore seemed doable, to some even fair. I remember discussing the need to decrease salaries for every employee, and although it was far from a done deal, there was a general understanding of the need for the actions.

Almost all the corporate and private borrowing had taken place in euros, thus currency devaluation should have generated additional bankruptcies and an additional shock to the financial industry. In addition, Latvia's export sector was small, limiting the effects of such a devaluation as exporting oneself out of the problems would be a very slow process.

'Devalue or not to devalue that is the question, whether it is nobler by thousand cuts to suffer' remains a question until this very day. To a large extent, it is a matter of belief. The fact that the IMF has used Latvia as a success story among all of their bailout programmes, shows that there were good arguments for Latvia's chosen path. I vividly remember the IMF disbelieving that Latvia would fully manage to recover only with internal devaluation. That was the situation up until early 2010, when data showed that Latvia had almost closed the current account gap. The retail and real-estate sectors had decreased in size, salaries had been slashed and exporters' situation had improved.

To help the IMF understand Latvia's opportunity for internal devaluation, I gave the following explanation. In the early 1990s, I worked on a potato farm for a few summers. The worst outcome I could see for myself was that happening again, but this time without Russian tanks and shootings on the streets, meaning that the worst outcome was still relatively good. My father-in-law, working as a professor at Riga Technical University, had a salary cut of 70 per cent. Still, he remembered the 30 per cent pay hike, plus the 30 per cent salary increases he had the two previous years. For him it was even easier to compare with Soviet times, and an Internet with free access to information and knowledge (unthinkable in the Soviet Union) would not be taken away from him during this crisis. And both my grandfather and my wife's grandfather did not even understand what the fuss was all about. Both had barely survived Soviet gulag camps and reflected that often the potato peels had been the best food they got there. They thought that the consumer orgy would stop, but that the food would still be there, so why all the stress? The event did not even register in the top of the worst events that they experienced during their lifetime.

Another thing that was difficult for the IMF to understand, was the inability of the Latvian government to collect taxes. When new car sales stopped, consumption dropped by 30 per cent and real-estate sales plummeted, so did the VAT contribution. The Latvian government started to investigate taxation of, for example, real estate. I showed the IMF a tax calculation I had just received from the local municipality, asking me to pay 17 eurocents for a house worth approximately €100,000. The irony was that the calculation was sent by post and the postage stamp cost 25 eurocents. Much has happened since then, and today I pay close to €200 per annum – still low by international standards, but an increase of more than 1,000 times.

The thing that Latvians, and people in the other Baltic countries, mourn the most is that many fellow countrymen and women had to go abroad in their search for employment and higher salaries. That was a very bitter and painful reminder of Soviet occupation, when many people had to flee to the West and others were instead sent in the opposite direction – to Siberian gulags. This development still creates frustration and anger among local politicians and can easily turn any rational 'what if . . .' discussion into a highly emotional one.

The recovery of the Baltic countries was one of the swiftest that the world has ever seen and can, in short, be explained by the following factors. First, a willingness and ability to redesign the insolvency law and remodelling of the entire governance structure, following the best of the IMF and the World Bank's advice. Second, government mis-management was greatly reduced, creating the right incentives for recovery and investments, for example, by redesigning the taxation framework. Third, EU funds were diverted to boost export capacities. Fourth, the burden of losses in the financial sector was shared with Sweden, as banks were swiftly re-capitalized and helped with liquidity. Fifth, the fact that leverage and borrowing was not evenly spread increased losses for the banks, but also helped with the recovery. It has been estimated that close to 80 per cent of the Baltic population had no significant amount of loans. Almost every household had some debt-free asset as a result of the collapse of the Soviet Union, such as woodland, farmland or a small apartment in a Soviet-built high-rise. Six, strong family ties (the only safe harbour during Soviet occupation) and links to subsistence farming allowed many to survive without creating an additional strain on state budgets. And finally and most importantly, the collective memory of harsh life under Soviet occupation as well as the 'Wild Wild East' of the 1990s helped to maintain social solidarity.

The Baltic countries have had their own Great Depression and have experienced the bitter taste of challenging economic cycles. That makes them among the most resilient to future crises. The post-Soviet mentality and ability to reflect on the harsh Soviet occupation will surely fade with time, but more sound and professional macro policies, as well as companies and individuals, are undoubtedly assets to count on. The Baltic economies have a good starting point for managing another international crisis, and also avoiding another severe domestic crisis. At the time of writing, however, COVID-19 is to provide a very harsh test of this statement.

Concluding remarks

It is not unusual for a bank to be facing a crisis in one form or another. What seems to distinguish different banks' behaviours in a time of crisis is the culture of the firm. In

SEB's case, a well-grounded established risk culture was, and is, the key component of how a financial crisis is worked through. Choosing customers with a long-term risk-based view, being prepared to support the customers in both good times and bad, has been at the core of this culture. Both the Baltic crisis and the Swedish crisis during the 1990s have proven that the best interest of society is aligned with the best interest of the bank, and we assume that this is true also for the currently ongoing crisis.

9

The Legacy of the Global Financial Crisis: The View from Greece

George Papaconstantinou

Introduction

The Global Financial Crisis of 2007–09 is etched into our collective memory as a crisis rooted in financial markets malfunctioning within an environment of regulatory forbearance. A lack of robust regulatory oversight in the US banking system resulted in extensive financial engineering and contributed to the creation of a housing bubble. Housing prices rose sharply as borrowers took advantage of low interest rates and easy lending conditions. Meanwhile, lenders masked the riskiness of their loan portfolios by issuing mortgage-backed securities and by 'packaging' problematic loans into synthetic financial assets such as collateralized debt obligations, which were then rated highly by credit rating agencies. These higher levels of subprime lending, together with speculation on residential housing, drove prices higher and increased the indebtedness of households.[1]

When in 2007 the bubble burst and housing prices collapsed, borrowers with variable rate mortgages found themselves with negative equity, unable to refinance their loans and meet obligations. Mass foreclosures ensued, coupled with a sharp decline in the value of securities backed by housing loan portfolios held by financial institutions, followed by the collapse and takeover of Bear Sterns in March 2008, the takeover of mortgage corporations Freddie Mac and Fannie Mae, the bailout of insurance giant AIG and eventually Lehman Brothers filing for bankruptcy in September 2008. By that time, credit had seized, household spending and business investment had plunged, and the US economy had gone into a recession. International financial markets responded by tightening credit globally and the US recession spread.

---

[1] The US financial crisis has been discussed from different approaches: some of the most acclaimed include Sorkin (2009), the interview-based classic; Geithner (2014), giving the view from one of the main government participants; and Sinn (2010) from a critical academic viewpoint.

Crossing the Atlantic

While the US administration was undertaking a massive bailout of its remaining banks, injecting almost $US 1 trillion into the economy, Europe was struggling to cope with its own problems. When the US subprime mortgage crisis hit, European banks were suffering from some of the same weaknesses as their US counterparts: insufficient capital and liquidity, as well as weak financial regulation and supervision. In many respects, this was the result of a number of years during which a benign attitude to the self-correcting power of markets had taken hold and dominated both economic thinking as well as policy responses in both the US and Europe.

European banks were hence vulnerable to the US-originated crisis because of their exposure to toxic US banking products but also because of their own weaknesses, which included excessive reliance on short-term loans from international markets. As the crisis enveloped the US, it quickly crossed the Atlantic and banks in a number of major European countries succumbed to difficulties. The first manifestation of the problem was a lack of faith: banks could no longer ascertain the financial health of their counterparts in other countries, so they stopped lending to each other, and the interbank market froze. As a result, in the summer of 2007, tensions emerged in European financial markets, but they were initially thought to be simply a liquidity shock.

It was, however, much more than that: the problems in the interbank market also laid bare the weaknesses of an incomplete European banking system. In an increasingly integrated European financial market, regulation and oversight remained at the national level. Lacking a supranational entity that could guarantee the health of banks exposed to each other on a European and global scale (or take appropriate measures where this was not the case), banks retreated from the market and liquidity quickly dried up. The situation deteriorated despite the efforts by the European Central Bank to counteract the rapidly worsening liquidity conditions in the interbank markets by introducing long-term refinancing operations for commercial banks.[2]

When Lehman collapsed in the US in September 2008, in Europe liquidity concerns had already mutated into concerns about the solvency of major European banks. One after another, European governments were then forced to provide assistance to their exposed financial institutions in order to contain the systemic risk by putting in place massive bank bailouts. In October 2008, the UK announced a bailout package for its banks totalling £500 billion. It included short-term loans, funds for recapitalization as well as guarantees to enable inter-bank lending.[3] Soon after, eurozone countries had to follow suit. Their response was similar to that in the UK, with bank bailouts taking place on a massive scale. By 2009, they totalled around 8 per cent of GDP in Germany, 5 per cent in France and 12 per cent in the Netherlands.[4]

---

[2]   A brief account is given in Praet (2012).
[3]   Statement of the UK Chancellor Alastair Darling (8/10/2008) on the measures announced by the UK government: https://web.archive.org/web/20081011062730/http://www.hm-treasury.gov.uk/statement_chx_081008.htm.
[4]   As quoted in Draghi (2018). See also Stolz and Wedow (2010).

This first wave of bailouts in 'core' eurozone countries was subsequently followed by a second one in peripheral member states. Spain and Ireland were particularly affected, where the banking sectors were overexposed to a collapsing real estate market. In Ireland, this was despite the attempt to change expectations by offering a blanket deposit guarantee of all deposits in Irish financial institutions.[5] There was, however, a big difference between the first wave of bank bailouts in countries such as Germany and France and those in Ireland or Spain. In the former case, the governments putting the assistance packages in place were in a robust fiscal situation, and as a result the bailouts did not greatly affect sovereign borrowing costs. In the latter case, given underlying weak fiscal positions, markets quickly responded by widening the spread on sovereign bonds (the difference between a country's borrowing costs and those of Germany, reflecting the risk premium): the doom loop between banks and sovereigns was thus quickly established.[6]

Greece lights the fire

During 2008, public deficit positions had worsened throughout the eurozone as counter-cyclical expenditures increased and revenues collapsed in the recession, prompting an attempted EU-wide response through the December 2008 European Recovery Plan (European Commission 2008). In 2009 the crisis exposed weaker EU economies to much higher deficits, and at the same time higher borrowing costs. In that single year, the public deficit in the euro area widened by four percentage points and the gross public debt by ten percentage points of GDP, while at the same time economies were contracting significantly.[7]

Ireland had come already close to triggering a eurozone sovereign debt crisis in 2008 as the deposit guarantee of all deposits in Irish banks instituted by the government effectively meant the state had taken the liabilities of the banking system on its balance sheet. Instead, the catalyst turned out to be Greece and the revelations by the newly elected government in late 2009 of the true size of the country's fiscal deficit: they triggered a repricing of sovereign risk, with markets realizing sovereign debt was no longer (near) risk free.

Over a period of six months, from October 2009 to May 2010, as Greek sovereign debt was being priced out of international financial markets, the eurozone was forced to confront what until that time seemed unthinkable: a euro area member unable to service its debt in international financial markets at sustainable interest rates and forced to default on its sovereign obligations. More broadly, to confront the undeniable fact that as long as the European and Monetary Union was not complete, the common

---

[5] For an account of the events surrounding the Irish deposit guarantee, see Cardiff (2016) and Honohan (2019).

[6] On the relationship between banks and sovereigns, see Mody and Sandri (2012).

[7] For the eurozone as a whole, Eurostat data (as reported in 2019) show that the government fiscal deficit widened from 0.7 per cent of GDP in 2007 to 2.2 per cent in 2008 and to 6.2 per cent of GDP in 2009. Gross government debt jumped from 65 per cent of GDP in 2007 to 68.7 per cent in 2008 and 79.2 per cent of GDP in 2009.

currency could not any more in and of itself mask the different risk profiles and characteristics of its member states.[8]

Eventually, the eurozone reluctantly came to the conclusion that to preserve the common currency, the rest of the euro area needed to create a 'financial backstop' to ensure Greece would not end up in a disorderly default. The result was an ad hoc and idiosyncratic construction, the Greek Loan Facility (GLF), a financial support mechanism composed of €80 billion from euro area countries and €30 billion from the IMF, accompanied with strict policy conditionality. It was initially thought to be confined to the case of the specific country only; instead, as a number of eurozone countries ended up requiring financial support, it evolved into a mechanism with permanent characteristics.

The chain of events that was set in motion in Greece in October 2010 ended up impacting financial and economic conditions in Europe and the world, forcing the EU to confront and eventually attempt to repair some of the design flaws in its institutional architecture. At the same time, it also greatly impacted the direction of EMU reform, with a strong emphasis put on fiscal consolidation and austerity measures, and a delayed acceptance of the origination of problems in the banking sector. In this sense, Greece acted as a conduit between the 2007–09 global financial crisis and the ensuing eurozone sovereign debt crisis, fundamentally influencing the latter's 'policy narrative'.

Systemic euro area risk

After Greece, there was contagion to all vulnerable sovereigns with high public debt levels, a lack of fiscal space and low growth. Sovereign risk was then transmitted back into the banking sector via bank exposures to government bonds, and negative confidence. The distinction between banks with and without high sovereign exposures disappeared and financial markets fragmented along national lines. Cross-border funding dried up and defensive risk management by banks and ring-fencing of liquidity by supervisors in core euro area countries ended up exacerbating the problem. The result was a 'bad equilibrium' trap caused by the links between sovereigns, banks, and domestic firms and households.

The contagion was apparent immediately after the decision to support Greece with the GLF in May 2010, as market turmoil continued. To stem it, barely a week after the GLF was agreed, EU leaders supplemented it with a more general financial support instrument. The European Financial Support Framework (EFSF) was billed as 'a European stabilization mechanism to preserve financial stability in Europe' (Euro Summit 2010). Technically, it took the form of a special purpose vehicle (SPV) backed by a joint guarantee by eurozone governments allowing it to raise €440 billion of market funds. To this would be added €60 billion of an existing mechanism

---

[8] Papaconstantinou (2016) gives a detailed account of this period, seen from the viewpoint of a policy participant.

administered by the Commission. This €500 billion total was supplemented by €250 billion by the IMF, making a grand total of €750 billion, a sizeable 8 per cent of Euro area GDP.

The creation of the EFSF was an important milestone in the eurozone crisis, and not only because it marked the first time that a general-purpose financial backstop was created for sovereigns. It was also the first step to revisiting the institutional architecture of the eurozone since its inception. At the same time, and perhaps more crucially in terms of the final impact on the markets, the ECB had organized its own response: to activate 'exceptional measures' – secondary-market sovereign debt purchases through the Securities Market Programme (SMP). It was the beginning of a clear shift in the policy of the eurozone's central bank, and one that would evolve further in response to the crisis in the coming months and years.[9]

Important as they were, these decisions did not manage to stop contagion. Instead, the situation was exacerbated by an ill-designed attempt to address the issue of debt sustainability in late 2010. In what is now known as the 'Deauville decision', in a bilateral meeting between Angela Merkel and Nicolas Sarkozy, a deal was struck. Germany agreed to back down on automatic sanctions for countries breaching fiscal rules and accept 'qualified majority' decision-making, which gave discretion to governments. In exchange, France accepted a German proposal for a limited EU treaty change that would, as of 2013, turn the temporary bailout fund into a permanent mechanism. Crucially, that decision involved the possibility of a country defaulting on its debts. In such a case, private investors would participate in the eventual bailout, taking losses through a 'haircut'.

While there was a need to create a permanent bailout mechanism, the decision reached in Deauville failed to take into account market reaction. European banks received it as a preannouncement of future possible losses on the Greek bonds which they had decided – in a gentlemen's agreement with governments – to retain only a few months earlier. The logic extended to other peripheral countries, so spreads ratcheted up for the bonds of all vulnerable sovereigns. Eventually Ireland – the country where the 'doom loop' between banks and sovereigns was most evident – and a few months later Portugal were also forced to apply for official financial assistance from the EU and the IMF. Whatever its intention, the Deauville decision helped transform a crisis which could have been contained into a fully systemic one.[10]

Greece's unique position

The prevailing narrative of the eurozone sovereign crisis focuses on the role of Greece as the crisis trigger while also stressing the unique 'fiscal profligacy' characteristics of

---

[9] The ECB decision was not unanimous. Internal criticism was blunted by the conditions attached to the decision taken on 9 May (the creation of the financial backstop by Ecofin) and the fact that the intervention was 'sterilized' by operations to re-absorb the liquidity injected by buying bonds, and therefore did not represent monetary easing.

[10] Most commentators would agree that the 'Deauville decision' drove spreads higher, forcing the hand of Portugal and Ireland. This is not a consensus view, however. For a more sceptical viewpoint, see Mody (2014).

the country when the crisis hit. Nevertheless, Greece was not alone in facing a difficult fiscal situation at the time. In 2009, Ireland, Spain and the UK also had double-digit deficits; Italy was flirting with debt at 120 per cent of GDP, Belgium was above 100 per cent, and even France and Germany were around 80 per cent. Greece's borrowing spreads were about the same as Ireland's.

Greece, however, was unique at that point in facing a triple deficit. It was facing a fiscal deficit which after successive revision rounds was revealed to exceed 15 per cent of GDP. Its external account was consistently negative over many years and had grown to double digits, revealing a persistent competitiveness deficit. Last but not least, data misreporting to Eurostat as well as repeated backtracking on policy reform commitments had added a serious credibility issue vis-à-vis both its European partners and the international markets. To that should be added a large public debt overhang which in 2009, following the economy collapse, had shot from 109 per cent to 127 per cent of GDP. Hence taking all indicators together, Greece was by far the weakest link in the eurozone chain. This led many to believe or at least to behave as if the problem were essentially only about Greece and could be contained there.

Subsequent economic developments underline the country's unique position. The Greek economy contracted by 4 per cent in 2008, at the same rate as other euro area countries; however, it then decoupled from the rest and went into a deep recession: from peak to trough, GDP declined by 27 per cent, on the back of a dramatic fiscal consolidation effort of over 15 percentage points of GDP. This is a recession whose depth is only comparable to the US Great Depression, while it lasted twice as long (Figure 9.1). Greece is also unique in the euro area in having undergone three bailouts totalling a disbursement of €289 billion (as an indication, at the end of the third bailout in 2018 GDP was €185 billion). Finally, Greece had the first ever and only debt

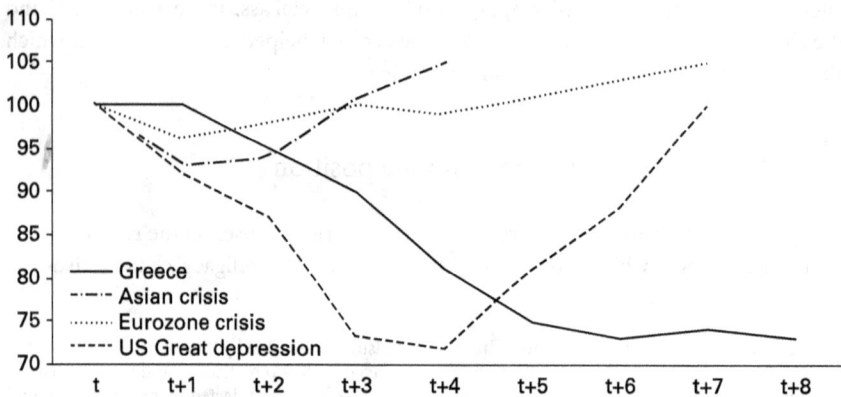

Source: Eurostat, IMF

Figure 9.1 Greece as an outlier. Note: Pre-crisis peaks are 2007 for Greece, 2008 for the eurozone crisis, 1997 for the Asian crisis and 1929 for the US Great Depression.

restructuring in the euro area: a nominal haircut of €100 billion, which still left the debt to GDP ratio at over 180 per cent of GDP by the end of the third bailout in 2018.

The analysis of what went wrong in Greece has focused on several factors. The extremely weak initial conditions explain much of the difficulty the country faced in regaining market access and restoring growth in the context of a severe fiscal consolidation effort. Nevertheless, a more complete explanation needs to include the flawed design of the EU-IMF support. Its initial harsh lending conditions (later relaxed) and the refusal to consider a debt restructuring exercise upfront (later reversed) contributed to making Greece's return to international markets impossible.

This combined with an excessively short path for fiscal consolidation (guided by the limits to the funding for Greece euro area countries were willing to commit to in 2010 rather than sound economic reasoning) which deepened the recession.[11] The macroeconomic projections of the adjustment programme were, as a result, way off the mark (Figure 9.2). Finally, and importantly, one should not underestimate the impact of internal political opposition to consolidation and reforms which reinforced a redenomination risk in both euro area policy-making and international markets.

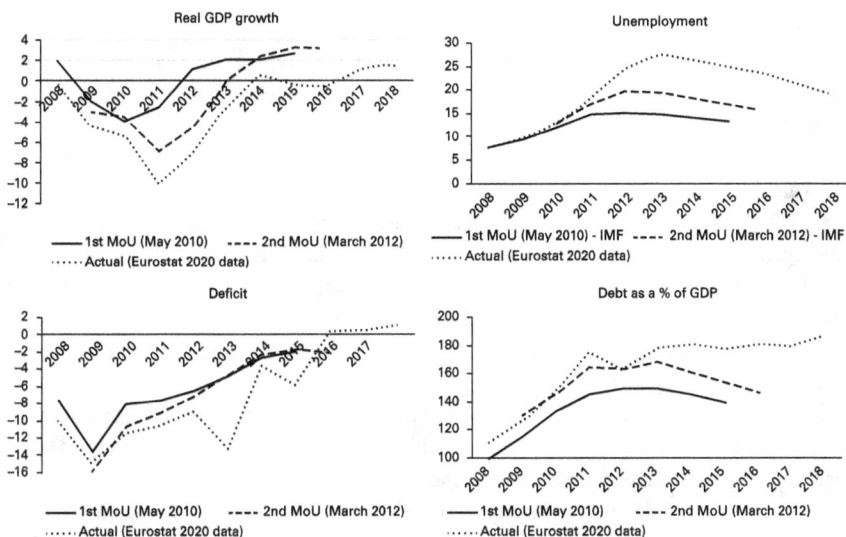

Sources: Greek Memorandum of Understanding (MoU; various issues); Eurostat

Figure 9.2 Getting it wrong: macroeconomic projections and realizations.

---

[11] Ex-post criticism has also come from the participating institutions as well as from EU perspectives. See for example the Independent Evaluation Office of the IMF (2016); and European Parliament (2013).

Focusing on moral hazard

The main apparent traits characterising the Greek economy and political system at the time of the start of the eurozone crisis – the triple fiscal, competitiveness and credibility deficit – played well into a traditional split in the European political economy debate that is philosophical and academic as well as geographical. In philosophical terms, it has been described as rules and rigour vs flexibility and adaptability, or as Kant vs Machiavelli (Brunnermeier et al. 2016). In academic terms, it is the distinction often stylized as rules vs discretion in economic policy making. And in geographical terms, it has been painted as a north/side divide.

The caricature of this divide is that the European north focuses on responsibility while the south on solidarity. More accurately, the first camp emphasizes risk-reduction while the latter risk-sharing. The first view believes that what is required is stronger enforcement of EU fiscal rules to rein in debt and deficits, and more market discipline. Avoiding bailouts is important, as they involve moral hazard. Regarding macroeconomic imbalances, the focus should be on shoring up the competitiveness of lagging countries with high external deficits through structural reforms. The contrasting view holds that there should be a distribution of fiscal efforts across countries to achieve an appropriate aggregate fiscal stance. Fiscal difficulties are perceived as liquidity problems which could be solved through financial assistance. Macroeconomic adjustment on the other hand should be symmetric in order to help weak countries and reduce the Euro area current account surplus.

This split explains much of the policy response in 2009, both in terms of its timing as well its substance in the case of Greece, that of other programme countries, as well as in the direction of the policy reforms that followed. In terms of timing of support, the reluctance to create a 'financial backstop' for a country unable to fund itself in international markets was apparent in the 'ultima ratio' doctrine that guided the German government's attitude to Greece in the first months of 2010. This ambivalence and delay increased the cost of overall support for the creditors as well as the economic hardship in Greece. Furthermore, when support came, its terms were punitive and laced with moral hazard rhetoric. Initial interest rates in official loans for example were set to be 'non-concessionary' at near market rates so as to encourage Greece to return quickly to market financing.

More generally, against this political economy background, Greece's characteristics helped paint the eurozone crisis as a moral hazard issue relating to governments, *not* banks. It was about irresponsible governments not reining in their finances, rather than about the need to address the failings of over-extended and under-regulated banking systems. Hence the policy response focused first and foremost on 'fiscal responsibility', then on backstops, before addressing banks and the financial system. This helps explain the severity (length and depth) of the crisis in a number of countries beyond Greece, and its huge economic and social cost.

This focus on fiscal issues goes beyond Greece and extends to other weak eurozone countries that were asked to tighten their fiscal positions in a recessionary environment. Unfortunately, it extended also to countries with had a sound fiscal position and fiscal space; instead of being allowed to use that space and act to counterbalance the (to an extent unavoidable) retrenchment in programme countries, they also embarked on a fiscal consolidation exercise.

The policy sequence – fiscal first

The policy sequence as a response to the crisis is evidence of the crisis narrative which prevailed. In the first instance, once the extent of the problems in Greece became apparent in late 2009, the response was to pressure the Greek government for the kind of fiscal consolidation that would ostensibly convince financial markets that Greece's debt was sustainable. Once that failed, and it was understood that markets were effectively looking for a backstop from the eurozone, the Greece-specific support package (the GLF) was put in place in May 2010. When in turn it failed to stem the tide building up beyond Greece, it was supplemented by a more generic backstop facility (again in May 2010), the EFSF. Even though its aim was to act as a deterrent, it quickly ended up being used in the cases of Ireland (in November 2010) and Portugal (in May 2011).

During the period between November 2010 and April 2011, markets kept pressuring not only countries in the eurozone periphery, such as Greece, Portugal and Spain, but also 'core' eurozone countries such as France and Italy. Spreads were rising everywhere, despite repeated attempts by targeted countries to show that they were taking measures to redress their fiscal positions. This suggests market concerns were broader and indeed varied: for Greece it was the necessity of debt restructuring, for Portugal growth prospects, for Spain and Italy an overexposed banking system. Once two more countries joined Greece in seeking official support, markets expected Spain to be next, with Italy also facing increasing pressure. In this environment, it was clear that the decisions to date had not addressed the problem of market confidence in eurozone sovereigns and banks.

Indeed, during all this time, in addition to putting in place a financial backstop, eurozone countries were realizing that there was a need for a broader reform of economic governance. The onset of the crisis had found the eurozone lacking the tools, and even the understanding, needed to address the problem of an asymmetric shock to the common currency area and the impact of one eurozone member defaulting on its debts. In addition to acting as the trigger for the crisis, Greece had also exposed the weaknesses of the common currency area and thereby prompted the search for a new institutional architecture (Papaconstantinou 2020). After initial denial and months of inaction came ad hoc solutions steeped in moral hazard rhetoric; eventually the response shifted from firefighting to create new tools and attempt to design a new architecture for the eurozone.

A reform agenda was already sketched out in the October 2010 Task Force report on the economic governance in the EU and its follow-up 2012 report.[12] As the initial

---

[12] 'Strengthening Economic Governance in the EU – Report of the Task Force to the European Council' (https://www.consilium.europa.eu/media/27405/117236.pdf) and 'Towards a Genuine Economic and Monetary Union' (https://www.consilium.europa.eu/media/23818/134069.pdf).

reading of the roots of the crisis was focused on a failure of fiscal discipline, it was on the fiscal front that most subsequent initiatives focused, starting with the main thrust of the 'Six Pack' set of legislative measures in 2011.[13] It was followed in 2012 by the 'Fiscal Compact',[14] with provisions related to fiscal discipline (notably the preventive arm of the Stability and Growth Pact) and rules and procedures for coordination and governance, and in 2013 by the 'Two Pack' directives,[15] aimed at reinforcing economic coordination and budgetary surveillance.

Collectively, this series of policy and legislative initiatives, adopted as a direct response to the Euro area crisis, strengthened the fiscal framework, though the new rules also increased the complexity and the opacity of the surveillance process. The rules also attempted through macroprudential supervision and the Macroeconomic Imbalance Procedure to detect non-primarily fiscal imbalances potentially leading to a banking crisis or a collapse in competitiveness.[16] The focus, however, was clearly on revamping fiscal rules: more attention was paid to debt dynamics, with some flexibility during a crisis as regards deficit limits. This reflected the belief in creditor countries that at the core of the eurozone crisis was a lack of fiscal discipline.

Importantly, reforms of the crisis prevention framework were complemented by the creation of a permanent financial 'backstop' to assist countries in danger of losing market access. As of 2012, the European Stability Mechanism replaced the idiosyncratic temporary support mechanisms created during the crisis – the GLF and the EFSF. Its creation represented a significant addition, both to the European institutional landscape and to the policy toolbox. It has since become central to the debate about the future of the euro area, with different views on its evolution, role and responsibilities.

Going back to the roots of the crisis

All these policy initiatives involved introducing a more robust framework for crisis management and support, gingerly moving towards creating a genuine 'fiscal union' by deepening policy coordination, as well as strengthening institutions for more effective governance. But in the policy sequence, the single moment which marks the inflection point in the eurozone crisis was in late July 2012 when the new ECB president made it clear the eurozone's central bank would use 'within its mandate' all the instruments at its disposal to preserve the integrity of the common currency area (Draghi 2012). Mario Draghi's 'whatever it takes' remarks succeeded where many previous attempts at staving off the crisis had failed previously; they set off a global market rally and sent the spreads on government bonds tumbling.

The Draghi pronouncement was successful not only because it committed the ECB firepower; it also came at the end of a long period in which eurozone countries had

---

[13] See https://www.consilium.europa.eu/uedocs/cms_data/docs/pressdata/en/ecofin/119888.pdf
[14] The text can be found in http://europa.eu/rapid/press-release_DOC-12-2_en.htm
[15] See http://ec.europa.eu/economy_finance/publications/occasional_paper/2013/pdf/ocp147_en.pdf
[16] This is examined in Papaconstantinou and Pisani-Ferry (2019).

gradually proved they not only had the political will but had also put in place economic tools to mitigate market concerns about the integrity of the eurozone. It came after the bailouts of Greece, Portugal and Ireland, and the agreements to lend money to Spain and Cyprus, as well as after the creation of the EFSF and its permanent successor, the European Stability Mechanism. Crucially, Draghi's words also came after it was eventually recognized that in most countries the origin of the crisis was not in the fiscal stance per se but lay instead in the banking sector, whose liabilities ended up on public balance sheets as governments bailed out the banks or guaranteed their deposits.[17]

Banking union was the forgotten element in the creation of a common currency, whose critical importance was demonstrated during the crisis. It was introduced in June 2012 with a Euro Summit statement whose first sentence read: 'we affirm that it is imperative to break the vicious circle between banks and sovereigns.'[18] European leaders decided to move ahead with the unification of the European banking sector under a single supervisory body (the Single Supervisory Mechanism or SSM) and to give the new European Stability Mechanism the power to recapitalize banks directly (Euro Summit 2012).

Following that, in 2014, supervisory authority and the power to grant or withdraw banking licences were transferred from national authorities to the Supervisory Board of the Single Supervisory Mechanism (SSM), a new structure within the European Central Bank (ECB). In 2015, the EU created the Single Resolution Board (SRB), a new Brussels-based entity which, together with national resolution authorities, constitutes the Single Resolution Mechanism (SRM). A Single Resolution Fund (SRF) financed by contributions from banks is being built up to support resolution procedures within the framework of the EU-wide Bank Recovery and Resolution Directive (BRRD). It was agreed at the Euro Summit in December 2018 that the SRF will be further backstopped by European Stability Mechanism (ESM) credit lines.[19]

In addition to the European Council decisions, the European Central Bank proved to be the most important actor in resolving the crisis. In response to the freeze of the interbank market, it extended liquidity to the banking system and further provided it on increasingly flexible terms, effectively rewriting the rules to accommodate a fast-evolving situation. Its 'Securities Markets Programme' of bond purchases from crisis countries since 2010 leveraged European Council decisions at a critical time and was followed by the 'Outright Monetary Transactions' programme of open-ended purchases in secondary sovereign debt markets, contingent on strict conditionality. The ECB was admittedly late in embarking on an unconventional monetary stimulus (which started in 2015 only), but its actions and words have been instrumental in defusing the crisis. They have also been the focus of intense criticism in a number of countries.

---

[17] For a discussion on identifying the causes of the eurozone crisis, see Pisani-Ferry (2011) and Jones (2015).
[18] See https://www.consilium.europa.eu/media/21400/20120629-euro-area-summit-statement-en.pdf
[19] See https://www.consilium.europa.eu/media/37268/tor-backstop_041218_final_clean.pdf

Concluding remarks

The roots of the Greek and broader eurozone crisis in the Global Financial Crisis took time to be understood. Throughout, Greece was considered a 'special case', and in a way it was. Its deep-seated fiscal problems allowed the whole crisis to be understood in terms of excessive deficits and debt and the policy response to focus on fiscal consolidation, and not only in the countries having difficulty to access market financing. Nevertheless, the country's unique characteristics that made it an outlier cannot mask the fact that it was simply the trigger of a broader crisis. Greece acted as the 'canary in a coalmine', exposing the weaknesses of an incomplete and deeply flawed institutional infrastructure and governance of the common currency area. At the core of that were issues related to the interplay between banks and sovereigns.

For Greece itself, what was originally seen as simply a tale of fiscal profligacy over many years was eventually understood to be a multifaceted economic, social and political crisis with deep institutional roots. However, this limited reading of the problem as high deficits and debt as opposed to focusing on the underlying causes led to many mistakes made by everyone involved – European and international institutions as well as the Greek government: on the appropriate size and timing of the fiscal effort, the policy mix, the question of debt restructuring, governance arrangements.

Debt management eventually came to be recognized as a central policy issue for the country, following the 2013 debt restructuring as well as follow-up decisions to help debt sustainability. An overhaul of banking supervision and governance took place, though with legacy problems such as high levels of non-performing loans. Financial regulation and compliance improved, after much restructuring and mistakes in the banking sector. Reforms in product and labour markets advanced, as well as in institutions, though with much more to be done. It was a crisis that defined Greece, its economy and polity. Though Greek democracy was challenged by populism, it proved resilient. But the high economic and social cost of the crisis has weakened the country significantly, perhaps making it harder to face up to the next crisis.

For Europe as a whole, Greece represented the perfect culprit,[20] allowing creditor countries to focus on the fiscal dimension of the crisis, to the detriment of understanding how the financial sector links to the Global Financial Crisis exposed the design faults of the common currency area. While EU crisis management proved the resilience of the European construct and its ability to invent new methods and solutions, much time was lost before moving to rebuild the institutional infrastructure and especially addressing the bank–sovereign nexus. In this context, one cannot help but wonder what would have happened if it had been Ireland – with its problems clearly identified with the banking sector – that first required financial support rather than Greece. A crisis narrative built on the need for austerity would perhaps have been harder to sustain.

There is no denying that once European policy-makers moved from firefighting to institutional rebuilding, much was achieved. Nevertheless, even the delayed move to a banking and capital markets union remains incomplete, with the glaring omission of

---

[20] The expression is used in Pisani-Ferry (2011).

the third pillar and the European Deposit Insurance Scheme that would prevent the 'flight to safety' we witnessed during the crisis and destabilized both financial markets and sovereign debt markets. To that should be added a long list of reforms that are either incomplete or yet to be tackled, including a central fiscal capacity, a safe asset and a rewriting of the currently outdated fiscal rules.

Given the fact that – as Jean Monnet wrote – 'Europe will be forged in crises, and will be the sum of the solutions adopted for these crises', these further necessary reforms will have to wait for the next crisis to finally have a hope of advancing. The robust EU response to the economic fallout of the COVID-19 pandemic seems to support this thesis, exhibiting at least some movement in the direction of the required reforms to the EU economic governance infrastructure.

References

Brunnermeier, Markus, Harold James and Jean-Pierre Landau. 2016. *The Euro and the Battle of Ideas*. Princeton, NJ: Princeton University Press.

Cardiff, Kevin. 2016. *Recap: Inside Ireland's Financial Crisis*. Dublin: The Liffey Press.

Draghi, Mario. 2018. 'Risk-reducing and risk-sharing in our Monetary Union.' Speech at the European University Institute, Florence, 11 May. The text can be found at: https://www.ecb.europa.eu/press/key/date/2018/html/ecb.sp180511.en.html#1

Draghi, Mario. 2012. Speech at the Global Investment Conference in London, 26 July (https://www.ecb.europa.eu/press/key/date/2012/html/sp120726.en.html).

European Parliament. 2013. 'Report on the enquiry on the role and operations of the Troika (ECB, Commission and IMF) with regard to the euro area programme countries, 2013/2277(INI).' Brussels. http://www.europarl.europa.eu/sides/getDoc.do?pubRef=-//EP//NONSGML+REPORT+A7-2014-0149+0+DOC+PDF+V0//EN

Euro Summit. 2010. Statement of the Heads of State or Government of the Euro Area, 7 May 2010. http://www.consilium.europa.eu/media/21430/20100507-statement-of-the-heads-of-state-or-government-of-the-euro-area-en.pdf

Euro Summit (2012), 'Euro Summit Statement', 29 June 2012, https://www.consilium.europa.eu/media/21400/20120629-euro-area-summit-statement-en.pdf

Geithner, Timothy. 2014. *Stress Test: Reflections on Financial Crises*. New York: Random House.

Honohan, Patrick. 2019. *Currency, Credit and Crisis: Central Banking in Ireland and Europe*. Cambridge: Cambridge University Press.

Independent Evaluation Office of the IMF. 2016. 'The IMF and the Crises in Greece, Ireland, and Portugal.' Washington D.C.: IMF.

Jones, Erik. 2015. 'Getting the Story Right: How You Should Choose between Different Interpretations of the European Crisis.' *Journal of European Integration*, 37 (7). DOI: 10.1080/07036337.2015.1079376.

Mody, Ashoka. 2014. 'The Ghost of Deauville.' CEPR/VoxEU. (https://voxeu.org/article/ghost-deauville)

Mody, Ashoka, and Damiano Sandri. 2012. 'The eurozone crisis: how banks and sovereigns came to be joined at the hip.' *Economic Policy* 27 (70).

Papaconstantinou, George, and Jean Pisani-Ferry. 2019. 'A big leap forward: Institutions and policies for a viable Euro area.' Paper presented 22 March at the Lisbon 'Where is Europe Going?' conference organized by the Caloust Gulbenkian Foundation. (https://

content.gulbenkian.pt/wp-content/uploads/2019/03/21165801/Policy-papers_EN_
Para-onde-vai-a-Europa_web.pdf).

Papaconstantinou, George. 2020. *Whatever It Takes: The Battle for Post-Crisis Europe*.
Newcastle upon Tyne: Agenda Publishing.

Papaconstantinou, George. 2016. *Game Over: The Inside Story of the Greek Crisis*. Athens:
Papadopoulos Publishing.

Pisani-Ferry, Jean. 2011. *The Euro Crisis and its Aftermath*. Oxford: Oxford University
Press.

Praet, Peter. 2012. 'The role of the central bank and euro area governments in times of
crisis.' Speech at the German Federal Ministry of Finance, Berlin (https://www.ecb.
europa.eu/press/key/date/2012/html/sp120419.en.html).

Sinn, Hans-Werner. 2010. *Casino Capitalism*. Oxford: Oxford University Press.

Sorkin, Andrew (2009). *Too Big to Fail*. London and New York: Penguin.

Stolz, Stéphanie, and Michael Wedow. 2010. 'Extraordinary measures in extraordinary
times: Public measures in support of the financial sector in the EU and the US.'
Deutsche Bundesbank Discussion Paper Series 1: Economic Studies No 13/2010
(https://www.econstor.eu/bitstream/10419/37071/1/631858768.pdf).

Part Three

The Architecture of Control

10

The Danger of Raising and then Dashing Expectations: The Lesson from Lehman?

Thomas F. Huertas

In the economy, expectations exercise enormous effects. Indeed, in finance, prices and yields predominantly reflect current expectations about future cash flows and future interest rates. Change those expectations, prices and yields change as well. Change expectations radically enough, the attendant shift in prices and yields may be large enough to impact financial markets and the economy at large.

The failure of Lehman Brothers on 15 September 2008 is a case in point.[1] Prior to its bankruptcy, the economy was treading water. Thereafter it sank like a stone, until the massive stimulus programmes put in place by governments and central banks began to pull it back up again.

Any analysis of the Global Financial Crisis should explain the reason for this downward break in its course. Few do so explicitly.[2] Most focus on the ultimate causes of the crisis, be they fault lines in the economy (Rajan 2010), in financial markets (Tett 2009; Gorton 2010; Milne 2009), and/or in regulation and supervision (Financial Crisis Inquiry Commission 2011). Some ascribe a role to monetary policy (Taylor 2018). Others blame housing policy (Barth 2009; Wallison 2016). This chapter suggests that what turned the recession into the 'Great Recession' was Lehman's descent into bankruptcy.

This suddenly swung market expectations concerning government policy from 'too big to fail' to 'let the chips fall where they may'. Following Lehman's declaration of bankruptcy, panic ensued, as market participants rushed to adjust to the new situation. This set off a downward debt-deflation spiral that caused the world economy to contract rapidly. Only massive monetary and fiscal stimulus, together with explicit

[1]   For a chronicle of the events on the Lehman resolution weekend (12 to 15 September 2008) see Sorkin (2009). For the recollections of the principal decision makers see Paulson (2010: 173–221); Bernanke, Geithner & Paulson (2019: 65); Darling (2011: 120–7); Geithner (2014: 162–210) and Bernanke (2015: 248–69). For detailed analyses of the Lehman bankruptcy, see Valukas (2010) and McDonald (2016).

[2]   For overall assessments of the causes of the crisis, see: Financial Crisis Inquiry Commission (2011); French et al. (2010); Davies (2010); Turner (2009). Huertas (2011) presents my own views.

government support to systemically important financial institutions (SIFIs), arrested the decline and turned what might have become the Great(er) Depression into the Great Recession. This weakened economies around the world, leading to further crises and changes to the political landscape (Tooze 2018).

In concept therefore, allowing implicit guarantees such as 'too big to fail' to develop generates not only moral hazard but also creates what might be called public hazard. This is the risk to financial stability and the economy at large, if the government fails to fulfil the implicit guarantee, when called upon to do so. This is a lesson that governments would do well to bear in mind as they wrestle with how to taper off the massive support that they are currently giving to firms and individuals to enable them to offset the economic consequences of COVID-19.

The failure of Lehman

On Friday 12 September 2008, Lehman reached what later became known as the 'point of non-viability' (PONV). It was unable to finance itself in private markets. At the time, some portion of investors, counterparties and supervisors expected that the US authorities would engineer a 'global solution' to the Lehman situation, similar to that the US authorities had employed some six months earlier to avoid the bankruptcy of Bear Stearns. In that case senior creditors had been fully protected, and some portion of the market expected that the US authorities would also ensure that senior creditors at Lehman would emerge unscathed.

That was certainly the intention of the US authorities. In the recollection of the three principal decision-makers at the time:

> [W]e did not let Lehman fail on purpose. We didn't even discuss whether or not to try to save Lehman . . .; we knew we had to do everything in our power to try to prevent its collapse. But everything in our power turned out to be insufficient.
>
> Bernanke, Geithner & Paulson 2019: 62

Initially, US authorities worked to achieve a 'global solution'. Late on 12 September, the Federal Reserve Bank of New York persuaded the UK Financial Services Authority to permit Lehman's UK subsidiary, Lehman Brothers International plc (LBIE), to transfer several billion dollars to LBIE's account with the group's parent, Lehman Brothers Holdings Inc. (LBHI). This transfer permitted Lehman entities to meet their obligations to payment and securities settlement systems in the United States, averting Lehman's immediate failure and allowing US authorities to search for such a global solution.

But they were unable to find one. The US effort to create one depended on finding an acquirer who was also willing and able, as JPMorgan Chase was in the case of Bear Stearns, to guarantee the trades made by Lehman prior to the completion of the acquisition. This proved to be impossible in the time frame required. The one possible US acquirer, Bank of America Corporation, opted to acquire Merrill Lynch, a troubled and considerably larger stand-alone investment bank, in an unassisted transaction. The one possible non-US acquirer, Barclays Plc, was not able to commit to guarantee the Lehman trades and consequently never made an offer to acquire Lehman.[3] Finally, the US authorities determined that the Federal Reserve lacked the authority to lend to LBHI, as it judged LBHI to be insolvent and unable to provide collateral of sufficient quality and market liquidity. Consequently, the US authorities determined that in the case of the parent holding company (LBHI), there was no alternative to bankruptcy. Accordingly, they instructed the LBHI board of directors to file for bankruptcy. LBHI did so, but not until 01:45 New York time on Monday 15 September, well after the Asian markets had opened and shortly before London and other European markets were due to open.

Outside the United States, the failure of the parent holding company forced subsidiaries into administration and liquidation. In the UK, the bankruptcy of LBHI prevented it from returning cash that LBIE had sent it on Friday. Consequently, at Monday open in London, LBIE had no liquidity and it went into administration, as did Lehman's bank in Germany, Lehman Brothers AG. Inside the United States, Lehman subsidiaries also filed for bankruptcy, except for Lehman Brothers Inc. (LBI), the group's US broker-dealer subsidiary. LBI received lender of last resort assistance from the Federal Reserve, enabling it to continue operations and settle outstanding trades.

The Lehman bankruptcy undermined financial stability in three ways. First, it accelerated the decline in asset prices. Counterparties to LBHI sold the assets that LBHI had pledged to them under executory contracts such as repurchase agreements and derivatives. So did counterparties to LBIE and other subsidiaries, such as LBAG. The sudden and significant increase in offers to sell securities for immediate and certain execution depressed the price at which such assets could be sold, in some cases to fire-sale levels. This in turn forced all institutions holding such assets to write down their value. This further depleted capital at major financial institutions, undermining their ability to fund in the market.

Second, the failure of Lehman led to the failure of entities heavily exposed to Lehman. In particular, it led to the failure of the Prime Reserve Fund to meet its promise to redeem shares at a constant net asset value of $1. In other words, it had to 'break the buck'. This created fears that other money market mutual funds could do the same and therefore unleashed a wave of redemption orders for such funds. This in turn drained demand from other markets, such as commercial paper, where money market mutual funds had been large investors, and that placed pressure on large issuers of such paper, as well as on the banks who had given such issuers back-up liquidity lines.

---

[3]   The account presented here takes at face value the statement of the principal US decision-makers that Paulson's stance of no federal assistance was a 'negotiating tactic, not a policy decision' (Bernanke, Geithner, & Paulson 2019: 65). However, Tooze (2018: 177) casts doubt on this, citing the refusal of the US authorities to offer Barclays – either directly or indirectly via the UK Chancellor of the Exchequer (Darling 2011: 120–7) – the same type of loss-limitation assistance that the Federal Reserve had provided to JPMorgan Chase in connection with Bear Stearns.

Implicit guarantees induce investors to reduce risk premiums

Investors in financial instruments must form expectations, not only about the likelihood that a counterparty will be unable to meet its obligations in a timely manner, but also about the decisions that authorities will make – for it is those decisions that determine the loss the investor will incur.

To illustrate, take the case two banks, each with a 15 per cent probability that the bank will reach the PONV and require intervention. In each case, the loss to senior creditors given bailout is zero, whilst the loss given bankruptcy is 20 per cent. The only difference between the two banks is the probability of bailout given the event that the bank reaches the PONV. In the case of a 'too big to fail' bank, the probability of bailout is 80 per cent, whilst in the case of a bank that is 'too small to save', that probability is 20 per cent. The expected loss for a 'too big to fail' bank is 60 basis points. In contrast, expected loss for a 'too small to save' bank is 240 basis points.

Expectation regarding bailout determines expected loss

	Too big to fail	Too small to save
Probability of reaching PONV	15%	15%
Loss given bailout	0%	0%
Loss given bankruptcy	20%	20%
Probability of bailout	80%	20%
Expected loss	0.6%	2.4%

Shifting an institution from too big to fail to too small to save therefore substantially increases the risk premium it will have to pay to raise funds, if it can raise funds at all.

Third, and perhaps most importantly, the failure of Lehman abruptly contradicted the belief that significant financial institutions were too big to fail. The market had long held this expectation with respect to deposit-taking banks, and the rescue of Bear Stearns in March 2008 seemed to many to have extended this principle to major investment banks as well. As Lehman was significantly larger and much more interconnected than Bear Stearns, many in the market expected that the US authorities would similarly rescue Lehman. When they did not, questions arose as to whether too big to fail was still valid, and, if it was, what was the dividing line between 'too big to fail' and 'too small to save'. That radically increased the expected loss given default (see Box).

Taken together, the three effects led to an immediate spike in risk premia as well as a flight to quality and a flight away from weaker firms. Like dominoes in a row, the latter stood ready to fall over in swift succession starting with AIG, the troubled insurance company, then the two remaining systemic stand-alone investment banks, Goldman Sachs and Morgan Stanley as well as numerous non-US banks, such as RBS, that had borrowed heavily in short-term wholesale markets. In brief, financial markets and the global economy were headed toward meltdown.

However, concerted action by G7 governments averted total catastrophe. On 10 October 2008, G7 finance ministers and central bank governors stated that they would 'use all available tools to support systemically important financial institutions and prevent their failure' and 'take all necessary steps to unfreeze credit and money markets and ensure that banks and other financial institutions have broad access to liquidity and funding' (G7 2008). Governments started to recapitalize banks. Central banks flooded the market with liquidity, both in general via reductions in interest rates as well as via lending facilities to particular sectors or markets. In addition, governments applied massive fiscal stimulus. Together, these measures arrested the economy's descent. By the end of 2009, the global economy was on the road to recovery. What might have well become the Great(er) Depression went instead into the history books as the Great Recession.

Regulatory response

At the G-20 summit in Pittsburgh in September 2009, world leaders pledged to 'make sure our regulatory system for banks and other financial firms reins in the excesses that led to the crisis' (G20 2009). Reform focused on three objectives: making banks less likely to fail; making banks resolvable or 'safe to fail', and making markets robust.

To make banks less likely to fail, policy-makers completely revised the framework for prudential regulation. Via the new Basel III accord (BCBS 2020), regulators significantly raised capital requirements and introduced liquidity requirements. Supervisors became much more forward-looking and proactive, reinforcing the shift to stricter regulation.

Basel III increased both the quality and quantity of capital banks must hold. Regulators purged from the definition of capital items that could not bear first loss whilst the bank was a going concern. The new standard, Common equity Tier 1 (CET1) capital, is effectively a tangible net worth standard. The minimum CET1 ratio increased from 2 per cent of risk weighted assets to 4.5 per cent. In addition, regulators introduced a capital conservation buffer of 2.5 per cent of RWAs, effectively raising the minimum standard to 7 per cent of RWAs for a bank that wished to be able to pay dividends or make distributions to its shareholders. Revisions to credit risk, market risk and operating risk effectively made risk weightings 'heavier' and limited banks' ability to use internal models to reduce capital requirements. Macro-prudential buffers (counter-cyclical buffer and SIFI surcharge) added further capital requirements, as did bank-specific requirements under Pillar 2. Finally, regulators introduced a leverage standard as a back-up to the risk-weighted regime. Taken together, the Basel III reforms increased capital requirements for large, systemically important banks by a factor of ten (Cecchetti 2015).

With respect to liquidity, Basel III introduced for the first time global liquidity standards. Under the liquidity coverage ratio, banks have to keep high-quality liquid assets, such as cash and government securities, sufficient to meet the net outflow of funds that the bank expects would occur over the next thirty days under a stress scenario. Under the net stable funding, ratio banks have to limit the maturity mismatch between their assets and liabilities and reduce their dependence on volatile, short-term wholesale funding. In addition, authorities have introduced limits on asset encumbrance.

Supervision has become much more proactive and forward-looking. This reinforces the shift toward higher capital and liquidity requirements. Via stress tests, supervisors have effectively forced banks to maintain capital sufficient to meet not only the risks inherent in their current business, but also the risks that may arise if stress were to occur at some point over the three-to-five-year test horizon. If banks do not, they may not pay dividends or make distributions to shareholders. In extreme cases, the bank may be required to raise new capital immediately.

Resolution reform seeks to end 'too big to fail'. It is a recognition that bankruptcy does not work for banks, and that banks correspondingly need a special resolution regime. Bail-in is at the centre of this new regime and is akin to a pre-pack bankruptcy. If a bank fails, gone-concern capital is written down or converted into common equity so as to recapitalize the bank and allow it to continue to perform its critical economic functions. This would be done very quickly without taxpayer support whilst maintaining the bank-in-resolution's access to financial market infrastructures and service providers. Instead of a bailout, there would be a bail-in.

To make markets more robust, regulators introduced a variety of measures, including mandatory clearing for OTC derivatives, restrictions on the use of constant net asset value money market mutual funds and rules governing secured financing transactions, such as repurchase agreements.

The role of expectations

Expectations play a critical role in the new regulatory and supervisory regime. They are embedded in both the design and detail of financial services regulation and supervision, and they shape how regulation and supervision affect markets, financial stability and ultimately the economy at large.

A cursory look at the details of capital and liquidity requirements suffices to demonstrate the importance of expectations (see Table 10.1). Requirements for credit, market and liquidity risk depend on assumptions regarding the future course of market factors. If assumptions regarding the possible movement in market factors are wrong, capital and liquidity may prove to be insufficient. Current methods of estimation heighten that risk. For example, in determining both market and credit risk, the probability distribution of future values may be estimated as the frequency distribution of past values. This limits the weight that can be given to unprecedented events. That shortcoming is further heightened if the detailed rules implementing the regulation permit the bank to truncate the frequency distribution by excluding events in the more distant past and/ or to ignore extreme loss events. Even stress tests may have this effect. Although they require banks to prepare for an environment more troubled than the current one, they may create the impression that the stress scenario is the worst that can happen.

Whether guarantees are as good as promised also matters. Regulation therefore seeks to ensure that private guarantors are able to fulfil the guarantees that they give. That was clearly not the case with respect to the promise of money market mutual funds to maintain a constant NAV, and regulation now precludes such funds or requires sponsors to maintain capital to offset the step-in risk associated with making

Table 10.1 The role of expectations in regulation and supervision.

Credit risk	
Provisioning	Banks must take loan provisions in accordance with **expected** loss over the next year (for loans that are current) and over the life of the loan (for loans that are not).
Probability of default	Probability of default represents the **expected** likelihood that an obligor will fail to meet its obligations in full when due.
Exposure at default	Exposure at default reflects the **expected** timing of default as well as the **expected** changes in exposure that may result from movement in market factors, amortization/prepayment of credit, drawdown of revolving and/or back-up liquidity lines, etc.
Loss given default	Loss given default reflects the **expected** net present value of any recoveries that the bank may make.
Market risk	
Valuation	Valuation of a position in the trading book represents the **expected** price at which a willing seller could sell to a willing buyer within the **expected** time to liquidation.
Expected Shortfall	The Expected Shortfall (ES) or Conditional VaR (CVaR) is a statistic used to quantify the risk of a portfolio. Given a certain confidence level, this measure represents the **expected** loss when it is greater than the value of the VaR calculated with that confidence level.
Liquidity risk	
Liquidity coverage ratio	Ratio of high-quality liquid assets to **expected** net outflow of funds over next thirty days under **assumed** stress scenario.
High-quality liquid assets	Cash and marketable securities that are **expected** to be liquid under stress.
Net stable funding ratio	Ratio of funding **expected** to be stable and available relative to stable funding **expected** to be required.

such a promise (IOSCO 2019). Nor is it the case with respect to central counterparties (CCPs). Legislation imposing mandatory clearing was based on the premise that CCPs would absorb risk. In fact, they mutualize it, so that the CCP becomes a single point of failure. Consequently, policy-makers are now expending considerable time and effort to make CCPs resolvable.

Far more significant than private guarantees are the guarantees that governments give. As they come from government, they have a high degree of credibility. Therefore individuals, institutions and intermediaries rely heavily on such guarantees when assessing and pricing risk. Consequently, the risk premium for a guaranteed instrument will be smaller the stronger is the government's commitment, and the greater the perception that the government will be able and willing to meet that commitment.

As is well known, such guarantees create moral hazard, namely an incentive for the entity benefitting from the guarantee to increase the assumption of risk covered by the guarantee. But such guarantees also create what might be called a public hazard, namely the risk to financial stability and the economy at large, if the government fails to perform on the guarantee when called upon to do so.

In this regard, implicit guarantees are especially problematic. Governments may allow market participants to believe that they will stand behind the liabilities of specific institutions even though they do not explicitly guarantee such liabilities. Panic may ensue, as it did in the case of Lehman, if governments do not perform as expected when called upon to do so. Rather than create such a risk for the future, should not governments be more reluctant to set the precedents that will create the implicit guarantees that create moral hazard?

COVID-19

Indeed, governments should consider this issue as they wrestle with the problem of how to taper off – and ultimately unwind – the massive support that they are giving to individuals and institutions adversely affected by the lockdowns imposed to halt COVID-19. Two aspects deserve particular focus: how to preserve the progress made with respect to eliminating too big to fail for banks, and how to prevent the creation of a similar doctrine for firms.

With respect to banks, there is considerable evidence that market participants believe it is likely that authorities will – in the event a bank reaches the PONV – bail in rather than bail out investors. This is exactly the type of *ex ante* market discipline that resolution reform was designed to achieve. But there is also considerable scepticism that authorities will actually employ bail-in.

The current recession will put resolution to the test. The recession is likely to be far more severe than any hypothetical stress test that supervisors have imposed on banks. It is system-wide and the shock to the banking system is already on its way. For resolution, the recession comes squarely in the midst of what might be called a 'transition gap'. This is the difference between the market's expectation that a regulatory standard, once adopted, will have full effect, and the reality that during the transition period the standard is not fully applicable. With respect to the Basel standards for going-concern (CET1) capital, supervisors used stress tests to eliminate the transition gap. By defining the hurdle rate in terms of the final standard, supervisors accelerated the effective date of the final standard. In contrast, supervisors have not accelerated standards for gone-concern capital (additional Tier 1 and Tier 2 capital plus qualifying senior non-preferred debt). The standards remain subject to lengthy transition periods. In the euro area, for example, banks need not meet requirements for gone-concern capital until 1 January 2024 (SRB 2020: 34). Until banks do meet the requirements, there will not be enough gone-concern capital to recapitalize the bank. Consequently, resolution via bail-in may fail the public interest test required for its use, and that might allow the authorities to resort once again to a bailout. If so, that would reverse the progress made toward ending too big to fail.

What is needed is a strategy and a stratagem to flatten the curve of bank failures so that resolution cases come one-by-one to the resolution authority and come with a full complement of gone-in capital so that bail-in will recapitalize the bank. To this end, it would be advisable for authorities to introduce asset-protection schemes that would cap the loss that banks could incur on non-performing loans with a premium payable by the bank based on the risk to the scheme. Such premiums would be payable in either cash or equity (including gone-concern equity). That will delay and reduce the number of bank failures and help ensure that bail-in is a feasible method to resolve those that do fail.

Similarly, attention needs to be paid to terms on which aid is provided to firms under stress due to COVID-19. In light of the possibility that COVID-19 is *not* a one-time event, it is particularly important for governments to convince firms and investors that the massive support packages *are* one-time events. Governments will simply not be able to offset the effects of a possible COVID-21 or COVID-23. Unless and until science finds a way to control or abolish infectious fatal diseases, the world is likely to become riskier. This should imply higher risk premiums and lower leverage.

Care should therefore be taken that aid in connection with COVID-19 is either extended on commercial terms or refinanced on such terms. In particular, attention should be given to designing and implementing schemes, such as the recent SAFE Equity Fund proposal (Boot et al. 2020), to convert debt into equity. This will diminish the expectation that governments will necessarily bail out firms in the future.

Conclusion

In summary, expectations matter. It is dangerous to allow market participants to extrapolate decisions to save individual firms into an implicit guarantee. This not only creates moral hazard, but also public hazard, namely a tripwire to panic and financial instability, should the government not fulfil the guarantee as expected.

References

Barth, J. R. 2009. *The Rise and Fall of the U.S. Mortgage and Credit Markets: A Comprehensive Analysis of the Market Meltdown.* Hoboken, NJ: John Wiley & Sons.

Basel Committee on Banking Supervision. n.d. *The Basel Framework.* Retrieved from https://www.bis.org/basel_framework/index.htm?m=3%7C14%7C697

Bernanke, B.S. 2015. *Courage to Act: A Memoir of a Crisis and its Aftermath.* New York: W.W. Norton.

Bernanke, B.S., T.F. Geithner and H.M. Paulson. 2019. *Firefighting: The Financial Crisis and its Lessons.* London: Profile Books.

Boot, A., E. Carletti, H.-H. Kotz, J.P. Krahnen, L. Pelizzon and M. Subrahmanyam. 2020. 'Corona and Financial Stability 4.0: Implementing a European Pandemic Equity Fund.' In A. Bénassy-Quéré and B. Weder di Mauro, *Europe in the Time of Covid-19,* 48–56). CEPR. Retrieved from file:///C:/Users/thoma/Downloads/Europe_in_the_Time_of_Covid-19.pdf

Cecchetti, S. 2015. 'The Road to Financial Stability: Capital Regulation, Liquidity Regulation and Resolution.' *International Journal of Cenrral Banking* 11 (3), 127–39.

Darling, A. 2011. *Back from the Brink: 1,000 Days at Number 11.* London: Atlantic Books.

Davies, H. 2010. *The Financial Crisis: Who Is to Blame?* Cambridge: Polity.

Financial Crisis Inquiry Commission. 2011. *Final Report of the National Commission on the Causes of the Financial and Economic Crisis in the United States.* New York: Public Affairs.

French, K.R., M.S. Baily, J.Y. Campbell, J.H. Cochrane, D.W. Diamond, D. Duffie, A.K. Kashyap, F.S. Mishkin, R.G. Rajan, D.S. Scharfstein, R.J. Shiller, H.S. Shin, M.J. Slaughter, J.C. Stein and R.M. Stulz. 2010. *The Squam Lake Report: Fixing the Financial System.* Princeton, NJ: Princeton University Press.

G-20. 2009 (25 September). *G20 Leaders Statement: The Pittsburgh Summit.* Retrieved from www.g20.utoronto.ca/2009/2009communique0925.html

G7 Finance Ministers and Central Bank Governors. 2008 (10 October). *Plan of Action.* Retrieved 31 May 2020, from http://www.g8.utoronto.ca/finance/fm081010.htm

Geithner, T.F. 2014. *Stress Test: Reflections on Financial Crises.* New York: Random House Business Books.

Gorton, G.B. 2010. *Slapped by the Invisible Hand: The Panic of 2007.* Oxford: Oxford University Press.

Huertas, T.F. 2011. *Crisis: Cause, Containment and Cure.* 2nd ed. London: Palgrave Macmillan.

IOSCO. 2019. *Udate to the IIOSCO Peer Review of Regulation of Money Market Funds.*

McDonald, O. 2016. *Lehman Brothers: A Crisis of Value.* Manchester: Manchester University Press.

Milne, A. 2009. *The Fall lof the House of Credit: What Went Wrong in Banking and What Can Be Done to Repair the Damage?* Cambridge: Cambridge University Press.

Paulson, H.M. 2010. *On the Brink: Inside the Race to Stop the Collapse of the Glabal Financial System.* New York: Business Plus.

Rajan, R.G. 2010. *Fault Lines: How Hidden Fractures Still Threaten the World Economy.* Princeton, NJ: Princeton University Press.

Single Resolution Board. 2020. *Minimum Requirement for Own Funds and Eligible Liabilities (MREL): SRB Policy under the Banking Package.* Retrieved from: Minimum Requirement for Own Funds and Eligible Liabilities (MREL) / SRB Policy under the Banking Package (europa.eu).

Sorkin, A.R. 2009. *Too Big too Fail.* New York: Viking.

Taylor, J.B. 2018. *Government as a Cause of the 2008 Financial Crisis: A Reassessment After 10 Years.* Retrieved from https://www.hoover.org/sites/default/files/research/docs/govt_as_cause_of_crisis-a_reassement_10.pdf

Tett, G. 2009. *Fool's Gold: How Unrestrained Greed Corrupted a Dream, Shattered Financial Markets and Unleashed a Global Catastrophe.* London: Little, Brown.

Tooze, A. 2018. *Crashed: How a Decade of Financial Crises Changed the World.* London: Allen Lane.

Turner, A. 2009. *The Turner Review: A Regulatory Response to the Global Banking Crisis.* Retrieved from https://webarchive.nationalarchives.gov.uk/20090414155227/http://www.fsa.gov.uk/pubs/other/turner_review.pdf

Valukas, A.R. 2010. *Lehman Brothers Holdings Inc. Chapter 11 Proceedings Examiner Report.* Retrieved from https://jenner.com/lehman

Wallison, P.J. 2016. *Hidden in Plain Sight: What Really Caused the World's Worst Financial Crisis and Why It Could Happen Again.* New York: Encounter Books.

11

Governing EU Banks after the Global Financial Crisis: From Regulation to Governance

Agnieszka Smoleńska

Introduction

The Global Financial Crisis had a notable beginning. The day of the collapse of Lehman Brothers, 15 September 2008, became a watershed moment for markets, sovereigns and eventually citizens around the globe. It is much harder, however, to demarcate clearly its end. This is because at least in the European Union, the financial crisis has given rise to a second wave of economic and sovereign debt disturbance (Sandbu 2017). Furthermore, the regulatory wave that the crisis triggered and which sought to correct *ex post* the pre-crisis shortcomings never seems to have ended (Gortsos 2015). With the arrival of the COVID-19 pandemic in the winter of 2020 and the economic disturbance it has caused, the advent of a new financial crisis appears imminent (Jackson and Schwarcz 2020), once again prolonging the period of banking sector instability. In this context, it may appear that identifying the legacy of the Global Financial Crisis is quite impossible. Since the Global Financial Crisis appears not to have a clearly defined end from a regulatory point of view, how can we establish whether the reforms introduced in its aftermath have brought about a meaningful change in how the financial sector operates? And more specifically, how can we determine the causality mechanisms of any market impact of such reforms, especially given all the other factors driving change in the financial sector, such as technological advances?

This chapter will argue that one lasting legacy of the Global Financial Crisis has been the shift to bank governance as a key regulatory technique for influencing bank behaviour in the EU. Such governance mechanism is established by the ensemble of rules and prerogatives of supervisory and resolution authorities, which allows them to intervene and guide the behaviour of cross-border banks, also in areas traditionally conceived of in terms of autonomy of the business enterprise (Grundmann 2015; Smoleńska 2021). Such limitation is complemented with greater responsibilities for banks for public goals and objectives, both in terms of the regulatory processes and internal management (risk-management) requirements as well as observed bank conduct.

The outcome of such a paradigm shift has been visible since the onset of the coronavirus pandemic in the winter of 2020: not only do the states rely more broadly on the banking sector to implement and disburse the rescue aid to the economy (e.g. loan and guarantee schemes meant to keep the financial sector afloat), but crisis-response policies also emphasize the public responsibilities of banks. Banks introduce of their own accord credit holidays for their customers, even as bank management accepts cuts in pay and dividends to share the burden of the economic slowdown (Morris 2020). Such bank conduct may of course also be explained by clever public relations, especially as reputational damage control has been another of Global Financial Crisis's enduring legacies for the banking sector. Alternatively, *ex ante* cooperation with the government may work in the banks' favour given the rising likelihood of future bailouts once the economic crisis morphs into a financial crisis. Focusing, however, on the regulatory impact on bank management, this chapter explains the features of regulatory bank governance which reorient internal decision-making procedures to such outcomes. To this end, it outlines the features of the regulatory paradigm shift, which reflects the criticality and social functions of banking, actively blurring the distinction between the public (regulation) and the private (corporate) control. The chapter first revisits the narrative of the Global Financial Crisis caused by excessive risk-taking and governance failures. Second, the subsequent stages of the EU regulatory reform after the Global Financial Crisis are outlined as they were progressively more concerned with internal bank processes and governance, not just in the context of ongoing supervision, but also in the context of the forward-looking crisis prevention mechanisms (resolution). I then go on to identify the core features of bank governance and explain their impact on ongoing operation of banks. The final section of the chapter discusses the implications of the paradigm shift triggered by the new regulatory technique from the perspective of two specific explicitly pursued goals of regulators – limiting the concept of 'too big to fail' and breaking the excessive co-dependence of banks and sovereigns in the vicious doom loop.

Bank governance failures caused the crisis

Many accounts of the origins of the Global Financial Crisis point to the faulty governance of financial institutions, which resulted in the excessive risk-taking that led to the crisis (Ferrarini 2017). Implicit guarantees on banks' activities and misaligned incentives of the individual bankers meant that risk was not properly factored into the banks' activities, with the prevailing assumption that the sector could (as a whole) externalize any downside of its activities onto the public purse. Further shortcomings included misaligned compensation incentives, insufficient board monitoring of risk-taking by the firm and overly complex organizational structures which impeded informed business management. The consequences of such a framework for moral hazard have been broadly discussed since (Ueda and Weder di Mauro 2013; Allen et al. 2015; Haentjens and Wessels 2015: ch Conclusions; Ramos Muñoz and Lamandini 2016: 805).

As a result of such market and regulatory failures, bank behaviour and policies not only failed to properly account for negative externalities, but also did not properly account for the underlying risk of the activities pursued. Though numerous other factors led to the Global Financial Crisis (e.g. misguided economic policies, absence of crisis management tools, insufficient bank capitalization, excessive concentration of risk in unregulated market segments), much of the global reform in the aftermath of the crisis was focused on reducing incentives for risk-taking. As the next section discusses, the new regulatory requirements span capital, liquidity, structural or disclosure and are complemented by an expanded scope of responsibilities for bank boards for risk management as well as the widened role of the supervisors and other public authorities.

EU regulatory reform delves into the core of bank activity

In the EU, the regulatory reform after the Global Financial Crisis was progressively more concerned with internal bank processes and governance, not just in the context of ongoing supervision (micro-prudential regulation), but also in that of forward-looking resolution law (macroprudential regulation). In the flurry of new legislative activity, five distinct stages of reform in EU bank regulation can be identified: (a) the calibration of EU state aid rules to the banking sector (2008–10); (b) the first EU institutional reform (2010); (c) the first substantive bank regulation reform (CRD IV/BRRD) (2010–14); (d) the creation of the Banking Union and the second institutional reform (2013–18); and (e) the second substantive bank regulation reform (CRD V/BRRD 2) (2016–19).

Once the Global Financial Crisis struck in 2008, both the regulators and the banks themselves faced a lack of adequate cross-border instruments to govern the fallout. Specifically, there were no prescribed crisis-management procedures and uncertainty as to the respective roles of institutions prevailed – for example, as to the extent to which the ECB is the Eurozone's lender of last resort. Among the prevailing uncertainty, EU state aid competition rules were the only instrument at the disposal of European Commission and the member states to provide for some coordination in crisis management. These rules, established by the EU Treaties, required that any bank bailout be in line with the common rules. Since 2009 the European Commission adopted almost 500 ad hoc decisions allowing for aid to over 100 individual banks. These included €671 billion in capital and repayable loans and €1,288 billion in guarantees. The decisions included restructuring and orderly resolution of more than 100 European banks (Adamczyk and Windisch 2015). In the absence of specialized crisis-management rules, such as a resolution regime, the control exercised by the European Commission became increasingly more detailed, and also concerned banks' conduct (Laprévote et al. 2017). Problems of moral hazard arising from the distorted incentives of bank managers were tackled directly through the commitments required for a given bank bailout to be approved. Such conditions required (for example) a ban on dividends for banks receiving public support and restrictions on bank marketing. Burden-sharing and loss absorption by shareholders and debt-holders was required prior to receiving state aid (Smoleńska 2020).

In the second phase of reform, marginal adjustments were made to the pre-existing EU rules (e.g. greater coverage of depositor guarantees was introduced). In 2010, new EU agencies, including the European Banking Authority (EBA) and European Systemic Risk Board (ESRB), were created to facilitate the convergence and exchange of information across the EU. These new bodies, which are effectively secretariats for networks of national supervisors, were then tasked with developing the technical standards to be followed by national supervisors. Such agencies remained advisory in nature, however, with virtually no direct powers over banks.

The third stage of the reform, which introduced the backbone of the new bank governance regime, was put in place in 2013 and 2014. It consisted of the new capital rules (Capital Requirements Directive, CRD and Regulation, CRR) and the new framework for bank crisis prevention and management (Bank Recovery and Resolution Directive, BRRD). These new substantive rules applicable to the whole of the EU market were established to restore stability, safety and soundness of the banking system (the macro-dimension) and individual institutions (the micro-dimension). Though the core of CRD IV package and BRRD largely draws on the frameworks developed at the global level, namely by the Basel Committee in the case of the credit requirements and by the Financial Stability Board (FSB) for the resolution law, adaptation to the European context was required. As a result of the infusion of global standards with EU law principles, a bespoke bank governance regime was established, however. The substantive EU law framework developed in 2013–14 specifically laid down the foundations of a complex and multipronged regime for public intervention in the bank sector.

The main objectives of EU prudential rules are to improve the stability and resilience of the banking system and individual institutions by strengthening capital regulation, liquidity regulation and restrict certain activities., thus creating a level playing field across countries. Further, these laws seek to strengthen banks' corporate governance arrangements to better align the incentives of the bank management (e.g. introducing a 'fit-and-proper' test for directors) as well as to regulate bank conduct. In addition, the new tool of macroprudential policy creates a framework for addressing the stability of the banking sector as whole, the logic being that the instruments needed to tackle failures and risk associated with individual credit institutions differ from those required when the system as a whole is considered (e.g. in the context of build-up of asset bubbles). To this end, macroprudential policy is aimed at identifying, monitoring and addressing systemic risk, taking into account the financial cycle as well as the direction and scale of cross-border capital flows. In many jurisdictions these tasks are delegated to the central bank.

The novel resolution law is a set of rules and procedures for dealing with failing banks under the BRRD as a variant of such a macroprudential, systemic approach. Following the G20's Financial Stability Board principles for effective resolution (2014), BRRD establishes rules to ensure the continuity of bank's critical functions after it has failed, the protection of insured depositors, and a rapid return of segregated clients' assets, an allocation of losses in a way which is not more costly to shareholders and creditors than the alternative of insolvency. Also the moral hazard related to implicit subsidies is limited and the unnecessary destruction of value is avoided.

This framework seeks to ensure that crises are prevented and managed. As an approach, resolution first emerged in the context of the Asian financial crisis of the 1990s, where the lesson drawn from the multiple bank failures was that the regulators need specific tools to act countercyclically, that is to prevent the build-up of risks not just in a particular credit institution, but in the system as a whole (Crockett 1997).

The goal of the new policy is therefore to furnish the authorities with direct tools to take over the management of a bank once a crisis occurs with the view to protect the public interest, the bank's critical functions to the real economy and financial stability. Such rules are needed as an uncontrolled failure of a bank due to – for example – its insolvency, wreaks havoc on the entire financial system and comes at a high social cost and with a significant destruction of value in the economy.

Further the policy aims to curtail moral hazard by enhancing market discipline and creating incentives for market solutions to be adopted as an alternative to taxpayer bailouts. New regulatory requirements also include provisions for greater internal loss-absorption known as bail-in, by anticipating a contribution from the creditors of the bank, including in some cases the subordinated creditors, to the costs of bank resolution before other safety nets – including public funds – are resorted to. This is intended to bolster the monitoring of the bank by creditors, in addition to the shareholders. Resolution laws therefore aim to enable restructuring or liquidation of financial institutions in an orderly manner, limiting contagion effects in the financial system, and decreasing taxpayers' exposure to losses from bailouts, while maintaining continuity of banks' critical economic functions. In a cross-border context they seek to ensure the speed, transparency and predictability of the resolution process as well as exchange of information and cooperation between responsible authorities. As a result of such rules, a bank's market exit in crisis is to be made 'safe'. While the efficiency, or indeed the ability, of these provisions to achieve their ambitious goals has been widely debated, resolution law already impacts bank's operation outside of crisis.

Specific regulatory requirements are put in place to ensure that a bank is resolvable, and that is that it can fail (Huertas 2014). This is achieved through building up the *ex ante* resilience of banks through contingency planning or the preparation of so-called 'living wills' detailing the course of action should a bank be faced with a deteriorating financial situation. Such contingency preparation is considered to better align the incentives of bank management, which translates into a better internalization of the possible systemic costs of failure. The changed time horizon of regulatory intervention and the enlarged toolkit of public authorities marks the third phase of the crisis reform.

In the fourth stage of EU law reform, the focus shifted again to institutional matters, not least as this period (2013–14) coincided with the peak of the sovereign crisis in a number of Eurozone member states, a crisis which was inherently linked to bank oversight shortcomings (Sandbu 2017). With the creation of the European Banking Union (EBU) the responsibility for direct oversight over significant credit institutions in the Eurozone was conferred on the ECB (via the Single Supervisory Mechanism) and for the crisis prevention and management on a new EU agency, the Single Resolution Board (via the Single Resolution Mechanism). These authorities were granted far-reaching powers of direction vis-à-vis the supervised banks.

The final stage of the reform of EU banking regulation, which can still be perceived as a consequence of the Global Financial Crisis, has been the revision of the rulebook developed in the previous stages. Amendments to the prudential rules (CRR 2 and CRD 5) and resolution law (BRRD 2 and SRM 2) rulebook approved in 2019 cover new rules on risk governance, net stable funding ratio and a leverage ratio in line with international Basel standards for credit institutions. New rules introduced greater variability and proportionality into the banking regulation regime. Among the novel elements were new rules on the Environmental and Social Governance (ESG) aspects of bank activity, including as a measure of supervisory assessment. Such a shift marks a further step into the regulation of internal governance of bank's operations, which is indeed the principal hallmark of the new regime.

As a result of the ensemble of the ongoing reform at EU level, coupled with national policies and domestic implementations of the new rules, a granular rulebook for the banking sector operating in the internal market was established, one which was not merely concerned with the liberalization and opening-up of markets (Teixeira 2017). The focus is now placed on how banks behave, operate and essentially take decisions in the post-Global Financial Crisis world. The proliferation of new authorities at national, Eurozone and EU level created an extensive network of public bodies with either direct powers over bank behaviour or rule-making and standard-setting powers. Specific features of the ensemble of the new regime allow to identify bank governance as a distinct regulatory method which prevailed after the Global Financial Crisis.

Bank governance as a regulatory method

The new set of EU rules governing banking across the internal market, as described above, seeks to produce effects on the way decision-making within banks, as private entities, takes place. As a result, such rules mark a departure from a liberalizing regime oriented at creating an internal market for banking activity, towards a more positive integration regime. As a regulatory method of governance, the framework blurs the traditional line between what is understood as regulation, inherently public in nature, and what is perceived to be restricted to the sphere of private autonomy, namely corporate governance. Before reviewing the specific combinations of the new rules which lead to such an outcome, it is worth recalling the significance of the regulation – corporate governance distinction.

Regulation is generally understood as the set of public rules oriented at rectifying a given market failure or at facilitating a specific outcome considered desirable. Such rules are to be complied with as a matter of law, under the spectre of sanctions or other enforcement measures by the legitimate public authorities. Regulation understood in such terms remains external to the decision-making processes of the regulated entities.

Corporate governance meanwhile denotes the 'structure of rights and responsibilities' of various stakeholders to the extent these determine the way in which the company is controlled and operated (Wright et al. 2013: 23). Since the seminal work of Jensen and Meckling (1976), the primary concern of corporate governance, also in an economic perspective, has been shareholder protection (Kraakman et al. 2009; Deakin 2011). One of the ways of conceiving the distinction between regulation and corporate governance is seeing the former as determining the outer limit of the choice of a company, and the latter as guiding the choices within it. However, given the scope of the new EU banking sector rulebook, this distinction no longer appears to hold. In particular, given the aims of EU bank regulation and the specific features of its procedures, it is more appropriate to use the term 'bank governance', which undermines the dichotomies of public-private as well as regulation-corporate governance.

Some scholars have argued against such an approach as it blurs the lines between internal/external governance and may as a result obfuscate the interest in which the management of the company is to act, and therefore accountability (Wymeersch et al. 2012). However, it has long been argued that in terms of constraints of corporate governance, banking has always been somewhat particular not least given the special protection awarded to depositors (Marcinkowska 2014; Armour 2016). Further, given the role of public backstops in underpinning financial activity as well as expanding the money creation function of banking, Theory of Finance literature argues that hybridity (public-private nature) is an essential feature of contemporary financial systems (Pistor 2019). In this context, a growing infusion of private relationships with public interest has been identified, both in general terms, as a strengthened mandatory role of boards in risk management and assuring adequate controls (Gordon 2018), as well as specifically for bank boards (Grundmann 2015; Grundmann et al. 2017).

Consequently, whereas the pre-crisis regime of EU bank regulation was characterized by rigid jurisdictional lines and dichotomies, the new regime boasts transnational features and requires governance to be conceptualized as a joint feat of public and private actors under an institutional framework serving multiple stakeholder interests. Specifically, in addition to protecting shareholders and other stakeholders of the bank (depositors, creditors), the new regime places the public functions of the bank (critical functions, public interest in financial stability) at its core. Such a holistic approach appears to contribute to attainment of regulatory objectives, such as reducing bank volatility (Srivastav and Hagendorff 2016).

Five features of the new EU bank regulations allow to identify the hybrid bank governance regime, namely: (a) scope of regulatory objectives pursued by the regulation; (b) scope of directors' duties introduced; (c) scope of the powers granted to the public authorities; (d) rule granularity and institutional set-up; and (e) a specific concern with cross-border situations.

Broad scope of regulatory objectives pursued by bank regulation

First, the overall thrust of the post-Global Financial Crisis reform has introduced greater heterogeneity, but also greater concern with broader public goods, among the objectives of public intervention in the banking sector. Previously, the prudential regulations were predominantly focused on the safety and soundness and generic depositor protection, with an arms-length approach by the authorities. These objectives are reproduced under the new rules, but broader considerations are also included as regards financial stability. For example, the BRRD aims to ensure the continuity of the supervised institutions' critical functions in order to prevent contagion during periods of crisis, to protect public funds by minimizing reliance on extraordinary public financial support and to protect specific stakeholder groups (depositors, investors, client funds and assets) (Gortsos 2019).

Such objectives are much clearer than was the case pre-reform, as far as the function of banking they seek to protect is concerned, namely the critical functions, to the extent these are essential to the proper operation of the real economy (e.g. financing the real economy, financing SMEs). Following the onset of the Global Financial Crisis, scholars became more concerned with articulating the precise social value of finance, both in negative terms (high cost of bailouts) as well as positive (i.e. continuation of bank lending as an essential precondition for recovery) (Bernanke 1983; Zingales, 2015; Cerutti and Claessens 2017). Thus, though concerns about financial stability are not new for regulators in the financial sector (Diamond and Dybvig 1983; Swoboda and Portes 1987; Padoa-Schioppa 2005), the growing financialization of developed economies, as well as the increasing role of private debt in creating value has accentuated the need to refine the thinking about banking regulation beyond concerns about means of payment and (internal) stability of the financial system (Streeck 2011; Hockett and Omarova 2015). The new scope of regulatory objectives has permeated the obligations imposed on bank management, which – in the aftermath of the crisis – is required to integrate considerations of systemic impact of their activity in the daily operations of the bank.

Broad scope of directors' duties

The second feature is the new set of rules applicable to bank management teams, which goes beyond a mere regulatory requirement to be complied with and seeks to guide and influence how decisions within the bank are taken, that is their corporate governance. The scope of directors' duties is expanded – in line with the broadened regulatory objectives – to encompass the maintenance of (overall financial) stability. For example, Article 88 CRD IV requires that effective and prudent management of the institutions take due consideration of the broader macroeconomic context. Resolution rules meanwhile, further require such systemic stability considerations to be included in the crisis contingency planning. Embedding bank management in broader system considerations is one element assessed to meet the regulatory requirement of resolvability of the bank.

Such new 'public' duties imposed on bank directors interfere with the prevailing shareholder value paradigm and with the private relationships between bank management and the shareholders, thereby providing one example of the radical change of the scope of directors' action, which marks a departure from general company law and corporate governance.

To the extent that mandatory requirements are formulated with respect to risk management, they affect the core of company administration. Such regulatory effects blur – as anticipated – the line between what are the regulatory requirements and what is the corporate governance in the bank. Such an effect is reinforced by the broadened powers of the authorities to interfere in bank management decisions.

Broad scope of authorities' powers

A third feature of the new regime arises in the context of the broadened powers of the regulators, legitimated by the broadened regulatory objectives under EU law. Specifically, the new rulebook espouses a logic whereby the overriding public interest allows for interference with the general right to freedom to conduct business. Since the principal reason for the regulation after the Global Financial Crisis has been to re-align banks' risk-taking approaches, new microprudential regulations introduce specific governance processes (resolution planning, supervisory review) which affect bank behaviour and introduce reflexivity between public authority action and going-concern decisions of the management. Supervisors and resolution authorities at EU and national levels after the reform have acquired special discretion to calibrate the requirements to fully take into account the specific banking model and bank structure of the supervised entity.

The powers of resolution authorities responsible for ensuring banks are resolvable in crisis and for minimizing the costs of one should it occur, are particular in this regard. In the first place, resolution under the BRRD allows for a complete takeover of bank operations in a crisis. The rules create an administratively managed reorganization procedure for banks, which can lead either to restoration of viability or liquidation, as well as for crisis prevention tools, that is *ex ante* recovery and resolution planning. Resolution proper means that the resolution authority takes over the management of the bank with a view to using resolution tools to achieve its objectives. Such authorities – once specific triggers of failure are met – have the power to take control of an institution and exercise all the rights and powers of shareholders. They have at their disposal the special bank-funded resources like the Single Resolution Fund (Smoleńska 2019) created to ensure there are sufficient resources available to finance this process. Moreover, resolution authorities have competences to intervene and guide the behaviour of cross-border banks through ongoing oversight with view of attaining specific objectives. This occurs in the normal bank operations already, when banks must prepare their living wills, and where – in cases where the resolution authorities are not fully happy with bank's decisions – they may impose sanctions for non-compliance with the requirements, such as the prohibition of certain distributions, such as dividends.

The intimate relationship between bank management and the public authorities (and the ECB in particular) is marked not only by regulatory compliance and verification but as well variants of moral suasion and flexibility in the regulatory relationship (through so-called 'guidance'), making the disentangling between business and supervisory difficult. Consequently, the broad and incisive duties of the public authorities reinforce the hybridity of bank governance post-reform as identified above.

Rule granularity and institutional set-up

The fourth feature of EU bank governance relates to how the rules are made; that is, their progressively more granular nature through implementing and delegating acts developed by EU agencies. The granularity achieved through the Single Rulebook developed in such a way makes the regime a highly prescriptive one, thereby ensuring that the bank governance objectives – such as the increased co-responsibilities of bank management for the public interest – do not leave much leeway for interpretation. Bank governance therefore does not merely cover the specific corporate governance regime developed under secondary EU law, but the ensemble of rules and prerogatives of supervisory and resolution authorities developed at the tertiary level to intervene and guide the behaviour of banks, also in areas traditionally conceived of in terms of autonomy of the business enterprise.

The governance impact of rule granularity is reinforced by the institutional set-up. New EU banking regulations are applied by multiple authorities – supervisors, resolution authorities, macroprudential bodies and central banks at national, Eurozone and EU levels. While creating a rather complex regime, with ample space for bureaucratic politics and contestation, it likewise necessitates broad acceptance and ownership of the granular rules implemented by the authorities and bank management. This is particularly the case for cross-border situations.

A more prominent cross-border dimension of EU regulation

A final feature of the new EU bank regulation regime, which marks the shift towards bank governance substituting the pre-existing liberal regime, is the new concern with the internal organization of banks – including their cross-border activity – as a matter of prudential rules.

Crucially, this does not concern only the so-called Volcker Rule and its variants separating investment banking from retail activity (Gordon and Ringe 2015; Carr 2015), but rather the structural complexity and cross-border operation, which became the object of detailed bank regulation.

Since the Global Financial Crisis, complexity has been considered as a new risk factor, in particular where over the course of the crisis there was a lack of reliable information allowing to adequately assess and manage bank's activities which in turn increased the costs of failure. Academic scholarship supported this approach. Carmassi and Herring (2016) consider that complexity impedes proper governance of banks' activities where it prevents adequate capitalization and makes supervisory action ineffective in constraining risk-taking (in particular where there are no specific international arrangements, for example, for the exchange of information). Likewise, the lack of congruence between business and legal lines prevents the salvaging of a going-concern value once a crisis materializes. In the aftermath of the Global Financial Crisis, EU bank regulation increasingly treats opaqueness in banks' organization as a matter of supervisory concern, and responds to this risk inter alia by increasing the transparency of internal organization through specific reporting requirements. Further, complexity in banking is not only just a matter of informational asymmetries between parties. New crisis prevention requirements under EU resolution law increasingly differentiate between integrated (single bank) and (cross-border) bank group situations, prescribing different procedures, as a means of facilitating better governance and cooperation between authorities at national and EU levels.

To this end, the reform strengthened cooperation at EU level by creating new EU agencies (European Supervisory Authorities) and establishing a dedicated structure for cooperation between national authorities ('colleges') for the oversight of cross-border bank groups operating within the EU (Lintner 2017; FinSAC 2019). Through this regime, authorities at home and host level acquire new prerogatives vis-à-vis the supervised bank. In so doing, it lays down the foundations for a model of cooperation between authorities which seeks to preclude the benefits of ring-fencing within cross-border groups, and therefore to facilitate cross-border bank activity also in crisis.

The five features identified here have broadened the scope of objectives of EU banking regulation, including the duties for directors and supervisors, and blended the line between the public and private activities creating a hybrid regime. Such a new bank governance-oriented regulatory method in the EU supranational jurisdiction context is further underpinned by a detailed and granular rulebook, increasingly concerned with cross-border entities. Such features of bank governance mark a departure from the pre-crisis regime oriented towards market-opening and liberalization and accordingly make the greater embeddedness of the banking activity in public interest through bank governance a notable legacy of the Global Financial Crisis reforms.

Bank governance before a new crisis

This chapter has shown that though we may be far from being able to fully assess the legacy of the Global Financial Crisis, in regulatory terms it has led to the emergence of a novel EU regulatory technique – bank governance as a tool for ensuring financial stability and protection of critical bank functions.

Such a regulatory technique was developed through subsequent reforms from 2008 onwards and can be identified through its features relating to the scope of objectives pursued, the duties of bank managers and supervisors, high rule granularity and an institutional set-up tailored to cross-border (EU) banking.

Bank governance emerged as a result of efforts to curtail the shortcomings of the pre-crisis regime, in particular with respect to the moral hazard problems it raised. By improving the decision-making and re-aligning the incentives, the objective was to break the excessive tendency of banks to shift their negative externalities onto the public purse. Likewise, by looking to bank complexity, structure and resolvability, EU legislators had hoped to diminish the scope of too-big-to-fail problems. Early evidence suggests that the new regulation has indeed changed somewhat bank culture – more and more banks refer to their social functions and engage in ESG. As already noted earlier, in the face of the economic turmoil caused by the 2020 pandemic, banks appeared to take responsibility (and action) for stability. EU governments have relied extensively on banks to distribute the guarantees and crisis loans to businesses, making lenders the transmission mechanism for public aid (Crow et al. 2020). The ECB, the Eurozone's bank supervisor and monetary authority, further utilizes the banking infrastructure to stabilize the economic situation. Such an increased interdependence between supervisory and bank management decision-making in the EU may in the long-term jeopardize the goals of the new regime, especially as financial troubles and corporate insolvencies materialize (Perotti 2020) and sovereigns become increasingly indebted to pay for the economic stimulus.

References

Adamczyk, G., and B. Windisch. 2015. 'State Aid to European Banks: Returning to viability'. *Competition State Aid Brief*, 1–7.

Allen, F. et al. 2015. 'Moral Hazard and Government Guarantees in the Banking Industry'. *Journal of Financial Regulation* 1 (1): 30–50.

Armour, J. 2016. 'Bank Governance'. In J. Gordon and W.-G. Ringe (eds), *The Oxford Handbook of Corporate Law and Governance*, 1–27. Oxford: Oxford University Press.

Bernanke, B. 1983. 'Nonmonetary Effects of the Financial Crisis in the Propagation of the Great Depression'. *The American Economic Review* 73 (3): 257–76.

Carmassi, J., and R. Herring. 2016. 'The Corporate Complexity of Global Systemically Important Banks'. *Journal of Financial Services Research* 49 (2–3): 175–201.

Carr, A. 2015. 'Bank structural reform: Too big to fail, too big to save and too complex to manage, supervise and resolve?' In M. Haentjens and B. Wessels (eds.), *Research Handbook on Crisis Management in the Banking Sector*. Cheltenham: Edward Elgar Publishing.

Cerutti, E., and S. Claessens. 2017. 'The great cross-border bank deleveraging: Supply constraints and intra-group frictions'. *Review of Finance* 21 (1): 201–36.

Crockett, A. 1997. 'The Theory and Practice of Financial Stability'. *Essays in International Finance*: 203.

Crow, D., S. Morris and L. Noonan. 2020. 'Will the coronavirus crisis rehabilitate the banks?' *Financial Times*, 1 April 2020.

Deakin, S. 2011. 'Corporate governance and financial crisis in the long run'. CBR Research Programme on Corporate Governance.

Diamond, D.W., and P.H. Dybvig. 1983. 'Bank Runs, Deposit Insurance, and Liquidity Douglas'. *Journal of Political Economy* 24 (1): 14–23.

Ferrarini, G. 2017. 'Understanding the Role of Corporate Governance in Financial Institutions: A Research Agenda'. ECGI Law Working Paper Nr 347/2017.

Financial Stability Board. 2014. 'Key Attributes of Effective Resolution Regimes for Financial Institutions'. Basel: Financial Stability Board.

FinSAC. 2019. *Banking Supervision and Resolution in the EU: Effects on Small Host Countries in CEE and SEE*. Washington, D.C: World Bank Group.

Gordon, J., and W.-G. Ringe. 2015. 'Bank resolution in Europe: The unfinished agenda of structural reform'. In D. Busch and G. Ferrarini, *European Banking Union*. Oxford: Oxford University Press.

Gordon, J. 2018. 'Convergence and Persistence in Corporate Law and Governance'. In J. Gordon and W.-G. Ringe (eds), *The Oxford Handbook of Corporate Law and Governance*. Oxford: Oxford University Press.

Gortsos, C. 2019. 'The Evolution of European (EU) Banking Law under the Influence of (Public) International Banking Law: A Comprehensive Overview'. SSRN Working Paper.

Gortsos, C.V. 2015. 'The crisis-based European Union financial regulatory intervention: are we on the top of the prudential wave?' *ERA Forum* 16 (1): 89–110.

Grundmann, S. 2015. 'The Banking Union Translated into (Private Law) Duties: Infrastructure and Rulebook'. *European Business Organization Law Review* 16 (3): 357–82.

Grundmann, S., C.-A. Petit and A. Smoleńska. 2017. 'Bank Governance.' In F. Barrière (ed.), *Le traitement des difficultés des établissements bancaires et institutions financières: approche croisée*. Paris: LexisNexis.

Haentjens, M., and B. Wessels. 2015. *Research Handbook on Crisis Management in the Banking Sector*. Cheltenham: Edward Elgar Publishing.

Hockett, R.C., and S.T. Omarova. 2015. 'Public Actors in Private Markets: Toward a Developmental Finance State.' *Washington University Law Review* 93: 103–75.

Huertas, T F. 2014. *Safe to Fail: How Resolution Will Revolutionise Banking*. Basingstoke: Palgrave Macmillan.

Jackson, H.E., and S.L. Schwarcz. 2020. 'Pandemics and Systemic Financial Risk.' SSRN Working Paper.

Jensen, M.C., and W.H. Meckling. 1976. 'Theory of the firm: Managerial behaviour, agency costs and ownership structure.' *Journal of Financial Economics* 3 (4): 305–60.

Kraakman, R.H. et al., ed. 2009. *The Anatomy of Corporate Law: A Comparative and Functional Approach*. 2nd ed. Oxford: Oxford University Press.

Laprévote, F.-C., J. Gray and F. De Cecco. 2017. *Research Handbook on State Aid in the Banking Sector*. Cheltenham: Edward Elgar Publishing.

Lintner, P. 2017. 'De/centralized Decision Making Under the European Resolution Framework: Does Meroni Hamper the Creation of a European Resolution Authority?' *European Business Organization Law Review* 18 (3): 591–616.

Marcinkowska, M. 2014. 'Zasady ładu korporacyjnego dla banków.' *Zeszyty Naukowe Uniwersytetu Ekonomicznego w Krakowie* 10: 93–105.

Morris, S. 2020. 'Santander chairman Ana Botín to donate half of pay to virus fund.' *Financial Times*, 23 March.

Padoa-Schioppa, T. 2005. *Regulating Finance: Balancing Freedom and Risk*. Oxford: Oxford University Press.

Perotti, E. 2020. 'The coronavirus shock to financial stability.' VoxEU Blog post.

Pistor, K. 2019. *Code of Capital*. Princeton, NJ: Princeton University Press.

Ramos Muñoz, D., and M. Lamandini. 2016. *EU Financial Law: An Introduction*. Milanofiori Assago: Wolters Kluwer Italia.

Sandbu, M. 2017. *Europe's Orphan: The Future of the Euro and the Politics of Debt*. Princeton, NJ: Princeton University Press.

Smoleńska, A. 2019. 'SRB: Lost and found in the thicket of EU Banking Regulation.' In S. Grundmann and H. Micklitz (eds.), *The European Banking Union and Constitution: Beacon for Advanced Integration or Death-knell for Democracy*. Oxford: Hart Publishing.

Smoleńska, A. 2020. *Law and governance of EU cross-border bank groups after the Great Financial Crisis*, PhD thesis, European University Institute.

Smoleńska, A. 2021. 'EU bank regulation after the Great Financial Crisis: swinging the regulatory pendulum into a new paradigm.' In Y. Cassis and A. Drach (eds), *Financial Deregulation: A Historical Perspective*. Oxford: Oxford University Press.

Srivastav, A., and J. Hagendorff. 2016. 'Corporate Governance and Bank Risk-taking.' *Corporate Governance: An International Review* 24 (3): 334–45.

Streeck, W. (2011), 'The Crises of Democratic Capitalism.' *New Left Review*: 5–29.

Swoboda, A.K., and R. Portes, eds. 1987. *Threats to International Financial Stability*. Cambridge: Cambridge University Press.

Teixeira, P.G. 2017. 'The Legal History of the Banking Union.' *European Business Organization Law Review* 18 (3): 535–65.

Ueda, K., and B. Weder di Mauro. 2013. 'Quantifying structural subsidy values for systemically important financial institutions.' *Journal of Banking and Finance* 37 (10): 3830–42.

Wright, M. et al. 2013. *Oxford Handbook of Corporate Governance*. Oxford: Oxford University Press.

Wymeersch, E., K.J. Hopt and G. Ferrarini, eds. 2012. *Financial Regulation and Supervision: A Post-crisis Analysis*. Oxford: Oxford University Press.

Zingales, L. 2015. 'Does Finance Benefit Society?' Presidential Address to the American Finance Association.

12

From Sets of Rules to Codes of Conduct

Jacques Beyssade

So many things have changed in banking over the last ten years. The aim of this chapter is to share with you the main ones that I have observed as an executive involved in running a bank before, during and after the Global Financial Crisis.

I acted as the head of trading floors in New York during the years where the financial bubble grew, and this gave me an insider's view of the mechanism through which the Global Financial Crisis progressively built up. I was based in Asia, still running trading floors, when the crisis erupted and I could observe how its impact was significantly different in sound financial markets, such as most of the Asian ones, as opposed to more fragile markets, such as the United States. I was then hired by a large European bank to sort out the damage on its books and in getting through these experiences, I developed a cradle-to-grave view of this major crisis of the early twenty-first century.

Significant changes occurred in our environment

The most visible element in that respect comes from changes in the regulatory environment that we must deal with. Conventional wisdom is that in order to avoid the recurrence of another financial disaster, authorities around the world imposed stricter regulation on banks, mostly through the obligation to set aside a much larger amount of capital to care for potential issues arising from capital market operations. Beyond pure solvency ratios however, new fields have emerged as major topics for stricter regulation.

First, banks had to reduce the amount of leverage or leverage ratio by increasing equity and reducing assets, irrespective of whether these were risk weighted or not. Over the last ten years, these requirements had an impact on banks' net profits: once they recovered after the crisis's early losses, the bulk of these profits had to be set aside to enhance equity levels. As far as France is concerned, the accumulated equity stemming from this accumulation moved overall reserves from 4.2 per cent to 6 per cent of the total balance sheets. For several years, these regulatory requirements to increase capital levels have resulted in banks paying dividends at much lower levels than before and affecting, up to now, the valuation of financial institutions in general.

Banks also had to address liquidity, in terms of quality and maturity. The general attention to liquidity in banks came from the observation, constant in the long history of banking but nevertheless regularly forgotten, that whatever the specific problems in a bank, it always fails because of a liquidity crisis. The 'Lehman weekend' served as a wake-up call.

Since the Global Financial Crisis, deposits from customers in French banks have increased from 40 per cent to 47 per cent of total balance sheets while credit exposures have been stable at 44 per cent. In this process, the banks became net lenders to the ECB for significant cash cushions – at a cost that further impacted the valuation of banks.

Just as with solvency, this effort on liquidity made the banks much stronger, but it came at a cost and ironically the result is that stronger banks are worth less, as valued by the stock markets.

The last point about regulation is the development of resolution planning. Here again, the Lehman story serves as an example of what not to do. The 'days after the weekend before' or rather the weeks, months and years after September 2008, proved that resolving a bank, or in essence liquidating its assets and liabilities as intelligently as possible, was a very complex operation that would benefit from an element of advanced preparation.

Hence the regulations passed to prepare the case when supervisors should intervene and prevent one bank's failure from creating repercussions across the entire system. Even if resolution planning is a sensible thing to do, the deployment of staff and energy dedicated to this task, both at the supervisory level and within the banks subject to this exercise, is very unlikely to be commensurate with the risks one tries to cover. Trying to imagine all possible situations and prepare for them, especially when dealing with a global systemic bank, is likely to be both theoretical and useless when it is activated. A more streamlined approach and the availability of a few high-level transition managers, able to take over control in case of trouble, may well prove less costly and more effective.

It would be superficial, however, to attribute to regulation all the changes that have impacted the financial system worldwide after the global financial crisis. Beyond the regulatory elements, several other changes on the business front have created new constraints.

The digitization of the financial industry's competitive landscape is certainly the most tangible one for all our customers. It is a technological change that has rapidly resulted in a significant number of newcomers entering the marketplace to compete with long-established financial institutions. The combination of much cheaper computer power and an exponential growth in available data opened the gates of the previously closed financial markets. This technological revolution could only be beneficial to consumers, including consumers of financial services, and was encouraged in Europe through the introduction of Payment Services Directive 2 (PSD2). It must be said that a consequence of these changes that goes beyond the arrival of new entrants on the financial services market, is also a progressive change in the behaviour of consumers of financial services. In addition to new competitors, existing customers of well-established institutions have forced them to shift to new ways of operating, challenging old habits as well as recurring profits.

The second change that has affected financial institutions in the Eurozone and elsewhere quite differently is the very low level of euro interest rates, which has lasted for a much longer period than in other western economies. It has resulted in an extremely high pressure on banks' commercial net interest margins. At the same time, commissions were reduced, mostly from competitive pressure by the newcomers surfing the digitization wave. Moreover, in several countries, margins and commissions were faced with a public backlash after admittedly improper treatment of some customers by banks that were more profit oriented than customer centred.

As a result, bank profits have decreased to some degree but have nevertheless proved resilient. Understanding this resilience to very challenging business conditions requires having a detailed look at banks' profit and loss statements. The impact is extremely visible on operating income levels, much less on net profit levels. This is entirely due to the cost of risk, the major factor influencing bank results in the short term, which currently stands at historically low levels, benefiting from the low level of interest rates. Although the correlation between the level of interest rates and the cost of risk is hard to measure precisely, it is quite obvious that servicing your debt is much easier when interest rates are close to zero than when they are at significant levels. Debt servicing in times of low interest rates, and abundant liquidity pushing most banks to finance or re-finance existing debts, is not an issue for borrowers, however fragile they may be.

All of these elements have resulted in banks adapting their business profiles including reducing expenses, increasing the proportion of fees as opposed to net interest income in revenues, revising overall the business models and aiming at keeping a very low cost of risk even in a cyclical downturn – as it seems clear that in the next financial crisis banks, with the current operating results, will not be able to resist similar cost of risks as ten years ago.

This change in the level of risks that banks can afford to take has led to heated discussions when International Financial Reporting Standard (IFRS9) standards were negotiated, or more recently in discussions about NPL provisioning, as the economy needs banks to take risks. Risks that are understood, obviously, managed and reported professionally, are necessary to fuel new ventures, support the development of existing operations and foster economic growth in general.

One common answer to these changes: 'just more'

It strikes me that such a major crisis as the Global Financial Crisis, coupled with game-changing technological evolutions, results in actions that are very much the same, having been applied over the preceding years and decades. Could it be that nobody did anything wrong, nothing has changed in the society around us, and therefore we should just have done a little bit more?

For example, just get hold of more capital both in terms of quantity and quality. The first general call, unanimously, has been for more capital, with the assumption that it is the best protection against potential losses. This has a mechanical consequence: the more equity you have, the lower your return on it. Obviously, the European model of financing, mostly through banks as opposed to capital markets, has been the most heavily penalized by this evolution: the Basel III finalization underlined this particular factor and was, overall, very beneficial to emerging countries' banks, neutral for US banks but detrimental to EU banks. This may be the result of long negotiations, where some actors get a better deal and others end up worse off, but let me come back to the basic question: is more capital, as detailed in the Basel III accord, a good protection? In other words, would the Global Financial Crisis that erupted with the subprime bubble have been avoided by such rules, had they been in place back then? I have not met anybody confidently saying so . . .

Another post-Global Financial Crisis response has been to obtain more solvency ratios. As I said, banks all started targeting more equity by accumulating profits and calling on investors in a frenzy of capital-raising. At the same time, profits are pushed downwards and investors have more attractive industries to look at – so we've moved from a logic of 'more equity to support my risk bearing business' to a logic of 'less risk with this equity' decreasing the balance sheets in order to improve solvency ratios. This is where microeconomics touches macroeconomics. When banks lend less, businesses invest less, and the economy slows down.

To some extent, banks can be substituted by other investors to support economic growth. Indeed, the European economy is more market oriented today in terms of financing than it was previously. The majority of financing still comes from banks but because banks have to reduce their balance sheet, because risk-taking is particularly penalized, we are moving away from our traditional model of banks financing the economy – a development that started in Florence at the time of the Medici when modern banking and modern accounting emerged. This model has dominated Europe since the fifteenth century; it failed but survived a few times since then. It is nowadays severely jeopardized by regulatory waves that placed specific constraints on banks. A part of the banks' role, still small but growing, be it in financing or in payments, is moving to unregulated players. Time will tell whether this has been a wise move, or whether an excessive regulatory focus on correcting banks' past mistakes unwillingly opened the door to less professional, more result oriented financial players.

Yet another outcome of the crisis was the idea to give more guarantees to the depositors, and more protection to the taxpayer. The post crisis backlash against banks was certainly fuelled by the losses incurred by depositors at some American and European banks. The fact that in several countries taxpayers were called not just to guarantee banks on a temporary basis, as was the case in France, but to absorb the losses of *any* failed institution, resulted in a public outcry. Parliaments and governments in democratic countries logically responded to their electorate's outrage and passed legislation in order to ensure that no banking crisis, or no financial crisis in general, should cost the taxpayer anything – and that customers' savings should be protected at all times. Beefing up deposit guarantee schemes at national level, or creating one at a supranational level like in the Eurozone, stems from this desire to protect customers, taxpayers and, critically, voters.

Many central banks – and more particularly the European Central Bank – have placed governance at the very forefront in their list of priorities. We should recognize that the boards of directors of financial institutions did a pretty poor job during the

Global Financial Crisis. It would be unfair to consider them to be the primary culprits in the mistakes that have been made, but they certainly did not perform their duty of oversight vis-à-vis management teams that made disastrous decisions. Governance is like a dam that should prevent major disasters, and governance did not work. This explains the requirements set by parliaments and regulators that all boards be better staffed, with people who both understand the financial markets and regulations, and are sufficiently determined and strong minded to efficiently challenge the top management of banks. This is not an easy goal to reach. I must confess that for a group of mutual banks and regional banks such as mine, it is a challenge to get such high level and powerful board members; but in general we have to recognize that the boards of banks today are much stronger than they were ten years ago at the time of the Global Financial Crisis.

And finally, more pressure by consumer groups. Consumer protection organizations are very demanding of banks. They were extremely hard on the industry ten years ago, sometimes with good reason. They are even stronger nowadays with the proliferation of populist movements which, together with the development of social media networks (Twitter and the like), offer any critical voice a worldwide platform and increased visibility. We see here a real change in our operating environment: reputation is something that all banks pay attention to. Cheaper bank services and less stringent loan criteria demanded by social media, are themes that across Europe, populist movements, including the fast-growing populist parties, embrace to rally potential voters, thereby putting an additional pressure on banks. Reputation is something volatile and prone to manipulation but essential in running a business. For banks, whose strength relies on the trust that depositors put in them, it is vital. In France, however, the level of popular trust in banks is back to levels last seen before the Global Financial Crisis.

Looking at the demands from European (EBA, ESMA, EIOPA) as well as global regulators, I have a feeling that there is some competition between them, as we have seen in the recent discussion around NPLs where a common position among the many stakeholders in terms of regulation has been hard to find. In addition, beyond regulators, we should not forget the supervisors who are constantly controlling us are increasingly moving from a very qualitative kind of supervision, at least in the southern part of Europe, to a much more quantitative approach. They rely less on on-site inspections and more on massive data collection, deep dives, specific reports requesting huge amounts of information in a very short time, along with issuing a suite of recommendations to be implemented in an equally short time. This brings us to the point where sometimes banks are spending more time answering regulatory questions than managing risks.

One important development arising from all of these public authorities telling the banks how to run our businesses (presumably better than in the past, and certainly better than many of our public institutions) is the focus on risk management itself – and in particular the demands to better link discussions on risk appetite with discussions around business models, budgets or strategic decisions. The control frameworks that have been implemented in banks around risk appetite, for instance, but also in supervisory practices via supervisory reviews like the Supervisory Review and Evaluation Process (SREPs), make a lot of sense. They force banks to focus on key risk areas.

At BPCE, a single risk mapping of all risks, including operational risk maps, compliance or reputational risks, is performed. This risk mapping considers the overall environment in which the bank transacts its business and the strengths or weaknesses of the current organisation, notably the control framework. This master risk map, which encompasses all of the more detailed risks, feeds into our risk appetite discussions, which are based on the materiality of such risks and also ties into our internal control framework in terms of permanent control but also periodic control, i.e. audit.

More capital, more solvency, more liquidity buffers, more regulatory powers . . . is it all more of the same? I do believe something had to change, and hopefully one thing has, and drastically: namely behaviour.

The most important issue for me, as Chief Risk Officer and Chief Compliance Officer, is to pay attention to the behaviour of our staff. Rules are important, of course, but they are only helpful if they are followed. Let us take a step back, outside of banking, and look at what our societies do when we face a dramatic event – the collapse of a bridge, a mass murder, a terrorist attack, or the calamitous distribution of contaminated food. Typically, governments and parliaments respond with alacrity and address public health and safety concerns by enacting new regulation. Was the previous regulation too permissive? Usually not; it is more often the case that it was only half-implemented, partly forgotten, or simply bypassed. The root cause of such dramas is more often to be found in bad behaviour than in bad rules.

Once this is acknowledged, the next logical step of any authority is to focus on rule implementation. Hence the focus on the various control mechanisms and the proper staffing of control functions. Let me just mention the increases in compliance staffing at HSBC and BNP Paribas, two large banks that came under the spotlight of regulators a few years ago. This focus on controls is particularly strong in the financial industry and has been theorized with the concept of 'three lines of defence'. The first line of defence should be the managers of whomever takes part in a transaction at a financial institution. Management is accountable for the actions of their teams and should, therefore, bear the primary responsibility for their staff following the rules. The second line of defence comprises people who are entirely devoted to controlling operations, on a permanent basis, hence their generic grouping under permanent control. In order to be really efficient, they have to be totally independent from the first line, and banking regulation all over the world has progressively imposed this type of organization, with Chief Risk Officers having to report to the CEOs or to the Boards of Directors, for instance, and never to a business line head. The third line of defence, independent from the first two, is devoted to periodic control. In other words, it does not control operations on an ongoing basis but on a case by case basis, usually linked to the level of risk perceived in each type of operation. This is the remit of internal audit teams.

What seems absolutely essential in this framework, long adopted by French banks and probably linked to their overall resilience in times of crisis, is to recognize that business lines are the real owners of the risk that they put on the books. This idea translates into two very important notions that are ingrained in our risk management practice:

- assumed risk: the amount of risk that you expect to take in line with your agreed risk appetite
- efficient interaction between first (those in business units) and second levels of control (those in risk departments)

Simply put, the overall control framework can only be efficient if there is, from the very beginning, a good first level of control within the business lines, under the full responsibility of the business managers. This explains the attention paid by regulators to the qualification and remuneration of front office personnel. Their knowledge of rules is checked, in many countries, by the requirement to have various types of licences before they can perform their role. Their personal alignment with the goals of their institutions is ensured by strict rules framing how much and how fast they can make money through specific transactions in a given year.

It all sounds fine, with progressive refinement in rules ensuring a better, more prudent, management of banks, but there remains, I believe, one complicating factor: the multiplication of rules, and the multiplication of procedures within a given institution, should not lead people to forget about their common goals – the basic principles that we have to follow and that we should remember every single minute of every single day in every single operation we do. This should translate, as a matter of good practice, into codes of conduct – or codes of ethics – with a particular attention to the culture that should be shared among the entire bank staff in terms of risk, in terms of compliance, and in terms of properly serving customers. Culture and control should go together:

- Culture is a matter of overarching principles, that everybody within an organization can understand, relate to, and turn to when in doubt. It comes from the top but should be shared with all staff, hence the necessity to keep it simple and general, but at the same time practical enough to relate to reality – using examples derived from real company cases is often a good way to make these general principles stick with operational staff.
- Control, on the other hand, is a matter of details that are specific to each job. It starts at the bottom, with every employee's tasks in what I described as the first line of defence, and it ends up at the top, with the CEO and the Board who must have a good control of the institution. For controls to work they have to be systematic, process related and, as far as possible, automatized.

At the crossroads between culture and control is compliance. This field has been an area of massive hiring in many banks, and often identified with control. The reality is, in my view, a bit different. Contrary to recurring definitions, compliance should be about respecting laws, regulations, and procedures but more fundamentally respecting the customers.

At the end of the day, customers are the ones who pay for all a company's costs. Start-up firms who raise equity regularly to grow operations around products that lose money should not forget it: in the long run, either customers are happy to pay for the products sold to them, or companies close down with angry investors having borne the weight of paying for unsuccessful ventures. In the long term, the interests of customers and those of investors are therefore more aligned than one may think, and of course quite coherent with the interests of employees and those of the company itself. Compliance, is therefore, all about caring for customers as the best long-term supporters of the company.

Rather than portraying compliance as a necessary burden the result of an ever-increasing string of laws, regulations, guidelines, recommendations and the like, which admittedly does not motivate staff very much, a more attractive way to develop it is to centre it on the means to keep and grow a bank's customer base. Everybody should more easily embrace such an ambition and realize that it is the best way to ensure the viability of the firm over the years. Having all staff understand this reasoning is where compliance touches culture – a set of large goals shared by all – and control – a series of detailed actions required to properly control operations and behaviours. Financial institutions who have understood this are obviously more likely to prosper and survive tough times, for customers' behaviour is always what can save or break a company in dire straits. A strong culture attracts and retains the staff. It also assists more effectively raising equity from long-term investors.

This applies to all companies operating in a competitive environment where customers are free to choose, but it is most significant for banks who rely so much on customers' confidence and by their very nature need a long-term relationship with them. Many of their products include a portion of risk that will or will not materialize over time. Today's sales results will only be measured at a later stage, unlike what is seen in many industries where future results are linked to future customers' behaviour, not past operations.

To sum up, as an executive involved in risk management from the beginning of the financial crisis, I have seen dramatic changes in regulation, supervision, consumer expectations, competition, human resources devoted to risk and compliance, data and artificial intelligence resources available to help us run our risks better, and sanctions catching the attention of our Boards of Directors and CEOs. But most importantly, I have seen positive and material changes in cultural behaviours.

What next?

One of the defining features of a crisis is that it happens when and where you did not expect it. This was the case with the Global Financial Crisis, which originated from an inventive financing system for home loans, that seemed very beneficial to people, that was part of the American dream, and that several countries even wanted to adopt in order to enable a large number of their citizens to own their homes. It will certainly be the same for the next financial crisis : it is unlikely to happen from the sudden burst of an asset price bubble (still thought by many CROs to be the most significant danger ahead of us) but it might come from a major cyberattack, a dramatic climate event, severe social unrest in a major economy, a health crisis affecting a continent, or the global escalation of a local military conflict, something that few people would seriously consider today to be a potential risk.

The COVID-19 crisis, with which we have now been living for over a year, provides a good example of how unprepared the financial industry is for dramatic events.

Nobody can be sure of its outcome and looking at past crises does not help identify future events. However, drawing lessons from the last big crisis can help us react appropriately to the next one, wherever and whenever it happens.

Among the lessons to be kept in mind, the role of individual behaviours is the first one. I have said that improper behaviours were behind the mismanagement of the otherwise safe home loan business and subsequent securitization in the years leading to 2008. Improper behaviour in another field, not necessarily a financial one, may well be at the source of the next crisis: improper behaviour of some industrial actors (such as the automotive or real estate fields) may create a string of bankruptcies or endanger human lives. Improper behaviour by some public officials (for instance in a highly indebted country) may be the trigger for a massive sovereign default. These are just scenarios intended to show how much disasters may find their source in human actions. On the other hand, behaviour can also be a critical factor in crisis management. The very different reactions of CEOs at major financial players in 2008 and 2009 largely explains why some of these institutions collapsed while others exited from the crisis stronger than ever.

In the case of COVID-19, while it is too early to assess whether improper human behaviour was at the origin of the problem, different government attitudes towards the crisis seem to explain the very different impacts observed in otherwise comparable countries.

Another lesson to be kept in mind is that money is not the only important issue when one tries to limit the damage. Having a plan, explaining it in clear terms, gathering support around it is just as important. It is obviously more difficult to repair the economy than to break it, and such repair requires many hands. An essential success factor resides therefore in aligning all possible actors in the crisis management effort: at a bank's level, or for that matter at any company's level, the staff has to be aligned with the corporate goals, the corporate goals have to serve the interest of the customers, these interests have to be coherent with all the other stakeholders, be they public or private. Once this alignment is assured, money can come and be put to good use. Otherwise, it is just a waste of resources.

A final point must be made when trying to prepare (not predict) for the next crisis. As explained earlier, banks and many other financial institutions have very significantly changed since 2008. One striking improvement is their strength, measured in terms of solvency or liquidity. Nobody disputes that.

The first consequence, evidenced in the COVID-19 crisis response, is that banks are no longer likely to be the origin of the next crisis and that the last ten years of regulatory and other measures have really strengthened the financial system.

The second consequence of the strengthening of financial institutions since 2008 is that they will be part of the solution to the COVID pandemic. Strong financial institutions are very necessary to enable the flow of money to continue, to channel resources from perennial savers (the individuals) to constant borrowers (the companies and, more and more, the governments) and to finance from their own funds all sorts of projects. These roles are essential in times where reconstruction work must be done, especially in the wake of COVID-19.

13

Risk Management and Corporate Governance

Laurence Bogni-Bartholmé

In the ten years following the Global Financial Crisis, banks' and financial institutions' balance sheets, liquidity and overall performance have greatly improved and strengthened, in part through the development of a more holistic risk management, material enhancements in risk and corporate governance and the embedding of a risk culture throughout the organization. In reviewing these developments, it is self-evident that much more needs to be done. The architecture of control needs to be further enhanced to sustain and strengthen the changes to risk management achieved to date and to ensure that the lessons learned from the crisis are not lost to the new generation of risk managers. This chapter is based on a practitioner's experience as an executive in a range of risk management and front-line roles in leveraged finance, corporate, commercial and asset-based lending as well as corporate and consumer credit in number of countries including the United States, Germany, Italy, France, The Netherlands and United Kingdom. It has been conceived primarily as a checklist of the principal advances in risk management and corporate governance achieved since the crisis, but also of the remaining challenges.

Developing a holistic approach to risk management

Pre-crisis, risk functions were mostly focused on credit risk and involved underwriting prospects, assessments of credit worthiness, developing cash-flow projections, performing portfolio monitoring of clients, and considering products and industry concentrations. It was not generally recognized, however, that most of the so called 'credit losses' had in fact operational, strategic or fraud-related root causes. Most of the risk teams were perceived (often for good reasons) as risk 'preventers' rather than safe business growth 'enablers'.

Following the Global Financial Crisis, the finance industry's focus has been on developing a risk universe and implementing specific risk programmes with business experts. Operational, strategic, financial, modelling and compliance risks have truly emerged as specific functions in addition to the traditional credit and market risk management. Developing operational risk management has been critical to strengthen processes and controls in the organizations. In particular, risk and control assessments, root-cause analyses, lessons-learned sessions, issues management and corrective actions have all helped to enhance risk and control processes, mitigate risk and support controlled growth.

Another change has been to hire risk managers from the first line functions with experience in managing incidents and recovering losses, who can support the function in understanding that risk is a business 'must have'.

Seven interrelated aspects of risk management have been developed: scenario analysis; capital risk management; liquidity risk management; strategic risk, modelling risk; compliance risk management; and financial crime risk.

First, scenario analysis. This mainly consists of forward-looking analyses leveraging past events to test future scenarios, with a focus on low probability/highly adverse impact events, and the inclusion of all functional leaders in the scenario workshops. Another key feature has been the evolution from contingency planning to full Recovery and Resolution Planning, driven by the EU's Bank Resolution and Recovery Directive (BRRD).

Second, capital risk management has been completely rethought, as regulatory capital requirements previously exceeded economic capital in most banks. To that effect, risk 'heat maps' with associated loss financial impact have been developed for all types of risk. They have helped to drive stronger risk mitigation and process improvements actions.

Third, liquidity risk management has been developed with calculations of future liquidity positions and the establishment of mainly regulatory-driven liquidity buffers. Liquidity monitoring has also been transferred from the Treasury function to Finance and Risk, to develop and adhere to proper segregation of duties principles.

Fourth, strategic risk has been developed with new product/initiative process and governance. A clear commercial benchmark has been set, measuring business performance against strategy and objectives, while M&A risk integration has been designed.

Fifth, modelling risk has expanded beyond straightforward credit scoring models and stress testing. Modelling activity has been designed to achieve business needs, including pricing, strategic planning and portfolio management. Decision science, big data and advanced analytics are opening new areas for more sophisticated models used in client relationship management, customer selection, Know Your Customers (KYC), and Anti-Money Laundering (AML) and fraud detection.

Compliance risk management is no longer limited to advising on regulations and avoiding penalties. It has been established even in non-regulated financial services. In many organizations, the function has now been incorporated into Risk. The function has therefore evolved to follow risk management processes, performing compliance risk control self-assessments (RCSAs), using risk management tools and techniques, setting their own risk appetite (or tolerance) levels and key risk indicators and recording the risk profile in the requisite registers.

And finally, enhanced financial crime risk programmes have been implemented in order to avoid the financing of terrorism and to prevent tax evasion and money laundering, but also to prevent fraud in order to protect customers and the integrity of the financial system.

Enhanced Risk and Corporate Governance

Before the crisis, Risk was an isolated function, not supported when looking forward and thinking outside the box. Fingers were often pointed at Risk for being merely a function raising problems or raising unlikely 'worst-case' scenarios. While risk analyses were performed with the associated metrics, there was no formal structured risk governance process and, in any case, it was not embedded in the overall organization.

The true risk-takers had neither formal risk framework and processes nor appropriate controls in place to report exposure and the level of risk being taken. The overall corporate governance was not documented with clear decision-making process and delegation and accountabilities were not sufficiently understood and quite often handed over to the risk managers. Pressure from management often led to compromises being made with respect to identified risks.

The post-crisis lessons learned, however, supported by regulatory obligations, have led to substantial improvements in controls and governance.

First, a practical risk appetite framework has been established, with a proper balance between quantitative metrics and qualitative assessments within the organization. This is now discussed and must be approved at board level and is embraced by the company executives as a key driver of strategic initiatives and decision-making.

A selection of meaningful risk metrics ('less is more' principle) have been combined with leading indicators that can provide an early warning of potential problems. It is essential here to monitor their trends and ensure that they can be calculated and reported in a timely manner. Associating risk-appetite metrics with the business' key performance indicators (KPIs) is the best way to ensure that financial institutions really embed risk appetite within their business strategy. Monitoring key risk indicators trends, ensuring they can be calculated and are reported in a timely manner, are critical success factors.

The risk identification step of risk frameworks has been strengthened and extended across all functions and is no longer limited to credit and underwriting areas. Using various techniques such as brainstorming sessions, workshops, interviews, questionnaires and so on has helped to ensure that many more risks (and potential processes issues) are identified.

The most optimized risk assessments also address both threats and opportunities. The development of risk tools to capture these risks identification has also been developed and most of the companies have now their proper risk registers.

Emerging risks and horizon scanning processes have also been implemented in most organisations. This has shifted the mindset to be much more externally focused when looking at our risk universe, and to ensure there is a proactive process to anticipate and respond to a threat before an event crystalizes.

Assessing the level of identified risks has also been a key milestone in developing enhanced risk management processes. This has helped to prioritize business response in accordance with their risk-appetite levels. Credit and market risks assessments were already well established and mostly focused on quantitative methods and statistical models. This has been extended to all risk types and includes qualitative methods. Generally, the assessments are matrix based, using probability of occurrence and monetary impact levels.

Comparing risk profile with risk appetite has led to structuring the risk responses in a more documented way and developing mitigations to prevent the same incident from happening again. Incident management has been developed to a stage where we need to do more than providing an instant action to stop the incident that is occurring and any immediate recurrence. Corrective actions to rectify impact, and root cause analyses to identify and address the underlying reason for failure, have been implemented to ensure the same could not happen anymore.

Formal issue-management processes have been developed to collate all the corrective actions and recommendations from audit and risk monitoring, including formal tracking of their implementation, to ensure closure within an acceptable timeframe. Development of sustainability reviews has even become a required procedure. This has provided better visibility to the boards and greater assurance of the risk mitigation's effectiveness.

The expansion of risk identification and measurement beyond credit and markets risks has supported the development of key process mapping in most of the functional areas. The development of integrated internal control frameworks, including key process mapping, has become as important as developing risk frameworks. This process-mapping exercise has led to establishing controls inventory. In addition, the first line functions are now developing assurance on control effectiveness and document the exercise. In first line functions like operations, information security and information technology, testing and validation has become the norm. In the second line of defence, monitoring and testing have expanded beyond the compliance functions. Disciplined internal control processes help to integrate risk management into day-to-day activity.

The three line of defence model has been installed with proper segregation of duties. All advisory, day-to-day business and functional management are the first line of defence and include Finance, HR, and Legal functions. Risk and Compliance monitoring are the second line functions with a full independent third line of defence, mostly in-house audit with internal or external co-sourcing being developed when specific technical expertise is required.

The risk function should be independent but not isolated and it should remain close to and understand business management. It should be independent from a reporting line standpoint, in a matrix organization with direct access to the board. Local risk teams, with market and regulatory expertise, close to the front-line risk-takers, are critical. This has been a key success factor in pro-active risk management.

Another best practice has been the retention of experienced risk staff, the communication of risk management objectives via in-house training and inductions programmes, and internal temporary placement/rotation (where risk managers work with first lines). Risk managers have also adopted a more business-oriented mindset, where they work in partnership with first and front-line managers, supporting them in effective risk management decisions. Hiring risk team members from the operations or with first-line trading and credit experience also had a positive impact.

Nominating board members with the required skills and the appropriate mix of technical and specialized expertise and directorship experience has become a key requirement. Board members are much more visible and accountability has been strengthened. Hiring Non-Executive Directors for key strategic roles (including the Chairman) to ensure independent thinking has been established more broadly across the industry.

Separating the Executive Management from the board has been a key milestone in ensuring transparency and the right level of controls in the organisation. The CEOs are 'employed' by the board and their performance needs to be evaluated constantly. Board members' increased accountability also reinforced their active engagement and time spent on providing effective oversight. They ask for proof of execution. It was frequently the case prior to the Global Financial Crisis that the statutory boards had no real effective governance oversight, and that they only signed off on the Group Executive decisions.

Corporate governance has been enhanced, with documented infrastructure to ensure that role and responsibilities between board and executive management are delineated. Policies, procedures, escalation arrangements, delegations of authorities and signature have been set up and clearly documented. Corporate secretary roles have expanded to ensure that meeting processes, agenda, board information, and attendance level are structured to allow adequate access to information and communication for informed and auditable decision-making. Developing self-assessment of board and committee effectiveness has helped to optimize governance.

It is also clearly recognized that the governance of Risk is a board responsibility. They will ensure the company has established a sound internal control system and the adequate risk oversight reflective of the board's risk appetite. Effective risk management is now considered as supporting better decision-making processes. Chief Risk Officers have taken an active role in providing corporate governance oversight.

Risk and audit committees chaired by Non-Executives Directors – as well as Chief Risk Officers' veto rights – have significantly strengthened oversight and execution and have reinforced the status and authority of the latter role. They now attend risk committees, investment committees and assets and liabilities committees and have significant authority in regulated and non-regulated firms alike.

Evaluating boards' and directors' performances has helped to assess whether firms are governed effectively, highlighting any gaps or weaknesses that need to be addressed. It ensures that corporate decision-making is consistent with the strategy of the organization. Using external partners is best practice but it is not yet fully established as a common practice. Actions and development programmes to correct the identified issues must be documented and monitored. In the UK, the Senior Managers & Certification Regime has helped to drive behavioural change and reinstalled control in the UK branches of foreign banks.

Embedded risk culture and corporate values

Pre-crisis, many banks and financial institutions had core values statements, thereby communicating their ethical way of doing business and how much they valued their clients and wished to ensure fair outcomes for customers. However, these statements remained at the conceptual stage: they were not really integrated into the operating model and therefore not cascaded across the entire organization.

The institutions that were worst affected by the crisis were those with a poor risk culture (sales-driven culture with strong pressure on revenue growth and aggressive sales targets) or those inadvertently exposed to risks they did not understand or did not properly measure, or which lacked an effective internal control framework.

Post-crisis, however, promoting an effective risk culture, ethical business practices and fair customer outcomes have become more effective. Generally, companies have established a conduct programme and complaints measurements, and have redesigned compensation schemes with key risk and compliance metrics.

A true 'tone from the top' has emerged, and this has now become part of leaders' DNA – leading by example and cultivating and promoting open exchanges of views. It has fostered changes in values and how they are applied. Culture surveys, seeking employee satisfaction and opinion, are critical to ensure that such values are spread widely. There will be confidence in the leadership if the right values are applied. The organization must be open to feedback and ensure the proper responses and corrective actions are implemented. Having a transparent spirit and code of conduct is not sufficient if it is not embedded and tested at every level of the organisation. There is no excuse for lack of integrity and conduct. Bad behaviours are penalized and communicating on the breaches is clearly what is now expected.

Second-line quality assurance and audits on culture and company practices via third parties have been established. Developing outcome-based testing in addition to risk-based testing is also helping organizations to develop greater ethical culture.

In-house as well as external communication campaigns have been launched on risk strategy and core principles, and training regarding risk values and expectations has become mandatory. Risk intranets have been developed and best practices shared in 'brown bags' sessions, with any risk events and incidents being transparently communicated. So-called 'lessons-learned' documents are now regularly written, with information on regulatory fines and examples of Do's and Don'ts.

A 'no blame' culture has helped employees to report any near-miss or future potential losses and to flag up potential issues. Measurement of the percentage of self-reported risk problems, in terms of time to escalation, has led to more transparency and earlier identification of risks and problems.

Mandatory training regarding policies compliance, regulatory requirements, ethics and anti-bribery, has been implemented and the quality of the programmes has increased. Tracking attendance and accomplishments has become a management accountability and including such metrics in the objectives has helped.

Real efforts have been made to establish whistleblowing policies and meaningful processes and/or ombudsman services. Testing that it works is becoming a 'must-have'. Boards have taken more responsibility for championing open and transparent channels for employees (and third parties) to raise concerns. Ensuring the process is handled in total confidentiality and independence to foster a 'speak up' culture will become standard.

Accountability regarding risk management has also been reinforced across organizations. Measurable risk objectives for all risk-takers, functional leaders as well as senior managers, have been established. Conduct metrics have been added and an annual performance review in line with risk management priorities is now required. Policy owners have been asked to ensure their policies are adhered through self-attestations processes. Annual objectives include the timely closure of corrective actions and internal audit recommendations.

The compensation structure has been redesigned: it has been aligned with risk-adjusted metrics and rewards long-term success rather than short-term gains, including individual and firm-wide objectives. Proper governance has been established through Board RemCo (Remuneration Committees). Chief Risk Officers participate to ensure incentive programmes promote ethical behaviours and are aligned with regulatory requirements.

Environmental, social and governance (ESG) factors have been incorporated into investment practices. Many organizations have become more cautious when underwriting deals, investing in companies or contracting with clients. They want to ensure they are entering in relationship with firms who have a high level of ethics, values and conduct.

Business models have been built around customers' satisfaction and fair treatment and market outcomes, with the result that detriment to either market and customer is no longer acceptable. New products should be developed and sold only if they respond to a customer or market need. Several organizations are not including the returns details in their loan-approval process and want to ensure that the product they offer does solely respond to their client requests.

Fair and responsible lending practices have been developed with transparent pricing, while measures ensuring customers (including vulnerable ones) are treated fairly have been implemented. The conduct principles edited by the Financial Conduct Authority have been expanded beyond the UK in some organizations to ensure no action can be taken to customers' detriment, or that has an adverse effect on market stability or effective competition.

Comprehensive conduct frameworks, including conduct dashboards, have been created to ensure that business areas can identify, manage and mitigate potential emerging (and crystallized) conduct risks more effectively – by measuring and reporting against agreed tolerances, triggers and thresholds in a timely manner. Greater focus on sales practices and customer complaint management has been part of the journey.

Continued challenges

This is a long list of specific measures which, taken together, amount to significant enhancements in risk management functions and corporate governance, and which have placed a stronger focus on customers' and markets' needs. However, these developments have not yet proven to be sustainable, as many have been implemented only recently.

These enhancements and changes to this architecture of control have been driven mostly by the regulatory landscape and legislative obligations. Risk leaders are still frequently using the 'excuse' of regulatory obligations to drive change or to enhance the firm's risk management processes. There is a need to ensure that the Chief Risk Officers' opinions and advices are being listened to, respected and not challenged in a confrontational way or that they are viewed as merely representing regulatory requirements.

Thus, in many organizations, risk assessments are still too academic. The embedding of risk appetite into business decisions has not yet been achieved fully everywhere and demands constant focus. The use of enterprise-wide risk management frameworks is difficult to implement effectively. All of this requires significant additional allocated resources, which have a cost that companies are not always willing to pay unless there is a mandatory requirement from the legislator or the regulator.

It is important to understand the limitations of risk systems and measures, and the balance between qualitative and quantitative assessments, in all risk disciplines. Many risk programmes remain too academic. Some organizations have been so focused on following a strict methodology, documenting risk identification and ensuring that they can demonstrate they have a risk management framework, that they did not realize there was some disconnection between the assessment results and their real risk profile.

Focusing on completing risk registers, rather than identifying process improvement and associated control weaknesses, has also led to an inability to drive effective risk management and embed it in the decision-making system.

Emerging trends (in politics, economy, climate, demography) and associated risks are insufficiently assessed. Risk assessment remain too internally focused. Financial firms are still in a reactive rather than a proactive mode. It is thus hard to catch management attention regarding hypothetical changes – see for example the initial reluctance to address or assess the impact of Brexit on the UK consumer lending sector.

Banks' stress testing results are not fully satisfactory, and the recovery and resolution planning process is not mature enough. Stress testing and recovery and resolution hardly exist in the non-regulated sector due to lack of expertise.

Both the level of operational risk and the proportion of risk incidents remain high given the persistence of manual processes and the lack of integrated systems in fast-paced and/or group organizations. With additional detective and corrective controls, these are mostly 'near misses', but it is still necessary to identify and correct root causes to avoid any occurrence.

On the other hand, in some areas, the level of digitization and the use of new technologies have created reliance on systems which are not fully understood. This, combined with the growth in social media use, has heightened the level of data and information risk.

The wider application of models, and our reliance on them, require stronger controls and governance. This has brought into focus the need for a complete model risk management. Whilst significant efforts have been made to develop state-of-the-art models, the model risk frameworks have remained immature: there are limited exhaustive models inventory, models' lifecycles have not been documented fully, risk appetite and materiality assessment for each model remain limited, and business impact analysis has not assessed for all models. Often, model validation is either performed by the first lines (thus without proper segregation of duties) or there is a heavy reliance on external consultants.

Internal control frameworks, despite significant enhancement, are still primarily focused on compliance monitoring and financial reporting. The extension to all risk types, processes and associated controls is not a common practice across every financial service.

The risk and conduct 'culture' tends to be taken for granted and we cannot simply assume that the company's culture and values are what is said on the packaging. They must be assessed and tested through regular surveys and reviews to sustain the cultural change.

Risk is about ethics, conduct, integrity, 'lessons learned' from crises, incidents, and frauds. Financial institutions need to sustain the work performed over the last ten years and educate people from an early stage – from university. For too many students, the motivation to join banks is still the large compensation package.

The complexity of cross-border groups is a growing concern, with their multiple jurisdictions, legal entities and business lines. Isolated second lines of defence remain a key risk there. In many firms, the risk function is based at headquarters, and thus far from front-line execution. Some banks have created a so-called '1.5 line of defence' to provide operational assurance and reporting within the first line of business. However, this runs the risk of removing the real accountability from the business and does not help to integrate and to really embed risk management in the business' core processes and decision-making.

Whilst regulatory pressure has definitely helped to drive risk enhancements, together with increased pressure from investors, regulatory changes cannot be underestimated as banks have the tendency to spend more time on managing stakeholders and regulatory changes than focusing on managing portfolios and other core activities.

Finally, it's important to add that future developments in risk management probably need to take more account of human behaviour. This would imply that reliable ways of measuring risk attitudes will need to be developed.

Index

www.ingramcontent.com/pod-product-compliance
Lightning Source LLC
Chambersburg PA
CBHW050429280326
41932CB00013BA/2049